Pushkar Dhami

Pushkar Dhami

The Vibrant Heat of the Himalayas

Sambhawana Pant

Published by
Rupa Publications India Pvt. Ltd 2025
7/16, Ansari Road, Daryaganj
New Delhi 110002

Sales centres:
Bengaluru Chennai Hyderabad
Jaipur Kathmandu Kolkata
Mumbai Prayagraj

Copyright © Sambhawana Pant 2025

Photographs courtesy: Sambhawana Pant

Copyright of the photographs vests with the respective photographer/copyright owner.

While every effort has been made to trace copyright holders and obtain permission, this has not been possible in all cases; any omissions brought to our attention will be remedied in future editions.

The views and opinions expressed in this book are the author's own and the facts are as reported by her, which have been verified to the extent possible, and the publishers are not in any way liable for the same. The publisher has used its best endeavours to ensure that URLs for external websites referred to in this book are correct and active at the time of going to press. However, the publisher has no responsibility for the websites and can make no guarantee that a site will remain live or that the content is or will remain appropriate.

All rights reserved.
No part of this publication may be reproduced, transmitted or stored in a retrieval system, in any form or by any means, electronic, mechanical, photocopying, recording or otherwise, without the prior permission of the publisher.

P-ISBN: 978-93-6156-152-8
E-ISBN: 978-93-6156-178-8

First impression 2025

10 9 8 7 6 5 4 3 2 1

The moral right of the author has been asserted.

Printed in India

This book is sold subject to the condition that it shall not, by way of trade or otherwise, be lent, resold, hired out or otherwise circulated, without the publisher's prior consent, in any form of binding or cover other than that in which it is published.

The late Sher Singh Dhami

Whose dreams could not be fulfilled in their entirety in his lifetime, and so he passed them on to his son Pushkar...

CONTENTS

Foreword   *ix*
Pushkar Singh Dhami: An Introduction   *xiii*

1. Result: A Glimpse into the Future   1
2. Oath: A Resolve for Public Welfare   31
3. Background: Laying the Foundation Stone   35
4. Evolution: Ascension of the Clan   47
5. Migration: A Path to Development   75
6. Education: A Chronicle of Struggle   86
7. University: A Nursery of Personality Development   104
8. Journey in Politics: The Enlightenment of Political Obligation   215
9. Public Acceptance: Fulfilment of Public Aspirations   232
10. Politics: A Labyrinth of Conspiracies   256
11. Chief Minister: Trendsetter for His State   268
12. By-election: Endorsement of the Accomplished Work   285

Acknowledgements   312
Felicitations from Well-wishers and Political Leaders   317

FOREWORD

Politics is generally believed to be a quagmire where lies, deceit and conspiracy often decide survival. It is seen as a den of duplicity where a wave of exaggeration is woven to camouflage and peddle vested interests. It is regarded as a world where ruthless crimes pave the way forward. Yet the same politics could also be a tool for development that is possible through disciplined practice of honesty, maintaining people's trust, exercising excellence with precision and ensuring total transparency. When politics is practised with a degree of propriety, it turns into a *pushkar* (reservoir) of welfare, widespread peace and prosperity.

Pushkar Singh Dhami, chief minister of Uttarakhand, is such a power personified that is serving the Himalayas. On the one hand, he is like a living pushkar—still, peaceful, clear-headed, unblemished and unperturbed by the chilling cold of the Shivalik hills, as if a furnace burns inside him. On the other, like a *singh*, a lion, he has courage, resoluteness, perseverance, dedication and awareness.

He was born into an ordinary family in a rural hilly area, but he was gifted with extraordinary talent to excel and march ahead in the labyrinthine terrain of politics. He attained a lofty rank by marching past all hurdles and relying solely on his tireless hard work. Climbing the stairs of Akhil Bharatiya Vidyarthi Parishad (ABVP) and Rashtriya Swayamsevak Sangh (RSS), he has ascended to the post of chief minister (CM) in his home state. He is the youngest leader to become CM of Uttarakhand and has only been a two-time member of the legislative assembly (MLA) so far. It speaks volumes about his political acumen. It is also evidence of his leadership range, his efficiency and a vast amount of patience in his character. Chief Minister Dhami's hold on politics and his relevance has been proved by the fact that despite losing in the Assembly elections, he was crowned the head of the state!

Therefore, it is proven that exceptions do not challenge the general rule of any field, but they demonstrate that the established rules can be breached if there is a genuine determination to succeed. Today, many may call the vibrant heat of Himalaya Pushkar Dhami's ascension to the throne of *mukhya sevak*, or chief servant, as a helicopter entry, but it is irrelevant to see his success in a swift series of events; rather his success must be viewed as part of a broad canvas of sustained and long-lasting struggles. It is exactly like asking in today's time whether the sun circles the Earth or the other way round. Who is revolving around whom? Today, almost all of us have the answer to the question that the sun is at the centre, but only Galileo and Copernicus would know how long and complicated has the journey been to realize this truth!

Sambhawana Pant, the daughter of *devbhoomi* Uttarakhand, has written the life journey of this immensely promising star, right from his origin to his luminescence on the firmament of Uttarakhand politics. Pant is a writer who often attacks all the valueless practices of fundamentalist, consumerist, market-oriented systems and champions the cause of a strategic counter to such cultures. The light emanating from author Sambhawana Pant's pen not only shines on paper but also dawns upon the soul and minds of the readers. Pant has established a wonderful harmony between the seriousness of political events and literary esotericism in this book. She has enriched literature by incorporating cultural landscapes and regional linguistic richness. She shows a mirror to society through her works, thoughts, poems, ghazals, speeches, articles, etc. Simultaneously, she also seems to be planting the seeds of futuristic ideas and axing trees of dogma and social anomalies. Pant has highlighted the *shukl* and *krishn paksha* of Dhami, Bharatiya Janata Party (BJP) and Sangh, as well as of Indian National Congress and other Opposition parties with equality.

The book *Pushkar Singh Dhami: The Vibrant Heat of Himalaya* begins with the warmth of the rising sun on 10 March with the announcement of the election results, highlighting the historical, cultural and political developments against the hilly backdrop of Uttarakhand; it then proceeds to the oath-taking ceremony of Pushkar Singh Dhami as the chief minister of the state. While the book has a vivid description of Dhami's childhood, education and migration, it has also captured his Lucknavi- Nawab-style mischiefs, his struggles and his understanding of active student politics and how that period changed him. The comparative manner in which Pant has exposed political conspiracies in Dhami's life journey is rarely seen in writings on political figures.

The book not only explains the political journey of Pushkar Singh Dhami but also highlights all aspects of human life. The vision, ideology, ideals and working style of Chief Minister Dhami have been kept as the focal point of this deliberation so that a harmony of understanding could be achieved. The impression of the ideas, teachings and training of the RSS on the personality of CM Dhami is clearly visible in his style of functioning. This book has not only presented the factual side of CM Dhami's work and plans but has also explained the ideological and emotional side of his personality. While the book reveals how Dhami imbibed punctuality and discipline from the teachings of his soldier father, it also narrates his father Sher Singh Dhami's courageous military duties and perseverance in the midst of life's struggles and challenges. The book makes it remarkably clear that a skilled leader-planner doesn't make his organizational structure strong solely *for* the public, but *with* the public.

The writer has maintained a sharp aesthetic sense while describing the beauty of natural scenes as well, which makes this book a valuable addition to the literary canon and points to its longevity. It has not only touched upon many untouched aspects of Pushkar Singh Dhami's life but has also done justice to them. The book successfully presents the journey of Pushkar to become a Dhami, *The Vibrant Heat of Himalaya* with the blessings of guardian-like Prime Minister Narendra Modi, Home Minister Amit Shah, BJP President J.P. Nadda, Defence Minister Rajnath Singh and Governor Bhagat Singh Koshiyari, along with all the countrymen and well-wishers. While the language of this life story is straightforward, simple and clear, it is also eloquent in literary terms!

My best wishes with these lines to Sambhawana Pant for writing this masterpiece:

Daal se bikhar jao vo pattee nahin ho tum,
Aththee se pichhad jao vo sattee nahin ho tum!
Ye duniya kitna bhee tumhein aag mein jhonke,
Mom see pighal jao vo battee nahin ho tum!

You have the ability to neither fall behind nor lose,
no matter how many challenges the world puts you through.

—**Sahishnu Samrat**

PUSHKAR SINGH DHAMI: AN INTRODUCTION

1. Born: 16 September 1975
2. Birth location: Pithoragarh (Tundi village)
3. Father: Late Subedar Sher Singh Dhami
4. Mother: Bishna Devi Dhami
5. Siblings: Three elder sisters, Pushpa, Nandi and the late Indra
6. Wife: Geeta Dhami (since 28 January 2011)
7. Children: Two sons, Diwakar (23 March 2012) and Prabhakar (8 November 2014)
8. Political Guru: Former Governor of Maharashtra Bhagat Singh Koshyari
9. Guardianship: Prime Minister Shri Narendra Modi, Home Minister Amit Shah and Defence Minister Rajnath Singh
10. Education:
    a. Primary: Tundi, Pithoragarh, Uttarakhand
    b. High School: DNCB, Sagar, Madhya Pradesh
    c. Intermediate: Tharu Inter College, Khatima, Uttarakhand
    d. Higher Education: Graduation and Post-Graduation in Human Resource Management and Industrial Relations (MHRM & IR), LLB and Diploma in Public Administration (DPA) from Lucknow University; Ph.D. thesis on Human Resource Management and Industrial Relations submitted at Lucknow University

11. Occupation: Active politics (chief minister of Uttarakhand since 4 July 2021)
12. Motto: *Sarve Bhavantu Sukhinah, Sarve Santu Niramaya*
13. Political Party: BJP via RSS
14. Important political posts: State-level responsible worker in the university unit, Bharatiya Janata Yuva Morcha, Uttarakhand; state president (2002–08), Urban Monitoring Committee Rank in Uttarakhand (2010–12); MLA for two consecutive terms, Khatima, Uttarakhand, (2012–17 and 2017–22), MLA (by-election), Champawat, Uttarakhand (2022–27); state vice-president, BJP (since 2016)
15. Sociopolitical objectives: With *Antyodaya*, taking development to the last man; resolution to make 25-year-old devbhoomi Uttarakhand become number one state on all parameters of development in India in 2025
16. Major honour: Received the Youth Icon Award twice; state-level best MLA award conferred by Governor Krishan Kant Paul in 2015; national level best MLA award conferred by President Ram Nath Kovind in 2020
17. Skin colour: Fair
18. Height: 5 feet 10 inches
19. Weight: 82 kg
20. Favourite food: Regional Uttarakhandi dishes
21. Favourite place: The green gardens of nature
22. Favourite dress: Indian-style kurta pyjama
23. Favourite colour: White, which symbolizes peace
24. Favourite idol: Swami Vivekananda
25. Favourite political leader: Shri Narendra Modi
26. Favourite movie: *Maachis* (1996), a political thriller written and directed by Gulzar
27. Favourite actor: Amitabh Bachchan, Manoj Kumar and Dharmendra

28. Favourite actress: Hema Malini and Rekha
29. Favourite song: 'Bedu Pako Baraha Masa' and 'Chappa Chappa Charkha Chale'
30. Frightful memory of childhood: One day, while sitting under a tree, a baby snake suddenly slithered from the side of his shorts. He initially ignored it, thinking it was a twig or leaf. However, on feeling a cold sensation near his stomach, Pushkar shook it off, realizing in shock that it was a snake

1

RESULT: A GLIMPSE INTO THE FUTURE

Determined people do not get upset with failures;
they move forward by learning from them.

The chirping of the early morning birds hadn't even ceased, and the green grass still appeared grey. The first rays of the sun had yet to emerge from the horizon and spread across the sky. Nonetheless, the sound of footsteps echoed through the streets—not just a few, but thousands in numbers. These were not the steps of schoolchildren or workers heading to factories, and neither were they the steps of those government employees who consider themselves pioneers of the nation-building process. They belonged to the people who were christened as the 'People of India' in the Constitution's Preamble by the Constituent Assembly of India. Today, these 'People of India' or the Indian public had taken to the roads, squares and streets in anticipation of the results of the largest festival of democracy—the elections. Some of them had made their way towards vote-counting centres, while others were heading towards their respective party headquarters. Among this multitude of Indians, there were infants with their parents, and there also were 90–95-year-old men who had been witnesses to a century of changes. There were impassioned young men who were ready to bear the nation's burdens and there also were women entirely dedicated to raise issues related to women and work for their empowerment.

A wave from this unfathomable sea of people also reached the Bharatiya Janata Party (BJP) headquarters, where some of the hardworking party workers were already making their presence known. While curiosity about the results lingered in the minds of all those present, a fear of defeat also simmered beneath the surface—the public's bitterness towards their representatives, palpable during the election campaign, was not a good sign for the BJP. The way this rhetoric was highly publicized and disseminated by the Opposition gradually made the common man realize that perhaps, this time, the winds of change might persist and the BJP would be ousted from power.

However, in stark defiance of this propaganda, the exit polls projected BJP gaining landslide majority. A reputed news channel aired the prediction of 43 seats for the BJP, 24 for Indian National Congress (Congress hereon), and three seats for others, suddenly dampening the morale of the opposition parties, especially the Congress party. The BJP workers became ecstatic, brimming with exultation and high on victorious fervour. Such was their confidence of an electoral triumph and a celebratory zeal that they had filled the BJP headquarters in huge numbers long before the official results were announced. Traditional sweetmeats of *boondi laddoos*, sent by the party high command to its workers, well-wishers and fans the previous day, were transported to the headquarters by enthusiastic party workers on their heads.

On this day, people from five provinces of Aryavarta Bharatkhand—Uttar Pradesh, holding the world's fifth-largest population; Punjab, a highly fertile region nestled amidst five rivers; Manipur, with an enriching tribal culture in the Northeast diadem; Goa; the biodiverse land within the Western Ghats, the smallest province in terms of area; and devbhoomi Uttarakhand, the meditation ground of sages and saints nestled in the foothills of the Shivalik range of the Himalayas—were waiting with bated breath: who will govern them for the next five years? Who will prioritize public welfare? And who will take on the role of Opposition in the House?

In such charged up moments, it was natural for anyone to be worried about his future. But amidst all this frenzy, current CM of devbhoomi Uttarakhand, Pushkar Singh Dhami, an epitome of the Himalayan blaze in action, kept a poised demeanour, his face reflecting the famed Rajputana glory. He still exuded the expected explosive energy in his speech for which Rajput rulers have been known for centuries. The day of declaration of results is an important moment in a person's life, irrespective of the fact that he is going to pass with flying colours or come out only average.

The incessant and accelerated pounding of the heart, the butterflies in one's stomach, the restlessness and anxiety—it's natural for every person going through such a pressure-packed situation to feel such turbulence of emotion. But not Dhami. Even on this day, as soon as the *tamasik triyama* or the time between midnight and 3 a.m. when negative energies are dominant ended, Dhami woke up and went about his day without any change in his routine.

Karmanyavaadhikaraste, maa phaleshu kadachana,
Maa karmaphalheturbhurma te sangostvakarmani

The meaning of the present verse mentioned in the holy book *Shrimad Bhagavad Gita's* Chapter 2, Verse 47, is that you have the right on your deeds, but not on its fruits; so you should not be attached to the fruits of your actions. It is possible that when Yogiraj Shri Krishna uttered these wise words, he not only dedicated them to Arjuna but he also devoted them to other men of action like Dhami.

The glowing dewdrops, resembling silver pearls on the leaves of plants, vines and green grass had evaporated from the heat of the sun and vanished into the horizon. On this day, the sun's life-affirming warmth was being dwarfed by the political fire, the flames of which were being stoked by the media. As astonishing trends had begun to emerge from all sides, most of the public was eager to capture the trends in their favour from the screens. In the first trend, the BJP seemed to be leading in devbhoomi Uttarakhand. As the party's numbers moved towards the much-desired destination, a wave of enthusiasm among the workers started pulsating. The BJP headquarter was suffused in saffron, with supporters, well-wishers and workers sporting the saffron colour. Those who weren't in saffron clothes had saffron stoles around their necks. In the joy of this astonishing rise of the BJP, everyone was seen dancing to the beats of drums, and in their exultation, feeding each other laddoos. Even the laddoos were imbued in saffron.

It was not just the party headquarter that was rinsed in the triumphant elation; the same fervour had engulfed the roads, crossroads, villages, streets, tea stalls and markets. Some people were taking their first sips of tea, while others were finishing their daily morning ablutions, and thus everyone, while doing their chores, was offering symbolic sacrifices of their emotions in the metaphorical *yajna kund* (a holy fire pit) of this historic verdict of ballots. Some eagerly anticipated the Congress' victory, recalling its role in winning independence for India from the foreign yoke. Others believed that the Aam Aadmi Party (AAP), renowned for combating corruption, sponsoring free amenities like electricity, promoter of quality education and healthcare initiatives, and inventor of odd-even formula for vehicles on the road, might sway the odds this time. Meanwhile, there were those who were confident of a significant victory for the BJP.

For some, this election was about focusing on state issues; for others, it was a glimpse into the 2024 roadmap; even others thought that it was also about what public thought of India's way of addressing international affairs and formulating its game-changing policies. Many dignitaries gathered at shops felt that on this day, as they sipped their tea, they had also been entrusted with the responsibility of presiding over an emergency seminar on some pivotal international topic. And why shouldn't they have felt so? After all, this was the people's mandate, where every vote would decide whose fate the key to power would unlock.

The graph of BJP continued to soar in all the trends being shown by various media platforms. As the number of seats showed an increase, there was a noticeable shift in the language of the dignitaries. As the beat of drums gathered vanquishing rhythms, those who were previously guarded in their statements, now confidently boasted of an imminent victory. It seemed that the BJP was poised to celebrate Jashn-e-Holi and Diwali together that year. Yet, there were still some politicians who were unable to digest the imminent victory of the BJP.

They felt, how could any party in power in devbhoomi Uttarakhand defy the existing myth that no incumbent shall return to power? How could this long-standing myth be shattered?

Suddenly, the political pundits were stunned by an unbelievable announcement—the chief minister, Himalaya's living legend Pushkar Singh Dhami, was trailing in his constituency Khatima behind his laborious Congress rival, Bhuwan Chandra Kapri, by about 7,000 votes. The setback for Pushkar Singh Dhami's figures in the Khatima seat, which is considered a VVIP assembly seat with 1,13,000 voters, sent a message of extreme distraction and discouragement to his supporters. This contrasted with the BJP's rising graph across Uttarakhand. The BJP was on ascent, but the man of action, Dhami, had been consistently lagging behind Congress' Bhuwan Chandra Kapri in Khatima. It was an unnatural turn of events; something unfathomable was happening; something unforeseen was unfolding.

Dhami was that head of the state who made every effort to fulfil the dreams of the people of devbhoomi Uttarakhand. He systematically launched, laid foundation stones and inaugurated schemes during his brief tenure. Simultaneously, he worked to reshape the historical trajectory of politics. How was it possible then that he was falling behind in the race? It was like the English writer Charles Lamb's situation of pathos and humour unfolding for Dhami in a single sequence.

This scenario led to a peculiar circumstance where, on one hand, Dhami received accolades from party workers, well-wishers and even the party's top leadership, while on the other hand, there was an unspoken undercurrent of regret. In this intriguing atmosphere, as the third hour neared its end, it became evident that Pushkar Singh Dhami had lost from his own Assembly constituency, Khatima, by 6,951 votes. The diligent candidate of Congress, Bhuwan Chandra

Kapri, had finally secured victory. **On this seat, the Bahujan Samaj Party (BSP) candidate, Ramesh Rana, had garnered 937 votes, and the AAP candidate, S.S. Kaler, obtained 764 votes. This figure further left everyone stunned.**

The election result in devbhoomi Uttarakhand was profoundly shocking. A minister who had led his party to a landslide victory under the Pundarik (lotus) symbol, adorned in the middle of the saffron flag, with the slogan, '*Vikalp Rahit Sankalp: Naye Irade, Yuva Sarkar*' (Resolution Without Alternatives: A Young Government with New Aims), throughout the state had ended up facing defeat in his own seat! How? A quick glimpse through the pages of history reveals that this incident is not entirely unprecedented. Only some years ago, a similar sequence of pathos mixed with humour took place when Shri Prem Kumar Dhumal, the BJP's CM candidate, had lost the election from his own seat in the 2017 Himachal Pradesh Assembly elections, while the Party romped to a majority. This trend was also observed in the 2021 West Bengal Assembly elections when the All India Trinamool Congress (AITC) secured a massive victory, even though Mamata Banerjee, the strong candidate who held the post of CM for years, couldn't retain her seat.

The astute leadership of the young leader in the young state was the centre of attention of a number of political enthusiasts. Thus, his unexpected defeat was unimaginable for them, as the BJP's easy march to majority with 47 seats out of 70, despite facing a wave of anti-incumbency, was a testimony that the party had showed exemplary resilience against Opposition's onslaught and several other odds stacked against it. It was in fact a lesson for both future leaders and young political observers in the face of adverse commentary by some political pundit.

After autopsy, a number of reasons were being cited for Dhami's electoral defeat. First, that he didn't give priority to his Assembly, instead focused extensively on ensuring the party's victory across the entire state. Second, Dhami had had limited time for showcasing himself as the CM. Third, some political experts attributed the defeat to party leaders' betrayal, suggesting their role in Dhami's loss. Fourth and furthermore, there was a belief among experts that the All India Majlis-e-Ittehad-ul Muslimeen or AIMIM (political outfit of Member of Parliament Asadudddin Owaisi) failed to appeal to Muslim voters, causing all the Muslim votes, approximately 9,000 of them, shifting towards the Congress.

In these assembly elections across all five states, it wasn't just the CM candidate Pushkar Singh Dhami who faced defeat. Several legendary figures also suffered losses. For instance, the CM of Punjab state, Charanjit Singh Channi, lost by a margin of 63,514 votes, and former Punjab CM Parkash Singh Badal also experienced a resounding defeat. Additionally, former CM of Uttarakhand Harish Rawat, a revered veteran and a prominent Congress leader, also lost his seat from Lalkuan constituency. According to political analysts, it was not just individuals but entire political parties that appeared to be faltering. The swift decline of both the BSP and Congress in these elections was particularly surprising.

Congress and BJP's Position Before Results

In a peaceful political environment, the monsoon winds of the exit poll survey managed to impact the stable branches of a banyan tree like the Indian National Congress; and it was not only the Congress whose spine had been broken but the whole Opposition edifice—with all its branches, vines and leaves—had crumbled. This upheaval was due to the visible progress of the BJP's victory chariot that was making strides in visuals of all television stations. The Congress dismissed these potential outcomes as 'speculative' because it firmly believed in the enduring nature of the years-old myth in this *tapasthali devbhoomi* of Uttarakhand (the holy land of penance for saints)—a belief that no government could repeat its success. News stations displayed the image of the indomitable and daring soldier Ajay Kothial alongside a summary of political experiences of Harish Rawat aka Harda. Between these two images was a larger and more captivating picture of Dhami, accompanying the BJP's historic victory. It was not something that the Congress had expected. The Congress believed that the exit-poll survey didn't align with reality because farmers, youth, women and the elderly all had expressed dissatisfaction with the BJP. This belief led to the perception that such exit-poll surveys disrespected democratic votes.

Amidst the chaos of these surveys, voters often make their final decisions, and at times, contrary to these surveys, our conscientious voters surprise the so-called intellectuals conducting them. Ignoring these exit polls, confident Congress started contemplating its strategy to secure victory by all means. Politics, after all, is synonymous with opportunism. It's challenging to determine when, by whom, where, how and why politics should come into play here.

> *Satyanruta cha parusha priyavadini cha,*
> *Hinsara dayalurpi cha arthpara vadanya.*
> *Nityavyaya prachuranityadhanagama cha,*
> *Varaanganeva nripanitirnekrupa.*

This is Verse 47 of Bhartrihari's Nitishatak. It says that truth and illusion coexist; its language is sometimes bitter, while sometimes is dipped in honey; it is violent at a place, and it showers as kindness at other; it devours as greed and it also spreads benediction in the form of charity; it is careless extravagance sometimes and becomes wealth accumulator in its other avatar. This politics changes forms to look attractive, just like a courtesan.

The Congress Party had got wind of the final results even before their announcement. It had begun preparing its future MLAs and senior leaders. In this regard, Congress convened an emergency meeting. Its state in-charge Devendra Yadav and his associate observer Deepender Hooda also participated in this crucial meeting. The meeting, shrouded in secrecy, reflected the Congress' unwavering confidence in forming the government. Only some distinguished personalities were privileged to attend this discreet gathering.

In the presence of Harish Rawat, Pritam Singh, Ganesh Kothiyal, Deepika Pandey and Yashpal Arya, among others, a crucial decision was made during the meeting—to invite the chief of the Chhattisgarh government, Bhupesh Baghel, to visit Dehradun on 10 March. He would be present at the state party office in Uttarakhand's capital city until the counting was over. This decision perhaps was aimed at discussing strategic issues beforehand, anticipating various scenarios that might have emerged after announcement of the results. If the result didn't show clear majority for Congress, Baghel would have been able to play a proactive role in ensuring numbers for his party through political machinations. This is what the Congress' state brass had planned.

After this meeting, Devendra Yadav, even though reluctantly, addressed the media: 'The tireless toil of Congress veterans and common workers is going to yield result soon. As it is said that when the crop is ready, it is only to be carefully watched over. Similarly, there have to be some pre-counting preparations. It also helps in deciding the post-poll steps, and thus we have shared inputs regarding all this in our meeting.'

The history of politics reveals that whenever emergency meetings are convened for the claim on CM's post, ministerial portfolio allocation or due to concerns about potential dissent among MLAs, it is publicly announced that the meeting is a courtesy call aimed at issuing important guidelines.

However, in some cases, the one for whom the message is disseminated understands more than who is disseminating the message. Or the receiver of the message is more astute than the messenger. Here, the receiver of the message was the general public that had been a keen observer and researcher of the machinations of the politics since ages. They knew how politicians make use of political situations to their benefit.

At that moment, a journalist who was present at the meeting posed a question: 'If you find yourself short of a majority and your party MLAs show an inclination towards the BJP, or if a situation of rebellion arises in any way, especially considering the presence of Kailash Vijayvargiya here...'

In response to this question, what congress leader Devendra Yadav said defied civilizational humility that is part and parcel of civility in public life. He said:

'Look, the Bharatiya Janata Party has ridiculed the democratic system, whether it is in Goa or any other Indian state! The BJP has been trying to subdue the Opposition for the last several years. Today we warn them through you that we will no longer allow this to happen. The gentle public of this hill state have now become sensible enough to well understand the difference between milk and water. Whichever party or candidate they must have given their mandate to, that party or candidate will surely be able to take their demands into account and work to fulfil them. Plus, they would be confident enough that their chosen candidates or party would secure majority. Therefore, we have full confidence that the Congress party is going to form the people's government for the welfare of the people, because while being in the role of a strong Opposition, we have always been the voice of the people. We have shared their happiness and sorrow alike. On the other hand, the BJP has dragged this young state into a dark abyss through its insensitive misrule in the last five years. This has upset people and out of anger and aspiration for change, they have put their trust in the hopes generated by the Congress manifesto. We swear here and declare that we will make every effort to live up to their dreams and present a strong government to the people as soon as possible.

'The atmosphere we've witnessed in these five years, from pre-election phase, campaigning up to counting, shows that both the people and Congress are confident of effecting change of the government.'

Meanwhile, when asked about his estimate of the post-poll survey, presumptive chief ministerial candidate Harish Rawat declined to comment and said that being crowned as CM would be his answer. He further claimed that his party had maintained selfless and disciplined work in public interest and that it would ensure that the Congress formed the government with a clear majority. According to him, the broadcasting stations had done their duties by airing their post-poll surveys, while the public had performed its role.

Meanwhile, Kailash Vijayvargiya, a passionate leader of the BJP from Madhya Pradesh, known for orchestrating consistent triumphs in assembly elections, had initiated extensive preparations to claim victory in devbhoomi Uttarakhand. An ebullient leader and party soldier that he was, he had manned the front trenches and conducted a series of meetings. He had made it clear to his party's state leadership and cadres that his party was marching towards majority in the state and that it had unsettled the Congress party. He had arrived in the state capital Dehradun well before the vote count; and in his capacity as the general secretary of the BJP, he had discussed the sensitive issues of state politics with Dr Nishank Pokhriyal, former CM and union minister for human resource development. Experts of Uttarakhand politics know that Dr Nishank has been an ace political player in the state and his experience and rapport with leaders across political lines make him a viable mediator should the party need external support in case of a lack of majority. Now, two of BJP's experienced figures had to play pivotal part in the party's hour of need. The duo had been active and come to their party's aid in 2016 as well and they had given Congress a run for their money, and now the Congress was very alert about their presence. Harish Rawat and other Congress leaders were in a fix because of BJP's 'awesome twosome', and memories of past defeats began to haunt them.

As the bustle in all political circles sprang up to become a roar, Pushkar Singh Dhami sensed signs of victory and he spoke up with an overwhelmingly confident and lofty voice:

> Thank you, godly people of Devbhoomi! Once again, the Bharatiya Janata Party is coming with an overwhelming majority. Friends, we will turn aspirations into reality with renewed vigour, youthful enthusiasm and unwavering commitment. We will in fact run the 'dream government'

of the youth. The BJP is not only the largest party of India but based on primary membership, it is also the biggest party of the world. [In his oration, he also dared the opposition that the BJP would form the government with a brute majority of more than 60 seats out of total 70.]

In general, the opposition parties have only been beating drums and blowing their own trumpets. The exit poll surveys are airing one after another, but I think they underestimate their results when compared to the toil with which our party has invested itself in the elections. I assure all our well-wishers, supporters and workers that the natural results will surpass the survey predictions. This is because our struggling workers have not only been devoted wholeheartedly to the people for twelve months but have also continuously stayed among them and stood by them in their every vicissitude. I express my heartfelt gratitude to the central supreme leadership, including the members of the state unit, my *panna* heads, booth presidents and everyone for their cooperation in this democratic festival. Under the efficient leadership of Hon'ble Prime Minister Shri Narendra Bhai Modi ji, the people of Uttarakhand have seen a remarkable pace in development projects during his prime ministership.

Whether it is the railways, road connectivity, hospitals, schools, tourism or religious places, the visible progress is not just on paper but it can be seen by everyone on the ground. In every field, we have done unprecedented work, and the people of Uttarakhand have acknowledged this work and cast their precious votes to let this caravan of progress march forward. We plunged into this election as humble soldiers of

Hon'ble Prime Minister Shri Narendra Bhai Modi ji, and we found no dearth of public blessings for our meek endeavour. Opposition parties, including the Congress, were jittery and stayed aloof from the electoral arena as they didn't have strong issues to talk about and neither did they have any appropriate strategy to face us. And now that the election is over, they are back to beat the same old drum of self-delusion. I sincerely request them to rest their drum, as it needs a break. Let it rest in the rest house for a long interval. The BJP will do the celebration with pomp and show on its own with *chholiya* dances [a colourful dress dance by local dancers of Uttarakhand] and music instruments that will reflect regional diversity on the beats of new drums. So don't worry about it.

After this, Pushkar Singh Dhami, the son of devbhoomi, was seen visiting the region's holy temples, gurudwaras and *dhaam*s or pilgrimage sites for solace and inner peace. Dhami, accompanied by his wife Geeta, paid obeisance at the Mahasu Devta temple. The temple, built by the majestic King Mihirkul of the Huna dynasty in the ninth century AD, sits in Hanol on the Tiuni–Mori Road near Chakrata, alongside the river Tons. Legend has it that Mahasu Devta fulfils the wishes of devotees who seek blessings at this holy site. Mahasu Devta is considered an incarnation of Lord Shankar and is a combined form of four brother gods known as Basik Mahasu, Pabasik Mahasu, Bautha Mahasu and Chalda Mahasu.

Following his divine visit, Dhami directed the setup of two control rooms by the BJP workers to monitor any conspiratorial activities of the Opposition during the counting of votes. These measures aimed to enable swift action in the event of chaos or disorder. The Election Commission also announced a ban on victory processions, considering the need to maintain order. Civil police were deployed to secure the outer boundaries of the counting centres, accompanied by the issuance of important guidelines. Within the inner circle, Provincial Armed Constabulary (PAC) forces and Central Industrial Security Force (CISF) personnel were assigned significant responsibilities of vigil and security. Director General of Police (DGP) Ashok Kumar publicly announced that only counting agents with valid permits would be granted entry into the counting centre, and any disruptions would not be tolerated.

The Dilemma

That which was absolutely unexpected had happened. Everyone was stunned how the charioteer of the party's victorious advance had been denied his own moment of jubilation. While his party's return to power had given him immense joy, Dhami was also perturbed with mental tumult of disappointment over his own loss in the election. However, these pangs of defeat were short-lived. The melancholy didn't hold back Dhami for long. Resolute individuals aren't disheartened by failures; they move forward, taking important lessons from setbacks. Dhami overcame this dilemma and chose to perceive the party's victory as his own success, deciding to move forward.

> *Sukha-duḥkhe same kritva labhalabhau jayajayau,*
> *Tato yuddhaya yujyasva naivaṁ papam.*

In Chapter 2, Verse 38, of *Shrimad Bhagavad Gita*, Lord Shri Krishna advises Arjuna not to be disheartened but to maintain a balance between victory and defeat, profit and loss, and happiness and sorrow, urging him to engage in the struggle anew. A determined individual, by striving, does not incur sin (or loss).

Naturally, it is understood that through the faculties of body, mind and intellect, one goes through various experiences in life. Experiencing favourable and adverse conditions, with either joy or disappointment, is actually the reaction of the inner mind of a man. Success and failure are both creations of the mind. If you are driven by the fancies of your mind, you are bound to exult at success and feel downcast when you face failure.

As soon as the afternoon of 11 March began, Dhami, along with Ganesh Joshi, Arvind Pandey and Satpal Maharaj, met the Hon'ble Governor of Uttarakhand, Lt Gen. Gurmit Singh, to submit his resignation letter. After meeting the Governor for about 15 minutes, he left Raj Bhawan. He encountered journalists outside and addressed them, saying:

> I express my heartfelt gratitude to the esteemed Prime Minister Shri Narendra Bhai Modi ji, Hon'ble Home Minister Amit Shah ji, party president Nadda ji, and Defence Minister Rajnath Singh ji, and all well-wishers. We were entrusted with a responsibility by our top leadership, and we have tried to fulfil that. Now the people of the state have given a new mandate by putting the stamp of consent on our public welfare schemes and development work, for which I will always be grateful to all the sacred people of the state. Furthermore, we are committed, in the public interest, to shoulder whatever responsibility our party high command assigns, taking note of all activities carried out during our short tenure and their results.

This statement had many interpretations.

Was Dhami not seeing himself as the Chief Minister?

Had the defeat of Pushkar Singh Dhami put a question mark on his political career?

Would the BJP high command bet on Dhami?

Would Dhami become the next Shri Prem Kumar Dhumal of Uttarakhand?

Amidst this curious situation, statements from eminent Uttarakhand politicians began to steer the political landscape towards a peculiar path. Within BJP's internal dynamics, discussions about the provincial presidency had intensified. While one section saw Dhami as their potential state chief, the tone of the other section appeared to have shifted in some other direction. Referring to the Vayu Purana and the historical significance of nine Nagavanshi kings and the city's medieval Chand kings, Kailash Chandra Gahtodi, MLA from Champawat, expressed a fervent desire on behalf of the people. He was convinced in body and mind and humbly requested the BJP high command to give Dhami the opportunity to serve as the CM again.

Brij Bhushan Gairola, who registered a sensational win in the Congress stronghold, the Doiwala constituency, by defeating his rival Gaurav Chaudhary 'Ginni' by a big margin of 29,021 votes, was in favour of former MLA Trivendra Singh Rawat from the same constituency. Now the political cauldron in the state began to boil. Even the snow of the Himalayas appeared to wilt due to the rising political heat. Suddenly Trivendra Singh Rawat, former CM of the state, decided to fan the heat down and addressed reporters. He cleared the air and said that had he had to become the

CM of the state again, he wouldn't have declined to contest the election. 'So I nurture no ambition or intention to take advantage of the favourable flow of the situation. I will accept all the responsibilities entrusted to me by fate, the creator and the party high command,' he said emphatically.

On another note, in 2009, a new face had emerged as the CM of Uttarakhand, marching past several political veterans. Dr Ramesh Pokhriyal Nishank was that CM and he later became an influential figure in central politics. Now when he was questioned about the chief-ministerial race, he carefully weighed the matter and stated, 'I don't personally engage in any race. My role, as an ordinary party worker, is to deliver results in whichever position and wherever the party places me. I've consistently provided results to my party through disciplined work.' This statement is enough to showcase his political vision. While on the one hand, he described himself as detached from the race, on the other, he was ready to undertake any significant responsibility entrusted to him by the party. Naturally, this statement reinforced the saying that it was better to drink milk than to break the pot, which meant one must find a way without causing harm.

To quell the speculations of conspiracies and political manoeuvres from different camps in the political sphere, BJP state in-charge Dushyant Gautam first congratulated and wished everyone for their victories. Then he assured all claimants and pleaded that they must wait for the decision of the parliamentary board of BJP. 'This is a momentous occasion to celebrate our historic victory. Thus, each one of us needs to exercise patience. Courage and patience have to be two crucial tools for any rational person. With their use, one can make impossible possible, and can also turn possible into impossible,' he said. While expressing joy over BJP creating history by dispelling myths, he also sympathized with Dhami over his election loss.

In devbhoomi Uttarakhand, where victory had been mixed with a tinge of defeat, the people of Uttar Pradesh, residing in the Ganga-Yamuna interfluves, were celebrating a historic victory under the saffron lotus banner with the able stewardship of esteemed saint of Hindutva politics, Mahant Yogi Adityanath ji Maharaj. Kanhaiya Mittal's famous bhajan was being recited in unison by the activists and Yogi followers all around, echoing like the verses from the Vedas.

Jo Ram ko laye hain,
hum unko laenge.
UP mein phir se hum,
bhagava laharaenge.

This time, the people of Uttar Pradesh will once again elect those who contributed to the construction of the Ram Temple in Ayodhya.

Address by Prime Minister Shri Narendra Modi

Hon'ble Prime Minister Shri Narendra Modi appeared on screens all over India with his statement about the election results:

> As we are marking the 75th year of Independence, the significance of these election results in the myriad colours of spring increases even more for all of us. Because we are going to enter the Amrit Kaal this year, these election results will write the growth story of the next two and a half decades. Despite adverse conditions, the way you

have strengthened us by turning the adverse winds in our favour, I firmly believe that in the coming time, we will be able to establish India as a superpower on the world stage. For the first time in the history of independent India, these elections were held at a time when the entire human race was fighting a terrible epidemic all over the world. To make the matter worse, at the same time, the Ukraine–Russia crisis affected the supply chain to a great extent. In such a transitory period, the work that India has done on the world stage is being praised by the whole world community today. However, even in such a time, whenever a corrupt person is arrested, some opposition parties start painting him with the colours of religion, state and caste. Even if the court's decision comes against the mafia, these people link it with religion and caste. In such a situation, I urge people of India who honestly believe in all those sects, castes and creeds that should try to remove such corrupt mafia and people's culprits from society, so that every individual, society and sect can be saved and its welfare can be ensured.'

The Next Day: 12 March 2022

The Uttarakhand unit of the BJP eagerly awaited PM Narendra Modi to return to his 7, Lok Kalyan Marg, residence in New Delhi after his address at a public meeting for the Khel Mahakumbh in Gujarat. Since he was heading the executive of the parliamentary democratic system in the country and was also taking care of the country's internal security as the *pradhan sevak*, or supreme servant, of India, not even a leaf moved in the BJP without his consultation or go-ahead. Hence, the entire BJP family anticipated the prime minister's arrival at his residence in Delhi soon, so that he could initiate the process of selecting the leader of the majority party in Uttarakhand as per his guidance.

Meanwhile, Union Minister Ajay Bhatt had held a meeting with the BJP's general secretary B.L. Santosh. He described the meeting as a courtesy call and expressed his wish to appoint observers for the hill state of Uttarakhand. When asked about the BJP's victory and Dhami's defeat, Ajay Bhatt responded, 'We all face challenges. We fought vigorously under the efficient leadership of the young Chief Minister Dhami ji. However, there might have been some shortcomings and drawbacks. Elections are such that both victory and defeat are usual outcomes. In a wrestling match, one wrestler wins while the other loses. Competent leaders may lose elections, but they remain leaders. Therefore, Dhami ji is our leader, and if he gets another chance, we have no objection to that, in my opinion.'

New Delhi, the capital of India and also occasionally the epicentre of the country's political turmoil, was also abuzz with the post-meeting activities. Different leaders in white clothes were meeting with various individuals. They all had their personal agendas and wished to push their political ambitions. They were trying every trick in their armour. The traffic between Delhi and Dehradun was on the rise. Upon the arrival of Ajay Bhatt, Satpal Maharaj, Madan Kaushik and other party veterans in Delhi, it was discovered that Rekha Arya was already present there. Each one was staking a claim and endeavouring to solidify their influence over the MLAs and top leadership.

Satpal Maharaj was actively reaching out to the central leadership, while Madan Kaushik was striving to garner support from the MLAs. Rekha Arya was leveraging her position within the Mahila Morcha. Surrounded by their supporters, each contender was confident in their claim to being the strongest candidate and the future CM. An adage advises against underestimating opponents and refraining from disclosing strategies to everyone. Whether facing a formidable opponent or a weaker adversary, a strategic approach remains the key is such situations. Therefore, this was the reason why prudent claimants did not consider it appropriate to take any risk by publicly stating their claim.

When a season shifts, the nature emits signs that we can see from the earth to the sky. The entire landscape changes colour, and it is visible in the songs and dances of birds and animals. In political realm, however, it is often ominous of a political storm. And what we were witnessing now was actually a time of whirlwind and counter-whirlwind, and the resultant dilemmas for the leadership.

And so it was seen that even the public opinion was swaying just as the branches of a tree move with the whip of the wind. The same public that had returned to their daily routines after offering their votes to their beloved candidates, the same people who had set out on pilgrimages to temples and mazars, or who had left for foreign tours, the same people now had a renewed zeal. The political fervour of the people has rekindled. Devbhoomi's atmosphere had again become political. With eyes transfixed on newspapers and TV screens, with questions flooding their minds with myriad possible answers, everyone was eager to see the name of the person who would become the CM of Uttarakhand.

As the suitable answer refused to make itself prominent, their curiosity began to slip away like sand and turn into dust. However, if one's faith in one's actions is unwavering, even dust can rise to become a mountain. With this belief

and hope, there was only one question on every lip:

Who would be Uttarakhand's CM?

People wondered who would stand at the forefront?

Upon their return from Saurashtra, who would the country's leadership and their advisors endorse?

On the one hand, strong senior leaders like Dr Nishank, Satpal Maharaj, Vijay Bahuguna, Dhan Singh Rawat, Madan Kaushik, Trivendra Singh Rawat, Anil Baluni and Vishan Chufal were striving to enhance their chances. On the other, proponents of women empowerment had also taken the initial step towards their ultimate goal and heralded their arrival. As the BJP's Mahila Morcha echoed the name of a female chief minister, influential leaders like Ritu Khanduri, Rekha Arya and Rekha Verma had come forward with assertions.

There were so many contenders for the post of CM in this relatively small state—a situation that surprised everyone. What was even more surprising and indeed heartening was that despite being a remote mountainous region, such political awakening signified a positive sign for democracy. This time, the BJP was determined not to repeat the mistake of 2017 at any cost. Back then, Trivendra Singh Rawat had been appointed as the CM for a five-year term, but three CMs had to be changed midterm. It not only made them the target of the Opposition, it even created a sense of anti-incumbency against the BJP government. Recalling this, BJP spokesperson Shadab Shams, mentioned that the Congress made N.D. Tiwari the CM of Uttar Pradesh three times, yet he couldn't complete his term even once. 'This highlights how most crucial decisions in politics are taken by the high command, as they sometimes read the true nature of the ground situation more clearly than individual representatives. So the BJP workers trust their leadership and they believe that whatever their senior leadership will decide, it will be the best for them,' Shams said with the confidence of a devoted worker.

On the other hand, Dhami's situation resembled that of a driver who safely drove all passengers home but found himself ensnared in the complexities of political routes, erasing the footprints of his initial successful journey. Dhami contemplated relinquishing the rewards of his work and struggles, distancing himself from political intrigues and surrendering to the will of a higher power. However, five MLAs publicly announced their voluntary resignation from their assembly seats in support of Dhami. They declared Dhami as the most suitable person for the multi-layered development of the state. They asserted that it would be in the public's interest for Dhami to lead them.

Atmaartham jeevlokesmin ko na jeevati manavah,
Param paropkarartham yo jiwati sa jiwati
Paropakarasunyasya dhik manushyasya jivitam,
Jivantu pasavo yesam charmapyupkarishyati.

These two common Sanskrit aphorisms imply: who, in this world, doesn't live solely for oneself? It is the one who lives for charity who embodies truth. And that a human life devoid of charity is considered condemned, contrasting with animals who are blessed even after death as their skin is used for various purposes.

This exceptional declaration of sacrifice and dedication, akin to the vibrant colours of *gulaal*, illuminated Dhami's illustrious nature. Defying disappointment, forsaking deceit and rivalry, everyone embraced the festival of colours, showcasing an exemplary spirit of brotherhood. Common folk greeted each other warmly. The elite visited their kin and relished traditional Holi sweetmeats such as *gujiya*. While children eagerly anticipated water-gun battles, elders advised them to stick to dry gulaal. Thus, everyone was brimming with enthusiasm during the sacred festival of Holi, not only in devbhoomi Uttarakhand but throughout the country.

The sun of politics rose once more in a tranquil environment from behind the clouds. The train of speculation resumed its journey along the political tracks, and politicians once again began delving into the bottomless sea of politics. They started preparing anew to row the boat of destiny with the roar of identity by neglecting the theory of determinism expounded by the ancient philosopher Ajita Kesakambali.

One Week Later: 19 March 2022

On 19 March, the seven mythical horses tied to the chariot were eagerly waiting for the divine sun to climb the horizon. However, oblivious to the sun, former CM Trivendra Singh Rawat had been present in Delhi since dawn. He had met B.L. Santosh and party president J.P. Nadda; soon, the state president, Madan Kaushik, also reached Delhi in the afternoon. Unaware and away from these meetings, Dhami was still in Dehradun. The sun's rays were radiating westwards at a rapid pace from the peaks of trees on mountain peaks in sunset during that beautiful moment in time called *godhuli bela*. These rays, though radiant, were taking away the hope of Dhami. He was fighting a duel between hope and despair when suddenly the his mobile phone buzzed from the table behind him. With this sudden ring, the mobile vibrated like a spinning top. The sound stirred Dhami from his thoughts, creating a sensation in his body like the waves of an earthquake. As the two-to-three-minute conversation came to an end, the depression washed away and Dhami's face shone with happiness. He immediately started making preparations.

At his home, his mother Bishna Devi and wife Geeta Dhami had spent the whole day envisioning a hopeful future for him. As the day progressed, Bishna Devi remained absorbed in prayers, discussing her son's promising prospects with God in the bhajan room. Unaware of her son's arrival at the door, her attention was entirely devoted to her prayers. Meanwhile, the arrival of Dhami brought a glow in the eyes of his children and wife, who eagerly welcomed him. Noticing her son's presence, Bishna Devi gestured to him to join her, while Geeta, observing her husband's visible concern, waited impatiently. Responding to his wife's quiet worry with a compassionate smile, Dhami, aware of the limited time he had, went to his mother to share the news of the invitation he had received to travel to Delhi. He sought her blessings before leaving. In response, Bishna Devi took a marigold flower from the pooja *thaali*, placing it behind her son's ear, and conveyed, 'Your fate will unfold as destined. What is written will come to pass, and I firmly believe that what fate has in store is what everyone eagerly awaits!'

Moved by his mother's words, Dhami expressed, 'Mother, you once mentioned that fate implies compulsion and incompetence, but I don't feel unsupported or incapable! I've faced life's struggles and want to achieve something. One failure doesn't define my entire life. So I must leave now. Please bless me.'

In response, Bishna Devi conveyed earnestly: 'Hope and faith are powerful weapons. Give it time, and the Supreme Father, God, will soon ease your overwhelming sorrow.'

At eight o'clock at night, Dhami, burdened with anticipatory questions, departed for Delhi on a chartered plane. The phone call that he had received could mark a pivotal moment in Uttarakhand politics. His being abruptly summoned to Delhi underscored his significance in Uttarakhand politics, yet it also prompted some questions:

Was Dhami called to pacify a simmering situation?

Was there a plan to integrate him into central politics?

Or would he be entrusted with the historic responsibility of Uttarakhand once again?

Upon Dhami's arrival in Delhi and his entry into Uttarakhand Sadan, he discovered that Trivendra Singh Rawat and Madan Kaushik were already there. It seemed the party high command was careful this time not to repeat past mistakes. There were speculations that not only the seat of the CM but also the entire cabinet could have been decided in one go. So, even those politicians who hadn't reached Delhi yet began to move towards the national capital. By the time everyone gathered in Delhi, the Uttarakhand BJP had divided into two factions: one in support of Dhami and the other against him. When his supporters advocated for his case, his opponents argued that when Mamata Banerjee had become CM despite her election defeat in West Bengal, the BJP had termed that against democratic principles. They also rued over the fact that in 2017 when, under the leadership of Ajay Bhatt, they had won 57 seats in the state, why had they not been given a chance? Such intra-party ramblings continued. Consequently, an emergency meeting was convened at Home Minister Amit Shah's residence to address and resolve these contradictions.

The party ensured that those leaders who were prone

to revolt, or may cause a split, must be specifically invited to this meeting. Hence, veteran leaders like Satpal Maharaj, B.L. Santosh, Pushkar Dhami, Madan Kaushik, Trivendra Singh Rawat, along with party chief J.P. Nadda, attended the meeting. After this meeting was over, another urgent meeting occurred at Dr Nishank's place. However, in an unexpected twist, Satpal Maharaj suddenly left from there, with his resentment evident. His abrupt departure hinted at growing political unrest.

Meanwhile, Defence Minister Rajnath Singh and Minister of State for External Affairs and Culture Meenakshi Lekhi were present in Dehradun as election observers of devbhoomi Uttarakhand. In their presence, a crucial decision was made that the following morning, all the MLAs would take the oath under pro-tem Speaker Vanshidhar Bhagat. At approximately 5 p.m., a legislature party meeting was convened, attended by Rajnath Singh, Meenakshi Lekhi and all the newly-elected BJP MLAs.

Addressing the gathering, Rajnath Singh stated, 'As the largest democratic party in the country, after thorough consultations with all the MLAs, MPs and senior leadership, it has been observed that frequent leadership changes disappoint the people. For the first time in Uttarakhand's history, our government has secured a significant majority due to its resolute governance approach. Hence, Pushkar Singh Dhami has once again been entrusted with the opportunity to lead the state! Pushkar Singh Dhami has been declared as the Chief Minister of Uttarakhand and the leader of the legislative party.'

The news that the press corps had been eagerly searching for for the past dozen days, scouring source after source, was broken so surprisingly. It was soon broadcast across all news channels as breaking news. As soon as the news reached the broadcasting stations, the party high command reaffirmed Pushkar Singh Dhami's name as the next CM of Uttarakhand. This declaration set the hope and aspiration vibrating in the hearts of the people. Elderly hands rose in blessing, while the youth enthusiastically waved their hands in the air with exuberance and joy.

There was an eruption of jubilation! **A roar kicked off:**

Pushkar Singh Dhami, Zindabad! Sabki Hami, Pushkar Dhami!

Long live Pushkar Singh Dhami! Everyone assents to Pushkar Singh Dhami as the chief minister!

2

OATH: A RESOLVE FOR PUBLIC WELFARE

I will bear true faith and allegiance to the Constitution of India as by law established, that I will uphold the sovereignty and integrity of India!

Workers began preparing for the oath-taking ceremony scheduled on 23 March, Wednesday, marking the sixth day of Krishna Paksha of Chaitra month as per the Vedic calendar. However, an issue emerged concerning the ceremony's venue, keeping in mind the rules set out by the Third Schedule of the Constitution for the oath of office and the oath of secrecy.

Due to the expected crowd, the Parade Ground of Dehradun was chosen as the most suitable place. Consequently, the Public Works Department (PWD) and the Dehradun Municipal Corporation began preparations accordingly. Contractors engaged with the PWD diligently constructed the stage. Many officers camped at Parade Ground to oversee the preparations. In order to ensure a grand ceremony, 15 teams were formed, each entrusted with different crucial responsibilities. A team from the municipal corporation was dedicated to maintaining cleanliness inside and around the venue until the program concluded, realizing Gandhi ji's dreams through Modi ji's Swachh Bharat campaign. Slowly, the entire parade ground was adorned with festive arrangements. It was no less than an achievement and was possible only because of persistent enthusiasm and commitment of both the public and the administration that, despite being informed on a short notice at around 5 p.m. on a Monday, workforce was employed at war footing and a splendid stage for an extraordinary oath-taking of a CM was set up.

The administration was very alert about cleanliness, as Uttarakhand is a hilly town and heavy tourist traffic ascends to this devbhoomi. So, there couldn't have been any room for littering. Chief Town Health Officer Avinash Khanna mentioned that the responsibility of maintaining cleanliness inside and outside Parade Ground had been assigned to two cleaning inspectors, three supervisors, and 20 corporation employees. District Magistrate R. Rajesh Kumar stated that the district administration had initiated all necessary preparations for the final phase of the oath-taking ceremony. Additionally, BJP organization officials were informed about arrangements being made to accommodate 25,000 guests. The program was thus poised to be a grand and all-encompassing affair.

Security measures had been notably heightened. A dedicated security setup had been established to ensure stringent security for PM Narendra Modi, who was the chief guest at the event. The Special Protection Group (SPG) had assumed complete control of the security arrangements. Once the stage was set, strict directives had been issued to maintain a zero zone specifically for the PM.

As per the schedule, PM Modi was set to arrive at Parade Ground via air transport. Consequently, the entire area was being transformed into a cantonment. The traffic to and from the venue had been diverted to other routes. Given the PM's participation, a vigilant security system was in place to monitor the ground closely.

The final event saw the presence of PM Narendra Modi; BJP National President, J.P. Nadda; Home Minister Amit Shah; Defence Minister Rajnath Singh; Union Minister Pralhad Joshi; along with Himachal Pradesh CM Jai Ram Thakur and Haryana CM Manohar Lal Khattar. Plus, Uttar Pradesh CM Yogi Adityanath and other senior BJP leaders had also been invited. Following the *Sabka Saath, Sabka Vikas* principle, efforts had been made to involve people from all sections of the society. The event emphasized the ideology of Hindutva by including saints and *sanyasis*. On the morning of 23 March, Dhami visited Raj Bhawan to meet Governor (Uttarakhand) Sukhbir Singh Sandhu. His entry, accompanied by the heavy police presence, drew the attention of MLAs, workers and reporters. After the meeting, Dhami humbly acknowledged his imminent appointment as the twelfth CM of Uttarakhand as a reflection of this transformative phase and expressed that the day's events aligned with the transformative leadership of PM Narendra Modi.

With all guests in the state and preparations in place, Dehradun's Parade Ground was now set for Dhami's swearing-in ceremony. Thousands eagerly awaited the 'Living Heat of Himalaya' Dhami and the top leadership to grace the venue. The ambience was reverberating with drum beats. Suddenly, a convoy of vehicles arrived, acknowledging the people's greetings. All BJP leaders then took their seats on the stage, and with the Governor's permission, the oath-taking program commenced.

Before taking the oath, Pushkar Singh Dhami reaffirmed his promises to the public, pledging to fulfil them as the CM. He highlighted the BJP's pre-election commitments, including rolling out the Uniform Civil Code (UCC). He assured the formation of a special committee comprising legal experts, seniors and intellectuals to draft this law. The UCC, he said, would apply equally to every citizen in Uttarakhand, regardless of their religion or caste. It would ensure uniform laws in marriage, divorce and property rights for all.

Dhami arrived with his family at Parade Ground in Dehradun for the oath-taking ceremony. Around 2.30 p.m., thousands of supporters and esteemed personalities witnessed the oath-taking process as per the Governor's guidelines. He solemnly took the oath, reading the text enshrined in the *Constitution of India*, Schedule 3:

Oath of Office
I, Pushkar Singh Dhami, do swear in the name of God that I will bear true faith and allegiance to the Constitution of India as by law established. I will uphold the sovereignty and integrity of India, and conscientiously discharge my duties as a Minister for the State. I will ensure justice to all by the Constitution and the law, without fear or favour, affection or ill-will.

Oath of Secrecy
I, Pushkar Singh Dhami, do swear in the name of God that I will not, directly or indirectly, communicate or reveal to any person any matter that comes under my consideration or becomes known to me as a Minister for the State of Uttarakhand, except as may be necessary for the proper discharge of my duties as such a Minister.

3

BACKGROUND: LAYING THE FOUNDATION STONE

Aryavarta means the home of oldest and greatest civilizations that assimilated even unfamiliar cultures and kept its unique acculturation unscathed.

Let's talk about this nations myriad, mesmerizing features. Like the glistening silver Himalayas, the sun-kissed coastal plains of Kerala, the fertile Mahanadi basin in the east, the Brahmaputra region in the northeast, or the vast desert terrain in the west—each representing our diverse subcontinent.

But now, let's move away from the natural beauty of Aryavarta Bharatkhanda towards a quasi-rectangular piece of it. Nestled between the Himalayas and the Ganga, it holds mythological significance, a glorious history; it has been a region blessed with the sacred presence of sages and saints. In this godly hilly area, every being emits love, affection, faith and honesty. A deep sense of humanity flows along with the blood of continuous struggle in the veins of people of these hills.

Over time, this sacred land has witnessed many changes, which were effected by geological forces, while sometimes, glaciers changed the landscape—resulting in formations of hills, plateaus, ravines, terrains and lakes like Nainital, known as Rishi Sarovar in the Manas Khand of the *Skanda Purana*. Along the renowned Maa Nanda Rajjat Yatra route, you'll find the mysterious pool of Roopkund in Jeonragali Valley, Chamoli, and Sahastradhara in Doon Valley. Gomukh is the origin of Mother Ganga, while rivers like Alaknanda-Mandakini are such lively rivers as if they are young, dancing and joyful women. Beyond these aquatic landscapes, vast green pastures like the cattle-breeding bugyal attract tourists. Prominent among them are Bedni, Dayara and Dudhatoli, while Nandanvan beautifies Tapovan and the valley of flowers in Chamoli fascinates with its own charm.

Then, if you look upwards at the natural beauty, the rugged plains, the lofty Nanda Devi, Trishul, Panchachuli, and Kedarnath hills would be seen draped in lush greenery. Among them, you will come to picturesque places like Panchprayag, Panchkedar, and Panchbadri and Gangotri-Yamunotri. You will possibly encounter musk deers, Brahma Kamal and Buransh, which are official symbols of the state of Uttarakhand and have been attracting both local and global tourists who come to see them from close quarters in their natural habitats.

Besides nature's wonders, the area's craftsmanship, stone art and murals embody the essence of human civilization. Despite the global reach of art, this region has retained its vibrant cultural heritage. As a tourist destination, one cannot overlook the allure of Jim Corbett National Park, Nainital, Dhikala, Rajaji, Gangotri, Nandur, Vinsar, Askot and Patal Bhubaneswar. Local folk dances and songs, such as Chhaufula, Chholiya, Harul, Chapeli and Sherda, along with the humorous satire of Ramman (a UNESCO intangible cultural heritage), captivate visitors. The local sweet delight, Ghugutia, made of jaggery, sugar, pure ghee and flour, adds warmth to snowy nights in the months of Paush and Magha (January-February).

Traditional celebrations like Harela pay tribute to the natural beauty and greenery of the region, while festivals and fairs like Khatdwa and Phooldei are organized to keep the younger generation rooted to and informed about their original culture and traditions.

Similarly, Uttarani in Bageshwar connects modern generations with Bagnath Dham, while Jauljibi links them to India-Nepal border, and Gochar, Purnagiri, Somnath and Devidhura knit them into one cultural milieu. Then there is the annual Kailash Mansarovar Yatra from June to September and the Nanda Rajjat Yatra from Chamoli to Hemkund (termed the Mahakumbh of Devbhoomi). In this yatra, a special sight is that of a four-horned *chausinghakhaddu* sheep, which is believed to be born once in 12 years and leads the troupe of Mata Bhagwati. Another highlight is Hiljatra from the Kumaon Pithoragarh sub-region, in which the tableau of cultural affluence of this hilly state is displayed.

Nature has showered its bounties upon the state in abundance. Spirituality pervades its every rim. Its people carry its reputation in their character. This *Bhoomi*, this land is drenched with religion and purity. It has earned its epithet—Devbhoomi—because of these unique features. It was actually the most ancient of the Vedas, the Rigveda, that called it 'Devbhoomi'. Other sacred texts have also recognized its special place in Indian geography. It occupies a special place in epics like *Ramayana* and *Mahabharata*. In the 'Aitareya Brahmana', it's referred to as Uttar Kuru, while ancient scriptures like *Brahma Purana* have called it Kedarkhand (Kumaon) and Manaskhand (Garhwal). The *Skanda Purana* calls the Himalayas as Himwant.

If we peep into the history of the region through the prism of the present, the Kuninda dynasty was the first politically integrated dynasty in Devbhoomi. Inscriptions and coins of Emperor Ashoka kept in Kalsi and Dehradun provide information about that era. Literary works like Ved Vyas's *Mahabharata,* Panini's *Ashtadhyayi,* Ptolemy's *Geography* and Shiv Prasad Dabral Charan's writings such as the multi-volume *Uttarakhand ka Itihaas* furnish glimpses into the society of that period. Subahu was the most prominent ruler of this dynasty who initially ruled independently but later allied with the Pandavas during the war of Mahabharata. Kalkut was the capital of his empire. It is believed that the third phase of this dynasty's rule witnessed the maximum expansion of this empire, as it was during this period that the dynasty pursued the policy of expansion.

Amoghbhuti was another powerful ruler of this period. His influence and might was on the rise and he overran the plains of Yamuna and drove the Yavanas (Greeks) from there. But his successors turned out to be weak, and their weaknesses were exploited by the Shaka and Kushan rulers. Ultimately, the region fell to the expansion of famous ancient king Harshavardhan and came under his control. This was the time when the entire North India had come under the centralized control of Harshavardhan. Xuanzang, the seventh century Chinese Buddhist monk, scholar and traveller, writes about this period, saying that the Pauravas succeeded the Kulind dynasty and their ruler Vishnuvarman first showed inclination towards suzerainty under Harshavardhan. Pauravas were known for their strong army consisting of horses, elephants and an able infantry. King Basant Dev of

Katyuri dynasty is credited with conquering the Pauravas. The rulers of this dynasty are still known for their welfare policies and support for Brahmins. The Katyuri kings' successors expanded their empire and reigned for about two and a half centuries. They left a legacy similar to that of Emperor Ashoka's successors.

Veerdev Sahib, the final ruler of this dynasty, imposed harsh and absolute taxation on the people. It's proverbially said that an ant acquires wings as it nears its demise—*Ujdnya Mati Kirmul Pakh*. So, one of his attendants deceitfully assassinated him, akin to the death of Darius II. After his demise, the empire fragmented into smaller segments. Somchand, an illustrious ruler of the Chand dynasty, capitalized on this fragmentation and the Chand dynasty reigned over the remaining Katyuris in the Kumaon region from the eleventh to the eighteenth century. Originally from Jhusi near present-day Prayagraj, Somchand was deeply connected to Devbhoomi and its spiritual essence. He embarked on a religious journey to this region after hearing its glorious tales. During his visit, regional rulers honoured him, and a Katyuri ruler even accepted him as his son-in-law, granting him 15-20 bighas of land near present-day Champawat. The famous Rajbunga Fort is believed to be attributed to him.

Later, his successor Garur Gyan Chand attempted to solidify the dynasty's political power. However, Nasir-ud-Din Mahmud Shah Tughlaq from the Delhi Sultanate was ambitious to claim the area of the present Tarai Bhabar (Khatima), which was then under the control of the Rohilla rulers.

Fortunately, the Tughlaq Sultanate and the Rohilla's were at daggers drawn. Thus, the Sultan listened to the proposal of

Gyan Chand attentively and honoured him with the title of 'Garur/Garuda'. Later, we come across a name Bharati Chand who rose to become a prominent figure in the Chand dynasty. He defended the dynasty from a 12-year struggle against the Dotiyas. Bhishm Chand, another one of the rulers who followed, earned considerable renown for providing moral protection to a fugitive army man, Khawas Khan of the Sur dynasty. He didn't have any heir of his own, so he adopted Balo Kalyan Chand as his son. Upon his father's demise, Balo Kalyan Chand shifted the capital from Champawat to Khagmara, establishing the present-day city of Almora.

The growing dominance of the Chand dynasty caught the attention of the Mughal emperor Akbar, who launched a campaign to control the region. Considering his circumstances and farsightedness, the Chand ruler decided to safeguard his empire by submitting to the Mughal court. This decision was largely influenced by Rudra Chand's commander, Purush Pant, a fact documented in *Jahangirnama*. Shah Jahan, impressed by the bravery and determination of the Chands, conferred the title of Bahadur upon a ruler named Baz. Gyan Chand was the final ruler of this dynasty.

Around the same time, the '*Zinda Pir* (Living Saint)' Aurangzeb compelled Fateh Shah, the ruler of the Panwar dynasty, to vacate Srinagar. Aurangzeb was so moved by the honesty and simplicity of the hill rulers and locals that he donated the entire accumulated wealth and the entire Srinagar to a Brahmin as a gesture of respect and goodwill. Subsequently, Chanakya Harsh Dev Oli of Kumaon invited Lalit Shah, ruler of the Panwar dynasty, to attack Almora. Lalit Shah triumphed over the local ruler Mohan Chand and installed his son Pradyumna Shah on the throne as Pradyumna Chand. Lalit Shah then assumed governance of Srinagar and appointed Harsh Dev Joshi as the ruler of Almora. However, in 1788, Mohan Chand's assassination led Mahendra Chand to plot revenge, forcing Harsh Dev Joshi to flee to Srinagar for refuge.

The Chand dynasty wasn't autocratic and oppressive; it governed according to popular plans for public welfare, maintaining friendly, diplomatic and political relations with the Mughals. Over time, the dominance of the Gorkhas, also known as Nepalis, grew in the region due to their robust military administration. Overawed by their military supremacy, the Panwar rulers too bowed down before them. But caught in a continued phase of wars, Gurkhas couldn't maintain control on their administration and their grip loosened. As a result, Panwar ruler Pradyumna Shah (aka Chand) handed over the governance of Almora to Harsh Dev Joshi and occupied the throne of Srinagar himself. The Gurkhas however didn't dwindle completely, they challenged the Panwars. Pradyumna Shah's successor, Sudarshan Shah, had to wage incessant wars with them. Drained of resources, and as a new strategy, he even sought British assistance to get the better of Gurkhas. Unfortunately, Pradyumna Shah faced financial constraints and reorganized his army by selling his jewellery in Saharanpur, Uttar Pradesh. Tragically, his struggle ended with his martyrdom in 1804 during a decisive battle with the Gurkhas at Khurbura or Khudbuda Maidan in Dehradun.

Cashing in situations for maximum benefit is the civilizational trait of human beings. So, in order to assert more pressure, the Gurkha ruler imprisoned Pradyumna Shah's son Kunwar Pritam Shah and sent him to Kathmandu. His second son, Sudarshan Shah, turned to meditation and prayers at the city of Ganga, Haridwar, for the freedom of his brother and success in his struggle against Gurkhas. He also approached the *firangis* and petitioned them for the liberation of his land. His plea was accepted by Lord Hastings, leading to a military detachment sent against the Gurkhas in 1814.

Consequently, the crucial Treaty of Sangoli was signed in 1815 between Colonel Gardner and Bamshah. This treaty liberated Garhwal and Kumaon from Gorkha rule, placing them under British occupation permanently; although later, it was publicly known as the British conspiracy to colonize the hilly region. Historical documents show that the Gurkhas governed Kumaon for 25 years and Garhwal for 10.5 years. As the region grappled with regional upheavals, the nationwide Indian Rebellion of 1857 erupted. Initially, its impact was limited in the Kumaon-Garhwal area because the firangi rule seemed reformist compared to the unjust Gorkha regime. However, the wave of this revolution reached Vishung Lohaghat in Champawat district, where Kalu Singh Mehra became the first Uttarakhandi freedom fighter, leading a secret revolutionary organization called Krantiveer. The movement gained momentum when over a thousand revolutionaries took control of Haldwani overnight. Subsequently, various organizations in the region worked for social, religious and economic interests, fostering a sense of national pride and patriotism among the locals.

During this period, a wave of political awareness swept through the region, marked by the emergence of several newspapers and magazines. Pandit Govind Ballabh Pant, a political thinker, established the Happy Club in 1903, followed by the foundation of the Almora Congress in 1912. Inspired by Bal Gangadhar Tilak and Annie Besant, Victor Mohan Joshi, Badri Datt Pandey, Chiranjilal and some local individuals initiated the HR Club in 1916, igniting a colourful wave of patriotism among the populace. Enlightened leaders actively championed social, political, economic and educational reforms, with figures like Hargovind Pant, Govind Ballabh Pant, and Badri Datt Pandey playing pivotal roles in these endeavours. Simultaneously, resistance grew against the oppressive policies of the colonial rulers. The region became rife with revolutionary fervour against laws such as forced labour, the forest and land settlement system, and the Rowlatt Act. Regional revolutionaries actively participated in national movements, exemplified by figures like Anusuya Prasad Bahuguna and Barrister Mukundi Lal, who were involved in the protest against the Rowlatt Act of 1919.

The Non-cooperation Movement of 1920 received robust support from the local populace. They contributed to igniting the fire of this movement just as ghee and camphor contributes to fanning the fire. Angered by oppressive laws, around 40,000 freedom fighters, led by Badri Datt Pandey, Hargovind Pant and Chiranjilal, ceremonially buried all the English registers related to the Coolie-Begar system into the Saryu River of Bageshwar. In a historic visit between June and July 1929, Mahatma Gandhi and Pandit Jawaharlal Nehru were so moved by the spirit of the local people that they visited Kumaon. They held public meetings and instilled an unwavering sense of patriotism. During his 12-day stay in Kausani, Gandhi ji composed a commentary on the Gita called *Anasaktiyoga* and christened this holy region as the 'Switzerland of India'.

On 26 January 1930, the tricolour was hoisted in various locations across Uttarakhand (except Tehri state) during the Salt Satyagraha. It was a declaration of defiance against the British authority. Among Gandhi ji's 78 Satyagrahis, three prominent figures from Uttarakhand were Jotram Kandpal,

Bhairav Dutt Joshi and Gorkha Veer Khadak Bahadur Singh. People of all ages and backgrounds, including children, farmers, youth and women expressed their dissent against misgovernance of the British Raj. Simultaneously, revolutionaries revolted in Dugadda, British Garhwal. Even today a hotel that was then established under the leadership of Pandit Dhani Ram Mishra stands as a reminder of this historic movement, and it has been recognized as a national heritage site.

In April 1930, soldiers of the 2/18 Garhwal Rifles, led by Veer Chandra Singh Garhwali, refused to fire upon unarmed Afghan freedom fighters. This later became known as the Peshawar incident. Motilal Nehru celebrated Garhwal Day in acknowledgement of this act. While the nation was ablaze with the fervour of the freedom movement, Uttarakhand also remained an equal participant in it, with a series of protests reflecting state's resolve to side with their fellow countrymen to attain *swaraj* (self-rule). Revengeful British forces resorted to indiscriminate firing in Sult, Almora, leading to the martyrdom of Kheemadev, Gangaram and other locals present at the meeting. Women were actively involved in these movements, including notable figures like Kunti Verma, Durgavati Pant, Janaki, Tulsi and Bishni Devi Shah. Gandhi even inspired his two foreign disciples, Sarla Behen (Catherine Mary Heilman) and Meera Behen (Madeleine Slade), who established training centres called Lakshmi Ashram, Kausani, and Pashulok Kendra, Rishikesh.

On 25 July 1944, Shri Dev Suman, a pioneer of the Tehri state movement, passed away after an 84-day hunger strike. Eventually, weary of the revolutionary activities of the Indian populace, the British government made the decision to withdraw from the country. Under Gandhi's leadership, the

Quit India Movement bore fruit. At midnight on 14 August 1947, the country was liberated from two and a half centuries of oppressive British rule, marking its independence. This historic milestone is beautifully encapsulated in the lines of 'Dhwaja Vandana' by national poet Ramdhari Singh 'Dinkar'.

Namo, namo, namo...

Namo svatantr bhaarat kee dhvaja, namo, namo!
Namo nagaadhiraaj-shring kee vihaarinee!
Namo anant saukhya-shakti-sheel-dhaarinee!
Pranay-prasaarinee, namo arisht-vaarinee!
Namo manushya kee shubheshana-prachaarinee!
Naveen surya kee naee prabha, namo, namo
Namo svatantr bhaarat kee dhvaja, namo, namo!

Taar-taar mein hain guntha dhvaje, tumhaara tyaag!
Dahak rahee hai aaj bhee, tum mein bali kee aag.
Sevak sainya kathor, ham chaalees karod
Kaun dekh sakata kubhaav se dhvaje, tumhaaree or
Karte tav jai gaan, veer hue balidaan,
Angaaron par chala tumhein le saara hindustaan!
Prataap kee vibha, krishaanuja, namo, namo!

This poem glorifies the Indian flag, symbolizing freedom, strength and sacrifice. It embodies the spirit of martyrs who gave their lives for the nation. The flag represents unity, honor and the unwavering commitment of the people to protect its dignity. It is not just a piece of cloth but the soul of the nation, reminding every citizen of their duty. The poem ignites patriotism, urging people to stand together in devotion, courage and national pride.

The Tehri princely state was still under the rule of the illustrious Manvendra Shah. However, amidst the widespread

Prajamandal movement, Manvendra Shah felt the tremors of public pressure; and bowing to such pressure, he signed the document of merger with the Indian Union in 1949. It was a tumultuous era marked by some unsettling revolutionary movements. Independent India faced its greatest challenge—to steer the nation toward progress, preserving its unity in diversity, integrity and sovereignty. Life gradually returned to normal.

Governments came and went, but the educational sector saw little improvement. By the 1970s, there arose a clamour for universities to foster higher education in the region. Consequently, Kumaon University in Nainital and Garhwal University (now Hemvati Nandan Bahuguna Garhwal University) in Srinagar were established in 1973. Later, the Uttaranchal Parishad in Nainital decided to organize a massive *padayatra* or march to Delhi's Boat Club, reigniting the fervour of '*Dilli chalo* (march to Delhi)' in Devbhoomi. This time, the demand was not merely for rights and duties but for the creation of a separate state within independent India. Yet, the initial call for this demand was raised in the national convention of the Indian National Congress held in Srinagar in 1938 under the chairmanship of Pandit Nehru.

4

EVOLUTION: ASCENSION OF THE CLAN

*Extreme sorrow is nothing but the pangs
of labour for the birth of joy.*

It was the early hours of 18 March 1974 when the sun's rays had just begun to paint the skies with a golden hue. This early morning arrival of the bright sunshine heralded the fast pace of tumult in faraway Pataliputra, Bihar. People had stepped forward, crossing the boundaries of fear, their voices ringing out in protest towards the halls of law and governance. As the day progressed, the gathering swelled in numbers, drawing in individuals eager to join this mass demonstration. Some of them had just wandered into the crowd without a clear purpose, while others had their purpose clear to them. Some from this mass of people were also careful not to endanger themselves and stayed aloof in precaution.

It was a red-letter day in the splendid history of Bihar as it would see the commencement of the legislative session in the state. Hon'ble Governor Ramchandra Dhondiba Bhandare was ready in his ceremonial suit to address a joint session of both the Houses. However, the Local Intelligence Unit (LIU) suddenly informed the authorities that thousands of protesting students from Patna intended to block the Governor's entry into the Vidhan Sabha building. They had also planned to stymie the Governor's address with the support of some Opposition parties. Amid widespread opposition and protests, some lawmakers, however, rushed to assemble in the building at the crack of dawn. The administration also mobilized a heavy police force to ensure Governor R.D. Bhandare's arrival at the Legislature building, yet the enraged students persisted, their chants of '*sampoorna kranti zindabad* (long live total revolution)' echoing loudly. Students prevailed.

Ancient doyen of statecraft and ace philosopher Chanakya has said in his magnum opus, *Arthashastra*: '**Actions of a king are not deemed well when they result only in amusement for him and his queen; a king's actions are righteous when they beget welfare of people.**' In the Mauryan Empire, the king treated his subjects like his own children. He believed that his power came from the people and considered himself merely a servant of the populace, and not a representative of a divine being. He respected religious and social traditions. Chanakya also advised that a king shouldn't keep people waiting at his door for long. Sadly, our current political scenario often reflects a sense of neglect. Chandragupta, Chanakya's exemplary disciple, always listened to his people's grievances, even when they criticized him. Loknayak Jayaprakash Narayan, a champion of socialism in India, also envisioned a similar kind of governance. But in today's circumstances, achieving such a regime seems painfully challenging.

Since nothing is impossible, it's possible that someday this vision of 'Ram Rajya', or good governance, will materialize and become a reality. Upon witnessing Jayaprakash Narayan's immense popularity, the restless student leaders decided to give him control of this movement. Ultimately, this movement spread so widely across the nation that it fundamentally altered the political climate of the whole of India, much like a blazing fire. Millions and millions of Loknayak supporters began chanting '*murdabad* (down with)' and denouncing the government for maladministration. The governor's convoy was approaching, and the restless students immediately began yelling slogans, their voices similar to a lion's roar. This shocked the drivers, who pulled the governor's convoy to a stop. When the police personnel saw this, they were totally flabbergasted and were feeling desperate, with their anger on the verge of eruption. Soon the students and the police came face-to-face. The police began to use lathi charge and attacked the students.

The police was mercilessly beating the unarmed students with sticks. The news of students being caned spread far and wide. When it reached the ears of Lalu Prasad Yadav, the president of the Patna University's student union at the time, he joined the Maidan-e-Movement for Sampoorna Kranti, along with his supporters, against the oppression by the autocratic system. Student agitators were brutally suppressed: many suffered grave injuries, from broken bones to bloodied wounds; many others were trampled under the feet of their fleeing comrades. Seeing such a scene enraged the revolutionaries even more, and they were now charged up against the government. The police continued trying to subdue them using water cannons, rubber bullets and tear gas shells.

Amidst the smoke of debates and discussions, the movement spread in the month of Chaitra, alongside the onset of spring, the chirping of birds and the growing attraction of bees and butterflies towards the beautiful flowers. However, it was observed during this time that some elements of anarchy also started sneaking into this movement. In many places, the movement was leaderless and unwanted incidents of looting, violence and arson were reported. Making the movement an alibi, such hooliganism was happening under the nose of the police. Meanwhile, the police ended up detaining real student leaders instead. As a result, the lives of hundreds of students were devoured by the movement.

As a proficient leader, Loknayak J.P. stood firm without giving up, refusing to let his supporters falter. He unexpectedly made a peculiar demand: no one associated with a political party should partake in the movement. Taking his words literally, his supporters—including students with past ties to agitating political groups—promptly resigned and backed J.P. Aligning with the circumstances and their resolute intentions, they unified under the Bihar Chhatra Sangharsh Samiti (a student union) banner. Together, they vocally demanded the immediate resignation of Chief Minister Abdul Ghafoor. Simultaneously, J.P. voiced opposition against the central government. Under Prime Minister Indira Gandhi's governance, the entire country had suffered due to various authoritarian decisions, including inflation and unemployment, prompting widespread discontent among the people.

Loknayak J.P. penned a letter to Indira Gandhi, highlighting her tyrannical policies and striving to alert her to the dire situation in the country. He also wrote similar letters to other central leaders, warning them about impending threat of dictatorship to democracy. Loknayak's democratic demands sparked a clash between streams supporting socialism and those in favour of capitalism. Till now, no one had dared to challenge Indira about her policies that were hidden under the garb of socialism. Loknayak had moved beyond that threshold. He raised numerous ground-breaking demands, including Lokpal and Lokayukta, and vehemently debated against corruption and black-marketing. He urged for the relentless continuation of the movement until all demands were met. This rattled Indira Gandhi's hold on power, causing chinks in her political standing.

Soon, the movement's flames spread rapidly in all directions. However, disregarding the protesters' demands, Indira Gandhi declared a national emergency under Article 356 of the Constitution, citing internal unrest. This period came to be known as the Emergency.

Meanwhile, in a small village in devbhoomi Uttarakhand stood Havildar Sher Singh Dhami, clad in khaki uniform, his heart immersed in the glory of the tricolour, vigilantly guarding the borders. Unperturbed by news of his family's welfare, Sher Singh was renowned among his fellow soldiers for executing his duties with unwavering integrity. After a day-long vigil, as Sher Singh headed towards his quarters at night, a fellow uniformed man warmly greeted him with '*Ram-Ram* Dhami ji'. Sher Singh reciprocated the greeting, shaking hands and adding, '*Ram-Ram, Jai Hind,* Subedar Sahib.' During dinner with his comrades, Sher Singh would passionately extol the beauty, honesty and mystical allure of Uttarakhand. His enthusiasm made the soldiers from Manipur and Mizoram praise the natural splendour of their villages, ones from Rajasthan and Haryana share stories of the Murrah buffalo and its milk and ghee, ones from Himachal Pradesh reminisce their fresh fruits, and ones from Maharashtra sing glories of their lemons and oranges.

When they went to get a good night's sleep, Sher Singh tried adjusting the radio placed on the cot, using a button to tune it in, albeit in a hushed manner, as he was anxious to catch up on news from his home and village amidst the persistent disruptions in the country.

A broad-minded Maharashtrian soldier, known for his love of food and drink, was celebrating his wedding anniversary that day. To mark the occasion, a small gathering was arranged, with fish from the mess and a bottle of rum. But before the party could start, the radio blurted out. Soldiers were habituated to listening to the radio while being posted on the front, so everyone turned to it attentively. It was the eight o'clock bulletin:

> Prime Minister Indira Gandhi has declared a national emergency, citing internal disturbances across the country from today...

On hearing this, the Manipuri soldier remarked that even during the roll call, the battalion had been informed by Subedar Sahib.

Sher Singh shrugged his head and expressed regret at the development; this strange news disturbed the Maharashtrian as well, who became worried about his wedding anniversary. The discussion became very long; thankfully, no one had a night duty that day. So everyone got a chance to eat and drink till late at night and share their thoughts according to their understanding.

The Haryanvi was the only person who was not tired of praising Indira Gandhi's decision, which was initially supported by Rajasthanis, but he also moved away after seeing the majority in opposition.

Sher Singh delved a little deeper into the political matter and said, 'Brother, it is not appropriate to forcibly impose an Emergency-like situation in the country. It seems like a plot to make independent India a slave again. Listen carefully to the news of how governments are being toppled in states and leaders are being forcibly put in jail. In the name of population control, men are being forcibly pushed into sterilization camps like helpless animals. Understand, brother, the young students who are raising their voices are being lathi-charged, and bullets are being fired upon them. Should they not even fight for their rights in a democracy?'

The Himachali, shocked to hear Sher Singh's words, expressed concern for the future and opposed the dictatorial rule. Hearing the noise of this heated political debate, Subedar Sahib came there. He was about to go on pension that month. Subedar Sahib, who grew up in the soil of Mathura, was attracted to the words of Banke Bihari's verse in the *Shrimad Bhagavad Gita*.

He recounted the entire episode in one breath, addressing his young colleagues. He emphasized that whenever hypocrisy, arrogance and anarchy spread across the earth, a force inevitably descends for their total destruction. This sentiment is also echoed in Verses 7 and 8 of Chapter 4 of the *Shrimad Bhagavad Gita*:

> *Yada yada hi dharmasya glanir bhavati Bharata,*
> *Abhyutthanamadharmasya tadatmanam srjamyaham.*
> *Paritranaya sadhunam vinashaya cha dushkritam,*
> *Dharma-sansthapanarthaya smbhavami yuge yuge.*

In the Mahabharata war, when Arjuna gets entangled in the difference between self and others in Kurukshetra, Lord Krishna preached that whenever dharma declines and unrighteousness increases, He manifests, '*Yada yada hi dharmasya*' which signifies that whenever domination or conspiracies emerge, God intervenes for mankind's protection, restoring peace by defeating hatred, sin, domination and conspiracy. In essence, whenever religion is destroyed and unrighteousness prevails, He reincarnates for the salvation of saints, the destruction of evildoers, and the establishment of religion, being born in every age.

This holy land, devbhoomi, known for its sages and saints, and the religious austerity of millions, had reached a breaking point under the weight of such anarchy and tyranny. There arose a collective need to awaken social, economic, political, educational, cultural and religious consciousness in society. In order to dismantle casteism, nepotism, dynasticism, dictatorship and fanatical communalism, and to revive the ancient glorious rites, beliefs and dignity of Aryavarta, an infant was about to take birth.

During the Shravan month, on Shukla Paksha Dwadashi, a Monday, Bishna Devi, due to the temple's restriction on entry during pregnancy (8th month), stood by the door, worshipping Lord Shiva from a distance. Suddenly, electricity crackled in the clouds. Even before Bishna Devi could cross the courtyard and reach the atrium, rain showers drenched her. After receiving raindrops as blessings from Bholenath in Shravan, Bishna Devi lay semi-unconscious in a corner, neglecting her daily household affairs.

After about a month had passed, when Bishna Devi looked into the courtyard, she found the rain *of bhado* at its peak. The cows and buffaloes tied in the courtyard had not been sheltered and were chewing on grass straws. Witnessing Bishna Devi's condition, her mother-in-law, without disturbing her, brought the livestock inside. Soon the darkness of night approached. Admiring the serene glow in the dark clouds, Bishna Devi, lying in bed, drifted into sleep. The clouds that rained all night now rested, yet the cold air from the mountains chilled the valley. In this extraordinary, and perhaps providential environment, a sigh escaped Bishna Devi's lips as she woke up, her eyes scouring the surroundings right and left.

Bishna Devi, like any birthing woman, experienced the onset of labour triggered by hormonally driven processes. Consequently, internal pressure built, causing repeated contractions that dissolve the mucus plug. Panicked, Bishna Devi took deep breaths, attempting to manage the infant's movements with both palms on her stomach. In the courtyard, despite her in-laws being busy in gossiping with her husband's elder brother, *jethji*, she groaned in pain and weakly gestured to her mother-in-law. However, the elderly mother-in-law failed to comprehend her distress. In fear, Bishna Devi called her elder daughter Nandi inside. Nandi, absorbed in playing with a doll made of fabric clippings, heard her mother's voice and rushed out, clutching the doll. Observing her mother lying on the ground, Nandi insisted on sitting on her lap for milk, but her mother explained to her that the baby in her womb was getting ready to arrive soon, trying to make the little girl understand the situation. Meanwhile, her pain intensified.

Fearing the unbearable pain, Bishna Devi instructed her daughter to fetch a bottle of oil from the kitchen and call grandmother from the courtyard. Her mother-in-law rushed in and seeing her daughter-in-law's condition, she knew that arrangements needed to be made urgently. She aided her daughter-in-law in lying down on the bed and, taking the bottle of oil from her granddaughter's hand, gently rubbed it on her daughter-in-law's stomach. However, the pain continued to intensify, coinciding with the return of rain outside. Despite having endured three previous labours,

Bishna Devi felt this situation to be different. She requested to summon a well-known female midwife from the village for assistance.

The crooked wooden walls, covered with clay and dung, started collapsing due to the stormy rain. The front gate, facing a dark ridge, posed a risk of the water seeping in. A red clay-clad door adorned with slanted lines made of white clay, reminiscent of the regional Aipan art created the previous Diwali, decorated the entrance. In one corner, a hearth stood, accompanied by eight or ten wooden logs for burning. Nearby lay brass, bronze and silver utensils. Opposite the hearth, a bronze container (*kumbh*) held pure cold water from the local water source. Shivering in wet clothes, Bishna Devi endured both day and night in excruciating pain, awaiting assistance. The water subsided by morning as the sun rose.

The village midwife, summoned by young Nandi the previous evening, arrived and was greeted by her grandma in the courtyard. Informed of Bishna Devi's unbearable pain over the last two days, the midwife hurried inside. Assessing her condition, the experienced midwife, having assisted in the delivery of almost all women in the village, understood the urgency and acted swiftly. Quickly ordering a glass of warm milk with dissolved ghee and sugar, the midwife fed it to Bishna Devi and commenced a gentle massage with warm ghee on her belly and waist to alleviate the pain. During the delivery process, she positioned Bishna Devi on her back on the ground, providing support and continuing the gentle massage with warm ghee to ease the pain. Soon after, the amniotic fluid sac ruptured, marking the auspicious onset of labour. Enduring difficult labour pains with boundless compassion, invoking Lord Bholenath and Jagannath, a beautiful crying child emerged from the womb, connected by the umbilical cord, soaked in blood, catching Bishna Devi's gaze.

The midwife, with trembling hands, lifted the beautiful newborn. When she looked at the black-brown head of the child, Bishna Devi couldn't contain the tears of joy welling from her eyes. For Bishna Devi, who underwent unspeakable pain, was now blessed with equally rewarding fruit of her patience.

But actually, it was an ambivalent moment for Bishna Devi, a young mother, who was happy for her newborn but she was also worried for the future of her children.

On one hand, the elation of cradling her son, and on the other, the relief of a safe delivery under challenging circumstances by the middle-aged woman! This duality of emotions painted a picture of Bishna Devi smiling with happiness while simultaneously shedding tears, reminiscing about the hardships and struggles she had endured at a very young age. In the middle of the adversity both within and outside the house, Bishna Devi, although not directly connected to external emergencies, only comprehended the language spoken from the village house to the farm barns. Despite the joyful moment, she handed the child to his grandmother, giving her the responsibility and opportunity to care for him, and immersed herself back into her work as before.

One day, amidst weeding and hoeing the lush green aromatic basmati paddy and maize fields, Bishna Devi paused to pluck a cucumber from a nearby vine. She looked admiringly at the cloudy sky and then, a few steps away, washed the cucumber in a natural water puddle. Retrieving a sickle hanging at her waist, reminiscent of a soldier's gun, she made four incisions on the cucumber before tucking it back into her waist. It's common to see rural women with sickles and large ropes tied around their waists. While relishing the cucumber, Bishna Devi became lost in thoughts of her husband, who was serving in the armed forces and hadn't sent any letters for several months. Talking to another woman in the village, she recalled how she was betrothed at a very young age, and how she had spent early days at her parent's home. She reminisced her childhood. She shared stories of joyous moments spent with her siblings, recalling that although there was a trend of schooling in big cities, sending girls to school wasn't considered as important by parents in their village. Instead, children cherished their education at home without worrying for pen and paper or the strictness of teachers.

Her friend, who had been listening to her, got lost in these thoughts, engaging with every word, perhaps recalling her own cherished moments with her parents and siblings, a part of her life she hadn't pondered over deeply until now.

Bishna Devi told her village friend that her upbringing revolved around tasks like cutting grass, tending to the forests and looking after cows and buffaloes. As she reached the age of 13 or 14, both the household and village began seeking a potential groom for her. Neighbours often inquired, 'Your girl is growing up; how long will you continue to care for her?'

At that time, no one cared what kind of family they would be wedded into or how they would raise their own family, Bishna Devi told her friend. At that time, she recalled, marriage for girls meant that there would be merry-making, good food, good clothes and ornaments. Girls eagerly awaited their weddings, anticipating the chance to adorn themselves with new clothes, bangles and bindis, and celebrate with good food.

Similar to others, her household faced financial struggles. Her parents managed household expenses through income from cows, buffaloes and goats. On the day of Raksha Bandhan, her maternal uncle, noticing her, suggested to her father, 'Considering my niece's future, I have a boy in mind; if you agree, I can propose the alliance.'

Her father was pleased, especially upon hearing that the boy had recently joined the Indian army—an ideal match in their eyes. Concerns about meeting marriage expenses arose due to their financial situation. However, they didn't lose hope. The following day, after seeing the groom's family, they finalized the wedding date. For the wedding, they stored some grains at home and purchased more from the local market.

During the ceremony, people and relatives from neighbouring villages contributed milk, curd, grains and other necessities. It was the month of Ashadha (June-July), and back then, the village lacked proper roads. The wedding procession was modest, comprising hardly 10 or 12 people. There was no need for drums, bands or grandeur. Unlike contemporary customs of palanquins or horseback rides, the bride would walk alongside the groom.

Bishna Devi said to her friend, 'However, my Bapuji gave some five/ten rupees to the palanquin bearer. The palanquin, adorned with flowers, was carried some distance by my brothers. However, due to the heavy rain, they pocketed the money but refused to carry me further. So, late in the evening, drenched in the rain, the procession reached the courtyard on foot. The brave warrior had come on a month's leave, half of which had passed before our marriage. In the remaining days, we were just starting to understand each other when the day of his departure drew near. By the time the next holiday arrived after eight-nine months, I had almost forgotten his appearance. When I saw a man standing in the courtyard, I initially thought he was someone from the neighbouring village and hurried inside. He followed me, and then I realized that maybe this was my warrior.

'It was a different time, but things are gradually changing now!' Although life is getting easier by the day, remembering that day now makes it feel like everything is so much simpler today.

Mata Bishna's words were filled with depth and the genuine essence of rural life, drawing many women and children to gather around her. They listened to her words like the teachings of a *satsang* or the eternal truth from a great lady. This increased Bishna Devi's interest as a public speaker, knowing that people were listening to her. 'We're likely the last generation that has witnessed the transition from horse carts, bullock carts to trucks, buses, cars and trains. We used to travel far to write letters and then walk miles to post them with great pride and reverence. We waited for months for the postman to bring us a reply. In the barren village fields, we forgot hunger and thirst while playing games like chor police, hide and seek, gilli-danda, kho-kho, kabaddi and pitthu with our friends. We wrote in an unknown script with bamboo pens on wooden planks, later coating it with soot. There was scolding too, especially when our siblings found out and questioned how we wrote without the elder's permission! During weddings and fairs, all siblings wore matching outfits from the same stall, which made it easy for our parents to spot us from a distance, identifying who their child was and what they were doing.'

The arrival of a newborn in any courtyard is the happiest time for grandparents. Kheem Singh, Bishna Devis's father-in-law, alongside his wife, had spread a mat in the middle of the courtyard, relishing the joy of his grandson's playfulness, agility, smile and sharpness, reminiscent of their own childhood days. Meanwhile, the astrologer laid out his almanac and discussed with Kheem Singh the important rituals for the night—such as invoking the protection of Shashti Devi, the goddess known for safeguarding children and ensuring their long life. Astrologer Balkrishna Pandey, well-respected in the village for his teaching profession and his versatile and amiable personality, had earned unwavering reverence from the villagers. Hence, it was decided that the child's birth certificate would also be prepared according to his guidance.

This day marked the naming ceremony of the child, stirring excitement in both the household and the village since early morning. However, everyone could feel the absence of Havildar Sher Singh. The child was being bathed and dressed in attractive clothes. Bishna Devi, applying a black spot to the child's forehead for protection, gazed around repeatedly. Acharya Balkrishna from Sangari, Pandey from Gauch and Acharya Bhatt from Runda had arrived for the naming ceremony. People from neighbouring villages like Tundi and Baramon, as well as their native village Harkhola (Pithoragarh), had come to offer their congratulations. After the meal, all the guests' palates were sweetened with jaggery and sugar.

As per the renowned almanac of the hill-region and the predictions made by the acharyas, the chosen name for the child was 'Pushkar', starting with the Hindi letter 'p'. Pushkar signifies a reservoir or pond, suggesting that the child would always strive to bring fulfilment and establish peace and prosperity for the betterment of society and the nation. Born under the Virgo sign on a Tuesday, a day associated with Mars, this momentous and fruitful occasion aligned with the practices of Mata Adishakti Parvati and Pawansut Mahavir Hanuman. Coincidentally, it was also Parivartini Ekadashi, renowned for the powerful results akin to Vajapeya yajna, an auspicious day to obliterate sins.

Those who devoutly worship Lord Vishnu's Vamana avatar on this Ekadashi are revered across the *Triloka* (three worlds), including Brahma and Vishnu. Virgo's birth alignment suggests a highly religious inclination for the child, showing determination in accomplishing tasks while being conscious of health and beauty. Honesty, duty and an idealistic mindset were to define this child, who might be seen as steadfast but intolerant of restrictions. Adapting to the child's nature would be crucial, as their playful demeanour might lead to unexpected actions, though always imbued with wisdom and strength to navigate adverse conditions. Due to the influence of Mercury in the ascendant sign, he will easily be able to differentiate between right and wrong. This child would show a keen interest in studies and demonstrate a systematic approach to tasks. An occasional display of passion and enthusiasm might be accompanied by moments of anger, yet the child would strive to care for loved ones and foster a pleasant atmosphere. Adored not only by family but also by society, wearing an emerald gemstone in later years was to be considered auspicious. The child would invest time in exploring and learning new things. Such were the predictions of the astrologers.

The child's astrological alignment with Mercury, governing intelligence, indicated a strong potential for higher education. However, it was advised that when choosing a career or business path, following the heart without hesitation would lead to unwavering success. This child held the promise of excelling in professions like journalism, medicine, social work, engineering and politics, showcasing extraordinary talents. A love marriage was highly favoured, with the partner likely to be from the southwest direction of the district—a beautiful individual who would illuminate his life, help in progress and run the household.

The predictions were that, endowed with versatility, this child would display dynamism and inherit the potential for wealth, prosperity and fame—a potential luminary not only in the country but also on the international stage. The grandmother, exuding youthful joy at the arrival of a grandchild with such a unique destiny, engaged the child with popular children's melodies. Unfamiliar with their meanings, the child tried to move in rhythm with the tunes, displaying gummy smiles without inhibition, enjoying the innocent moments as the grandmother sang:

Ghuguti basuti... Ghuguti basuti...
Maam, kaan chha!
Ki laaloo... Dudu bhati...
Kooo khaloo... Lallaa hamaro...

Every Kumaoni mother lies down, seats her child on her legs so that the child's body rests against her knees, and sings:

Oh! Ghughuti bird
Child: Where is my uncle (Mama)?
Ghughuti: At his home.
Child: What will he bring?
Ghughuti: Milk and rice.
Child: Who will eat?
Mother: Our child.

Grandparents were captivated by the divine image reflected in the beautiful eyes and sweet smile of their grandson. Words failed to capture the depth of this affection. Born after three sisters, the child was cherished as a priceless gem in the family. This love evoked the vision of mischievous Krishna, a familiar image that every mother sees in her child, a sentiment echoed even by the renowned poet Mahakavi Surdasa:

> *Mukh dadhi lep kiye, sobhit kar navneet liye.*
> *Ghuturuni chalat renu tan mandit, mukh dadhi lep kiye.*
> *Charu kapol lol lochan gorochan tilak diye.*
> *Lat latkani manu matta madhup gan maadak madhuhin piye.*

> Surdas ji describes Bal Krishna with curd/butter on his face, charming cheeks, playful eyes, a sandalwood tilak on his forehead and curly locks swaying as he crawls.

As the child began to crawl and take small steps, Bishna Devi, much like Mother Yashoda, started tying small bells with black strings around his ankles and applying black spots between the wide eyebrows of the adorable face, enhancing the charm of the child's mischievous childhood. As his steps became steadier, the child's curiosity shifted to the cows and calves tethered in the courtyard, the sparrows pecking at grains, the mynahs, crows and the playful children in the neighbourhood. Animals and birds became friends through the gentle touch of the fearless child's hands. Like other children nearby, the child became enthralled with playing and breaking toys. Consequently, every year, various items like toy vehicles, toy guns, flute-like wind instruments such as *peepani* and *algoja*, and balloons were brought from the Chhadandev Fair for him to play with throughout the year. Engrossed in playing, the child became adept at dismantling them, as if a skilled surgeon was operating on a patient with a serious illness. The child did not relent or tire until the toys were completely disassembled. Mata Bishna Devi, despite her efforts to explain, eventually succumbed to the child's determination.

The family's financial condition wasn't strong. Pushkar's father Sher Singh joined the 5th Battalion of the Mahar Regiment in 1963 due to his penchant for hard work and physical fitness. This battalion was renowned globally for its soldiers' dutifulness and patriotic chivalry, and it had numerous accomplishments on the battlefield. Since its establishment in 1948, this regiment has been providing for the entire family through their dedicated service at the borders of Jammu and Kashmir and Sikkim. Despite this, Sher Singh, like any father, harboured lofty dreams for his children and was willing to go to great lengths to fulfil them.

Sher Singh sought his father Kheem Singh's permission to take two handfuls of land in Nagla Tarai Bhabar and construct a small house for the family there after returning home, having completed seven years of service (1963-70). Granting permission for his son's ambitious aspirations so that the future of his grandchildren should be brighter, the elderly father supported Sher Singh in pursuing this dream.

Pushkar's great-grandfather had grown up in a small village in the Pithoragarh district. Financial hardships had added to the challenges in his life. At the age of 11, he was married to a nine-year-old girl from Tundi village. A close relative had fixed this match. When the new daughter-in-law realized there was hardly any sustenance at her in-laws' home, she somehow managed to convey this news to her parents. Her narration of misery at her new home moved her parents so much that they set out for her village Harkhola and, traversing steep terrains, finally reached there. When fathers of both groom and bride couldn't arrive at any solution, her parents proposed the idea of bringing her husband to their home as an adopted son-in-law.

Those days, Tundi was geographically more favourable for farming than Harkhola. The primary income sources for villagers were agricultural land and livestock. They cultivated various crops like paddy, wheat, maize, barley, ragi (madwa), soybean and lentils such as *urad*. Alongside farming, they reared Murrah buffaloes, Jersey cows, sheep and goats. So the girl saw prospects for her family in this place and moved there with her three young sons, Kheem Singh, Dhan Singh and Hansa Singh, and her husband. They started living in a roof shed gifted by her father. The boys received warmth and affection in their maternal home (*nanka*). Education wasn't prevalent in the village at that time. As the boys grew self-sufficient, they actively participated in farming, managing barns and forestry. It was customary for sons to join the army to serve the country or, if not possible, gather resources locally for the family. Daughters were expected to take on family responsibilities at their in-laws' homes.

The education system was indifferent and so the people lacked awareness as well. The result was that venturing outside the village wasn't deemed auspicious and village life was preferred to be able to run the household. The three brothers efficiently handled their responsibilities, with the grace of their maternal grandparents. As the elder brothers got married, the family grew. Dhan Singh and Hansa Singh had three sons and three daughters each. Kheem Singh had two sons and three daughters. Running such a large family on charitable land was next to impossible if not outright difficult. The children were enrolled in the nearest primary school. However, there wasn't a specific admission process in the government primary school those days. Besides, such schools would often be quite distant. Initially, Kheem Singh would escort all children to school. Sher Singh and his cousin Gopal excelled in their studies. Upon completing eighth grade, due to the absence of further schooling opportunities, Sher Singh began working at home. In the meantime, father Kheem Singh, during a discussion with locals at a tea stall, learned about the Chinese army's incursion into the North-East Frontier Agency (NEFA) border (present-day Arunachal Pradesh).

The Chinese army had been consistently trying to encircle this area, which had been a disputed territory since the time of the British and Chinese Empires. Exploiting the vulnerable situation, around 80,000 Chinese soldiers attacked 22,000 Indian soldiers on 20 October 1962. The battle took a heavy toll on the people, with thousands from both sides being martyred, many declared missing or injured, and some taken as prisoners of war. Lasting for a month and a day, the war concluded with China unilaterally announcing ceasefire on 21 November. In its aftermath, China occupied about 38,000 sq. km in Aksai Chin, a part of India. The core reason behind the India-China conflict was the dispute over the sovereignty of border regions like Aksai Chin and NEFA. India viewed Aksai Chin as part of Ladakh, while China insisted it was part of its Xinjiang province. In 1958, India had protested against China's official map showcasing NEFA and parts of Ladakh. The year had also seen a Tibetan uprising, harshly suppressed by China, prompting the Dalai Lama to flee to India in 1959 with his followers.

Zhou Enlai, China's Premier, had first claimed around 103,600 sq. km of Indian territory in both Ladakh and NEFA in January 1959. Later, in 1960, Zhou Enlai unofficially proposed that India must relinquish Aksai Chin's claims in return for

Evolution: Ascension of the Clan

China dropping claims over NEFA, but Prime Minister Nehru rejected the offer, leading to escalated tensions and the subsequent war.

During this conflict, Nehru wrote two letters to United States (US) President John F. Kennedy on 19 November 1962. Nehru had sought 12 squadrons of fighter jets and modern radar systems. However, Kennedy was preoccupied with the Cuban missile crisis, where the Soviet Union was on the verge of deploying nuclear missiles in Cuba. Kennedy cautioned the Soviet Union against this and a catastrophic nuclear war was averted. But he couldn't entertain Nehru's request.

Sher Singh's determination to serve the nation led him to enlist in the army, seeing it as a way to honour his father's commitment to the country. His decision embodied the belief that achieving dreams requires a strong desire, which he turned into reality. He joined the 5th Battalion of the Mahar Regiment, got posted in Jammu and Kashmir, which paved the way for many others from his family to serve in the military. Despite lacking formal education or direct involvement in mainstream society, Kheem Singh endeavoured to instil a strong sense of patriotism in his children as well as the youth around him. While he lacked literacy, he fostered positive nationalistic ideals within the local community. He was looked up to as a torchbearer for progress with his humble village background. Individuals like him, though not academically accomplished, serve as societal assets, offering valuable insights and guidance for a progressive society.

The wisdom and forward-thinking mindset of elders like Kheem Singh not only inspire future leaders but also steer society in the right direction. Their accumulated knowledge and practical wisdom are invaluable assets, and these assets should be passed down to the younger generation. This transfer of progressive ideas contributes not just to individuals or families but to the intangible wealth of the nation, shaping a brighter future.

The Dhami family, resilient in their journey, continued to progress despite obstacles. Sher Singh, with support from relatives and friends, acquired land in Nagla Tarai Bhabar (now Sharda Barrage) and settled in Khatima. Life in a joint family, where dozens resided together, taught the younger children valuable lessons in familial duties. Among the brothers, Kheem Singh was beloved by the children—they would gather around him in the evenings to hear captivating stories. Sher Singh expressed his desire to relocate his uncle's family to Nagla Tarai Bhabar, but Hansa Singh advised patience, citing the challenges of leaving the village and adjusting to a new place. Dhan Singh echoed this sentiment, emphasizing the need to consider how people would manage to leave everything behind.

At just three years old, young Pushkar began showing his eagerness for learning, sketching at his brothers' slates and attempting to wear their pyjamas to 'attend' school in the morning. His father took advantage of the holidays to teach him the alphabet at home through engaging stories. By April, at the tender age of three, Grandfather Kheem Singh secured admission for Pushkar in an Anganwadi centre, kick-starting his educational journey.

The school was located about 4–5 km away from their house. Pushkar, without even washing his face in the morning, all ready to leave for school, would pick up his new bag, which his grandfather Kheem Singh had bought from the nearby market the previous month. This would upset his elder sisters, Nandi, Pushpa and Indra, as they didn't have new school bags. Consequently, conflicts arose among the siblings, and sometimes, Nandi, Indra and cousin Gopal took on the role of judges in these disputes. Their disagreements would last for hours and come to an end only when some elder would calm them down. Pushkar, along with his sisters and cousins, was determined to transition from the Anganwadi to a higher-grade school. This led to occasional sibling rivalries, making the household like a children's version of *Mahabharata*, where the elder siblings tried to mediate. School education commenced for all of them. But it would prove to be a daily arduous journey to school, leaving the children exhausted and sweaty by the time they returned home in the afternoon. They would throw their belongings in different directions and settle in their mothers' lap.

Even the mothers and elder sisters would get tired after a day of household chores; they would nevertheless set aside their fatigue to cuddle little ones in the family. Tiny tots were lucky that they were adored by their elders and would always be the centre of everyone's affection, despite their naughty streaks. Indra groomed Pushkar's hair, and Nandi helped with bathing and dressing him in fresh clothes. When Bishna Devi returned home, exhausted from her work in the farm and barns, she would feel relaxed seeing Pushkar's playful antics from his grandfather's shoulders. Little Pushkar would play with his granddad until he fell asleep on the bed.

As Pushkar grew, so did his mischiefs. Not only the household but even the teachers were not immune to the mischievous behaviour of young Pushkar. His teacher Acharya Balkrishna recalls that once a unique teaching approach was adopted in the school, teaching the Hindi alphabet using local items, starting from vowel sounds like '*a*' represented by *anaar* (pomegranate), '*aa*' by *aam* (mango), '*ee*' by *eekh* (sugarcane), etc., explaining their everyday uses. Pushkar and his classmates rebelled, demanding mischievously but assertively, 'We'll only study if we can eat sugarcane and mango!' In response, Headmaster Mohan Ram offered them orange sugar candies, but most of the children refused to budge from their demand. Some of them took them and eagerly waited for more. When the teachers declined further treats, Pushkar lay on the ground, crying loudly, and his classmates followed suit. A villager, thinking the children were being punished, intervened. To console them, a herdsman offered to share sugarcane from his field.

Pushkar admired all his siblings and preferred to memorize poems from his elder sister's book before doing so from his own book. Saturdays were eagerly awaited by the children. After the break, teachers and students would gather for a game of *antakshari*, a spoken parlour game, speeches, poetry, dance, singing, and small sports competitions. Everyone would eagerly prepare for this special day. Madho Singh would narrate inspiring stories from *Panchatantra*, and Gopal would share his favourite Kumaoni humorous poem composed by Sherda Anpadh, starting with:

> *Dai jasi gori ujai, aur bigot jai chitti.*
> *Hisau kilmodi jaisi, muni khatt muni mithi.*
> *Aaankh ki tari jaisi, aankhon men ley ritti.*
> *O dhei phuldei hai jo, jo dhei tu hiti.*
> *Hath patney harai janchhe, kai ryudi dhhon chhei tu*
> *Sur suri bayav jasi, o chiyapini kochai tu?*

The poet describes the young girl of his dreams—You are as white as curd, as sweet and tangy as Hisalu and Kirmodi fruits. Like the pupil of an eye, you dwell in mine. Wherever you go, you bring joy. You are truly as sweet as honey. Oh beloved, let me know who you are.

While Manoj would be seen dancing and singing a local *chapeli* (folk-lyric), young Pushkar would also resolve to participate in poetry recitation for Class III. He would earn a lot of praise by reciting a poem that he had learned like a parrot, flawlessly spouting it in a single breath:

> *Vah punyabhoomi meree, vah janmabhoomi meree,*
> *Vah svarnabhoomi meree, vah maatrbhoomi meree.*
> *Janmen jahaan thhe raghupati janmee jahaan thheen seeta,*
> *Shrikrishna ne sunaee vanshee puneet geeta,*
> *Gautam ne janm lekar jiska suyash badhaaya*
> *Jagko daya dikhaee jagko diya dikhaaya.*
> *Vah yuddhabhoomi meree, vah buddhabhoomi meree,*
> *Vah janmabhoomi meree, vah maatrbhoomi meree!*

The poet describes some of the great heroes like Ram-Sita, Krishna and Gautam, who were born on this land. Ram's righteousness, Sita's ideals, Krishna's selfless action and Buddha's wisdom and compassion have made this nation glorious.

The Surname 'Dhami': Historical View

What's in the name, what's in the surname!

If we look back at human development on this earth, it seems that our ancestors started living on the continent of Africa about six and a half million years ago. The present mega human, commonly referred to as *Homo sapiens*, is believed to have originated from Neanderthals. The journey of human beings towards an evolving state, traditions, customs, religions, politics, social hierarchies, castes and creeds began with the Indus Valley Civilization, the Vedic period, and the epic period leading up to the present. Therefore, the historical roots of surnames are associated with these civilizations.

India's diversity is such that every object, person and emotion here holds a unique essence. People can belong to any clan. However, according to religious history, all Indians are considered the descendants of some sages, saints, or Manu (the apocryphal first man). Some scholars deny the trend of surnames in the Vedic period, asserting that surnames were introduced in the Smriti period based on ancestry. In support of this, only two ancient dynasties emerged: Suryavansh and Chandravansh. Over time, many sub-clans were formed under these dynasties, such as Ikshvaku and Agnivansh under Suryavansha; and Nagvansh and Yaduvansh under Chandravansh. Even today, Gautam Raja Raghu of the city of Ayodhya is considered part of the Ikshvaku dynasty.

As these dynasties grew, they split further, giving rise to various varnas, including Brahmins, Kshatriyas, Vaishyas and Shudras. Later, *gotras* or clan were created based on the names of the Saptarishi or the seven sages. Today, only a few tribes retain surnames; some societies use titles, while others identify themselves according to the trade they are associated with.

William Shakespeare, the famous English dramatist, once wrote, 'What's in a name?' If he were alive today, there might have been debates about his surname too. Numerous researches have been conducted on the origin and prevalence of surnames. A hefty budget of millions of pounds has been spent on only such research at the University of West England. In India, there is a vast sea of surnames, but we don't have to get lost in it.

The surname 'Dhami' is well-known in the lap of the Himalayas, and is often associated with expertise. Some believe it is a Nepali surname present in many parts of Nepal, symbolizing heroism with beautiful, courageous and fearless attributes, connecting it to the Rajput family. Others associate it with a remote Indian region and suggest migration from place to place. Some consider it a title rather than a surname, linking it to Lord Jagannath of Orissa, stating that initially, he was known as Kunwar and was declared the chief servant of Lord Jagannath due to his unique faith, eventually being named Dhami.

Looking back at Himachal's history, there was a small princely state called Dhami under Rana's rule. It shot to limelight when, in 1939, a horrific firing incident took place there. Gandhi and Nehru had condemned it. Some people believe that the king of the Dhami princely state was a descendant of Prithviraj Chauhan, the majestic ruler of Ajmer. Maharaja Dalip Singh ruled there from 1920-87. Experts of the Dhami surname suggest its origins from Pithoragarh in Uttarakhand, associating them with Bholenath, Harichandra-Balichandra and Lord Jagannath. They reside in various regions, including Kumaon-Garhwal and other lands such as Harkhola, Manmanle and Tundi. Other than Pushkar Singh Dhami, some notable personalities with the Dhami surname include British children's writer Narinder Dhami, Nepali politician Prem Singh Dhami, Uttarakhand politician Harish Dhami and Indian TV actress Drashti Dhami.

5

MIGRATION: A PATH TO DEVELOPMENT

Yojanon ke safar mein, main bilbilaata raha.
Chhale ghiste rahe, khoon behta raha.
Main rukne kee himmat, karta bhee kaise,
Do tukdon kee khaatir, paanv uthaata raha...

Here, duty is described as the true purpose of life. I am forced on a long journey, moving forward in distress, because if I stop, I will starve. So I must migrate to earn a livelihood.

One day, Kheem Singh informed the headmaster, Acharya Balkrishna Pandey, that he would be moving to Nagla Tarai Bhabar in Udham Singh Nagar district. Pushkar, who was shaping up as a promising boy, had forged close bonds with his classmates, friends and siblings. Hence, leaving the school and departing from the village was not easy for him. Assistant teacher Mohan Singh, who was a man of empathy and nurtured fondness for Dhami, explained the situation to the child. The headmaster, with teary eyes, handed over the transfer certificates of Pushkar and his elder sisters to their grandfather Kheem Singh. He expressed, 'Young Pushkar not only displayed courage as a class monitor but also actively participated in every school program. Last month, along with his classmates, he planted beautiful flowering plants like marigold, rose and dahlia, which he diligently cared for. Now I must entrust this responsibility to another child. I am confident that Pushkar will bring honour to our name one day. Given the chance to learn, write and take the stage, this independent-minded child will undoubtedly succeed. I wish a bright future for the talented Pushkar!'

With his brothers' blessings, Kheem Singh led his entire family towards Nagla Tarai Bhabar. After a brief rest to shake off the weariness, they reached Chharandev, the nearest station, after walking several miles through Gaenali, a small village. Eventually, they boarded a truck with their entire luggage. Amidst the feeling of leaving their village behind, there was excitement about embracing a new life among new people in a new place. As they journeyed, Bishna Devi peeked outside, her eyes moist with the sorrow of parting from her village. Pushkar, seated on his grandmother's lap, enjoyed the natural beauty of Rameshwar Ghat and the Saryu river visible in the distant valley. However, Grandma complained about the overpowering smell of the vehicle and burning fuel on the rough road. Kheem Singh took the boy on his lap. Grandma's condition worsened, and she started vomiting. Pushkar became restless and began to cry, and it took a while to console him. Eventually, like his elder sisters, he fell asleep as they reached around Barakot.

The sun sank into the horizon, casting its last rays. Pushkar saw a tonga and a *bhainsa buggi* (buffalo cart) running on the streets for the first time, as these were not seen in Tundi village. Previously, people primarily used mules to transport goods.

Seeing rickshaws, large Uttar Pradesh Transport Corporation buses and wide paved roads for the first time, Pushkar was captivated by their movement and speed. In a fleeting moment, he found himself lost in this new world. He observed a rickshaw owner pulling his rickshaw and noticed the hotel owner raising the shutter of the roadside hotel! Upon seeing his bus driver, he began dreaming of becoming a driver and for the next few moments, he got lost in daydreams.

Sher Singh transferred all responsibilities to his father as he was now posted far away in the east, newly assigned to the 15th Mahar Regiment. Kheem Singh got Nandi and Pushpa enrolled in the nearby Government Junior High School, Lohia Head, Khatima. However, young Pushkar and Indra were admitted to the nearest primary school, Nagla. Within a few days, Pushkar became immensely popular among classmates and teachers. His mischievous yet charming demeanour and alluring persona impressed everyone. The sorrow of leaving the village paled in comparison to the vibrant life he discovered among these young students. Even the simple wooden plank and bamboo pen of the village occasionally caught his attention, a reminder of his former home.

Setting out as per his school schedule early in the morning became his routine. In the evening, he would rush home, wash up, eat and engage in lively conversations with his mother Bishna Devi and his grandmother who would be in the fields. As time passed, Pushkar befriended the neighbourhood kids who would be enjoying their summer holidays by swimming, catching small fish and spending their days bathing in the nearby canal. It was natural that being a sportive person Pushkar would be drawn to these activities. One day, he managed to slip away from his family and ventured towards the canal. However, the sight of the rushing water made him a little fearful in the beginning. Meanwhile, other kids of his age were confidently swimming in the canal. Observing them closely, Pushkar stood silently along the smooth canal track, trying to comprehend their swimming techniques, until Kheem Singh noticed him. At one point, Nandi spotted Pushkar near the canal and, fearing for his safety, rushed towards him, trying to dissuade him from venturing into the water. She even tried to shoo him away by sharing how kids who went too near to the canals had fallen into danger.

The scorching heat of the Tarai Bhabar was now reaching its peak. Pushkar, now a student in Class VII at Lohia Head School, saw himself as a campus student. Most children who would be playing in the street, revelling in the holidays, would set up camp in the sprawling courtyard of their house. Among them, Pushkar assumed the role of an elder brother, and was thus often called Vinod Khanna of the locality. He always sported a long-collared shirt, trousers and belt over his lean waist, and shoes. He was the one planning and dividing teams before every game. However, Diwan and Indra, their neighbours, tended to stir controversy with policies that went against sportsmanship, despite their close friendship. During cricket matches, disagreements over batting often led to clashes. Tempers flared, resulting in angry strikes on waists and buttocks. But after some tears, and with the help of friends, peace was always eventually restored, but not without crying, complaining and a hard-won ceasefire. A distinct trait in Pushkar was his silence at home regarding these conflicts. He was not someone who wasted his time, unlike many other children who would often spend time observing women from the neighbourhood engaging in morning squabbles—over Golu's mischief against Chintu, Monu's theft of Sonu's ball, and the like.

Meanwhile, Sher Singh took on a new responsibility in the 15th Mahar Regiment, actively participating in Operation X (1970) and the subsequent Operation Cactus Lily from Brahminbaria to Raipura (December 1971). This operation was crucial in the context of India and Bangladesh conflict. Indian soldiers had bravely put their lives on the line to liberate Bangladesh from Pakistan. Meanwhile, the Pakistani forces were determined to quash the liberation movement in Bangladesh, leading to the daily killing of thousands of innocent Bangladeshis. This escalating crisis raised grave concerns for PM Indira Gandhi.

To address the worsening situation, PM Indira Gandhi penned a letter to General Sam Manekshaw, directing Indian forces to intervene in Bangladesh against Pakistan. However, General Manekshaw initially refused, citing the need for additional time to prepare militarily.

Surprised by the General's response, Indira Gandhi wrote another letter, summoning General Manekshaw for a meeting. At the scheduled time and place, they discussed the entire plan for deploying the Indian Army in Bangladesh. Indira Gandhi inquired about the duration of the war, to which the General responded, 'It will take about two months.'

In December 1971, the Indian forces were officially deployed in Bangladesh against Pakistan. Sher Singh, representing the Mahar Regiment, displayed tremendous courage in the battle. The Liberation Corps of Bangladesh also fought alongside the Indian forces. Interestingly, although General Manekshaw had estimated a two-month time frame for the operation, his diplomatic strategy led to a victorious outcome within a week. On December 16, Pakistan Army Commander Lt Gen. A.A.K. Niazi surrendered to Lt Gen. Jagjit Singh Aurora of the Indian Army, handing over his pistol as a sign of surrender along with more than 80 thousand Pakistani soldiers.

Kheem Singh, unaware of the ongoing border conflicts, learned from an Air Radio program that the current heatwave had broken all previous records. Concrete and asphalt roads absorbed vast amounts of sunlight. The severe heat was likely to increase disease and mortality. It would also affect people's work capacity, causing an economic downturn. Bearing the responsibility as the family head, Kheem Singh felt the weight of these challenges. Observing the absence of rain and the standing crops gradually fading in the fields, everyone feared the difficulty of feeding their families, as most relied on farming for their livelihoods. With no sign of rain, Kheem Singh began irrigating the fields from the canal.

When Pushkar would roam out, everyone would fear for his safety as the sun would be blazing, and the area would be full of wild animals, insects, snakes and scorpions. Particularly venomous green and black snakes emerged during this time and found shelter in the rice paddies. Despite the risks, one day, Pushkar ventured into the field, calling for his mother and grandfather. Engrossed in his own thoughts, someone began shouting at Bishna Devi while humming an old patriotic song.

Eeja...
Eeja...
Eeja...
Mujhe bhi aapke paas aana hai
Dada Shri ne dapatkar kaha...
Are o...o hoshiyaar!!!

Yahaan kya karna hai aakar beta???
Dekha karo zara, itni jhulsati dhoop hai yahaan!
(Nidaagh aur tapta sooraj ki oor ishaara karte huye!!!)

By calling his mother thrice, he expressed that he too wanted to come to her. But Grandfather said sternly, 'Oh, you naughty one! What will you do here, my child? Look around, it's scorching hot here!' (Pointing towards the blazing sun and intense heat.)

Upon seeing the water, little Pushkar couldn't contain his excitement. 'I too want to take a bath,' he exclaimed eagerly. Observing the child's curiosity and the scorching sun, Grandpa surrendered to his wish. He guided the child a little further and brought him to the water's edge. Witnessing this, Pushkar joyfully leapt into the water, bathing for about two to three hours. Eventually, he left for home without informing anyone, lost in his world.

Gradually, the summer vacation came to an end. Besides attending school, Pushkar developed a strong interest in sports and various competitions. In anticipation of the preparations for Independence Day, he diligently crafted a powerful speech with the guidance of his elder sister Pushpa and his teachers. His uncontrollable joy erupted when he learned that his father Sher Singh would also be on leave from 7 August. He rehearsed the speech countless times, even while eating and drinking. Listening to her son, Bishna Devi had almost memorized half of it herself. Finally, upon hearing the sound of his father Sher Singh's arrival in the courtyard, Pushkar dashed out of his room. He saluted his father and gestured to his elder sister Pushpa for water.

Sher Singh settled comfortably on the cot and began sharing anecdotes and various memories with all of them.

Suddenly, as if remembering something, Pushkar left the discussion and rushed inside, swiftly retrieving the page of his speech, and returned, holding it in both hands. He began to read it aloud. His father understood what the speech was for, took the page, and started reading from the beginning.

Bharat Mata ki jai! My greetings to the most respected gurus! As we celebrate Independence Day today, our country, on 15 August 1947, was liberated from the oppressive rule of the firangis. Therefore, for any patriot, the motherland holds greater importance than heaven. This is achievable only through the sacrifices, dedication and valour of patriots. It is now our responsibility to work towards fulfilling the dream of a developed and prosperous nation tomorrow. Disrespecting the tricolour, dishonouring the elders or disrespecting women are not part of our cultural values. Thus, this soldier's son earnestly requests you to honour the sacrifice of the millions of brave sons of Mother India. Let us all strive to become true patriots by fostering a beautiful, prosperous and unified democratic India, forsaking all forms of discrimination based on caste, religion or sect.

Jai Hind. Jai Bharat!
Thank you!

After a three-day journey from the far away northeast border, Sher Singh had arrived home, exhausted, among his children and elderly parents. Despite the oppressive humidity that seemed to suffocate all, Sher Singh was stunned upon hearing the talent and ideas of his only son, Pushkar! The fatigue dissipated as he felt immense pride in his child.

Sher Singh patted his son's back before the family, stating, 'My son will surely join the army and demonstrate his strength on the borders. But if for any reason that isn't possible, he'll become a son of Mother India, committed to the country's development.'

Sher Singh returned to his duties after spending time with his family. However, the nation suddenly became embroiled in internal conflict from the western direction. Subedar Sher Singh, representing the 15th Mahar Regiment, witnessed Operation Blue Star, which was organized to quell this turmoil. On April 1984, at PM Indira Gandhi's residence on Safdarjung Road, an unexpected event unfolded. A white Ambassador car arrived, from which a towering, wrestler-like man emerged. Rameshwar Nath Kao, a middle-aged spy and principal advisor to PM Indira, was pivotal in training the Mukti Bahini proxy warriors during the 1971 Bangladesh war through the Research and Analysis Wing (R&AW). His task was to resolve the Khalistan issue, spurred by escalating communal tensions led by pro-Khalistan Granthi Jarnail Singh Bhindranwale. In just two years, Bhindranwale's armed supporters had killed hundreds.

At midnight on 5 June 1984, dozens of commandos donned in black entered the Golden Temple covertly. Armed with AK-47 rifles, MP5 submachine guns, bulletproof jackets, night-vision glasses, and M1 steel helmets, they faced a shocking revelation of the extremists' true strength. A sniper's bullet struck a young radio operator's skull, creating panic. Despite the setback, the operation continued as commandos advanced through the temple's pillars. However, a rocket attack forced the army to halt near the Akal Takht. Seventeen army commandos sacrificed their lives for Mother India. The clash resulted in a bloody battlefield between the Akal Takht and the Golden Temple. Despite attempts, the para commandos couldn't breach the Khalistan supporters' defence. On 6 June, as dawn approached, R.K. Dhawan, PM's aide, relayed the news about the success of Operation Blue Star to PM Indira at her Golf Link residence in Delhi. However, the casualties among soldiers and civilians were extensive. Upon hearing the news, PM Indira's reaction was surprising. She exclaimed to Dhawan, 'Oh God! I was told there wouldn't be casualties, but what happened!'

The aftermath of Operation Blue Star led to unexpected consequences within the Sikh community. A discord erupted that caught everyone off guard. The army faced internal rebellion within its ranks. Tragically, within four months, PM Indira Gandhi untimely met her demise at the hands of her two Sikh bodyguards. The nation witnessed horrifying acts as more than 8,000 Sikhs fell victim to brutal violence, with 3,000 casualties in Delhi alone at the hands of enraged mobs.

Krur murdon ne, jindon ko murda banaaya kyoon hai!
Haivaanon ne rab ke bandon ko, rulaya kyoon hai!
Kabhi antaratma se ye poochhkar to dekho,
Insaanon ne insaaniyat ko, bhulaaya kyoon hai!

Oh! Why are cruel beasts in this world tormenting and killing innocent people! Do they never ask their conscience why they have abandoned humanity?

Sher Singh, who was involved in this, would remember those times later and tell his buddies that, in the history of civil struggle in independent India, this was an intense and bloodstained conflict. The revered Holy Akal Takht of the Sikhs had suffered greatly in this war, a fact that had brought regret to every religious individual, including those in the army. Sher Singh regretted his absence for an extended period and thus his inability to take care of his family. However, given the dire situation of the country, he believed it was essential to prioritize the nation's well-being.

Even the elderly, feeble grandparents understood that their son had to dedicate himself to the nation's service and instead looked at their grandson's bright future as their ultimate dream. But age took its own course and they suffered health-related complications. The doctors, despite their efforts, advised relying on faith. Bishna Devi wholeheartedly cared for them. Meanwhile, Sher Singh, after taking a few days off from duty, made every possible effort to alleviate their pain—from seeking help from fellow soldiers to knocking the doors of private hospitals. But ultimately, within a few months, the inevitable happened.

Now, in all practicality, the entire responsibility for the family fell on the shoulders of Bishna Devi and her son Pushkar. Sher Singh's next posting in the coming months was to be in Sagar, Madhya Pradesh. He assured his wife and son that he would try and assist them as far as he could. Pushkar started sharing the workload with his mother and sisters, taking on significant responsibilities at a young age. Their sense of duty helped them manage their studies and household chores systematically. Pushkar's exemplary conduct garnered admiration from the neighbourhood mothers, who encouraged their children to emulate his example.

6

EDUCATION: A CHRONICLE OF STRUGGLE

Door jaana door jaana, mat poochho kitanee door jaana!
Mat roko, mat roko bahut door hai mera thikaana!

To fulfil my dreams, I still have a long journey ahead, so don't ask how far I am going. Let me go, don't stop me, because my destination is very far.

—Pushkar Dhami

Fortunately, Pushkar's father Subedar Sher Singh was stationed in Sagar, Madhya Pradesh, and he had his family residing with him in the military cantonment. Plans were underway to enrol the children in the local school. Pushkar was enthralled by the captivating natural beauty of the cantonment. To add to his thrill, he was informed that he would also be starting school the following day!

'*Pitaji*, where's my new dress?' inquired Pushkar.

'*Beta*, first excel in the initial test!' replied his father. 'Tomorrow, the headmaster at the school will conduct your examination and then determine the next steps.'

Filled with confidence, Pushkar exclaimed, 'Okay, I'm ready! What kind of test will they have for me?'

'It will involve arithmetic, algebra questions, scientific definitions, and proficiency in Hindi and English,' explained his father. 'You should be familiar with these.'

Pushkar confidently responded, 'Absolutely! Pitaji, I've been the top student in all three of my previous schools. I always scored full marks in mathematics. I was the teacher's closest pupil, and was frequently appointed as a monitor.'

Seeing the child's confidence, Bishna Devi also intervened, encouraging Indra and Pushpa to study.

'Pitaji, let's revise some poems and be prepared for tomorrow,' Sher Singh suggested before leaving for duty. The following morning, Pushkar rose early and began studying from the worn-out books of Lohia Head School and 'UP Board' (Uttar Pradesh State Board of High School and Intermediate Education or UPMSB), motivating his three sisters to wake up too. Witnessing their child's determination and enthusiasm for learning, tears of love welled up in the eyes of Sher Singh and Bishna Devi. Despite having three daughters, the parents felt immensely proud to have a son, especially one who exceeded their expectations in promise and skill. Overwhelmed with emotions, his father embraced him, showering him with love and blessings.

Subsequently, Pushkar got ready, took a bath, borrowed a belt from his sister, and caught up in the rush of fastening his pants, tried to alert his mother in the kitchen. 'Mother, understand that today is my entrance exam for eighth grade! Hurry, look at the new clock from Khatima Bazar on my wrist, there are only eight minutes left until eight o'clock!' he said to her.

'Now that I've grown up, Eeja, I'll be studying in a higher class where questions span two to three pages instead of just simple answers. In Didi's notebook, the Revolt of 1857 covers more than three pages. Sometimes, success comes inevitably when there's no other option but to strive for it,' he reflected. Setting goals and pursuing them makes even the impossible achievable. With these thoughts, he started thinking beyond his years.

Sher Singh, attired in a deep green military outfit resembling a dedicated military officer, accompanied his son to DNCB Higher Secondary School, run by the Ministry of Defence and the Cantonment Council, Sagar, within the allotted time.

He answered almost all of the teachers' questions, but he didn't stop at that; he kept posing further queries, impressing them with his innovative and investigative nature. The teachers were surprised by his inquisitive mind. Recognizing the ambition and passion in his eyes, they admitted him to eighth grade. Sher Singh felt immensely proud upon hearing the teachers' feedback. On their way back, Pushkar received an ice cream and a new bicycle as per his request. Overjoyed, he brought sweets for his sisters and mother. After a meal and some rest, as Sher Singh prepared for his evening roll-call duty, Pushkar recounted the entire incident to his sisters, introducing them to his school activities.

Soon, he started commuting to school on his bicycle, being always punctual and diligent. His timely arrivals and dedication caught the attention of his teachers, leading to his appointment as class monitor and earning additional responsibilities and courses. With discipline and a sense of responsibility, Pushkar began to stand out. Adolescence is often a time of ecstasy and fervour, and Pushkar was no exception. Besides excelling in studies, he actively engaged in various competitive activities, displaying emerging masculine traits typical of adolescence. While he treated his classmates with respect akin to his three sisters, his charm, good looks, playful nature and thoughtful demeanour attracted attention from young girls. However, despite their admiration, most students viewed him as a responsible brother, or at times, a loyal friend referred to simply as Pushkar.

As Pushkar's presence became more prominent through daily morning prayer meetings and his active role in school life, a notable event occurred during the special assembly of the last Monday when the auditorium was packed. He recited poetry, particularly these lines by Dushyant Kumar, which were also first published in Pushkar's birth year, sparking an interest for Hindi poetry and literature among the entire school community.

> *Ho gaee hai peer parvat-see pighalnee chaahie,*
> *Is himalaya se koee ganga nikalanee chaahie.*
> *Aaj yah deevaar, pardon kee tarah hilne lagee,*
> *Shart lekin thee ki ye buniyaad hilnee chaahie.*
> *Har sadak par, har galee mein, har nagar, har gaanv mein,*
> *Haath leheraate hue har laash chalnee chaahie.*
> *Sirf hungama khada karna mera maksad nahin,*
> *Saari koshish hai ki ye soorat badlanee chaahie.*
> *Mere seene mein nahin to tere seene mein sahee,*
> *Ho kaheen bhee aag, lekin aag jalnee chaahie.*

The pain has intensified; a solution is essential. Covering up the problem won't help; it must be eradicated. People from every village and street must unite, and this revolution should spread across the nation. My goal is not just to protest but to find a solution.

Mr R.N. Tripathi was Pushkar's science teacher, known for identifying children's hidden talents and showcasing them in public forums. When he would teach, students would naturally feel compelled to ask questions related to the topic. One day, in the science class, they were commemorating the birthday of the great American inventor and businessman Thomas Elva Edison. Tripathi, the science teacher, mentioned that Edison was born on 11 February 1847, in Ohio, America. Despite enduring poverty in his childhood, Edison never lost courage. Tripathi credited Edison for the electric bulb, illuminating humanity's nights. He told the students that, at the young age of 10, Edison built his first laboratory. 'While children today ask for various gifts, Edison asked his mother for books, a gift that sparked his interest in chemical experiments, ultimately shaping his success.'

Atin Chouksey, a student in the class, asked, 'Sir, my uncle told me that Edison was so dedicated to his work that he sometimes forgot to eat,' interrupting the teacher.

The teacher acknowledged Atin's statement and asked another student, Sanjay Vishwakarma, where his attention was. Sanjay remained silent, causing the other students to laugh. Pushkar, noticing this, raised his hand to speak.

The teacher encouraged Pushkar to share his thoughts. Pushkar responded, 'Sir, this morning, the newspaper delivery person handed me the newspaper. Glancing at the headlines, I noticed an extensive feature on Edison. Due to time constraints, I couldn't read it all, but what I did read highlighted how Edison made his name, with nothing other than sheer hard work. Despite failing over 10,000 times while inventing the bulb, unlike how we tend to give up after one unsuccessful attempt, Edison saw those failures as discoveries. He said, "I found 10,000 ways that didn't work for me!"'

Upon hearing Pushkar's statement, a huge applause erupted, almost cracking the walls even before the teacher's acknowledgment. His friends Salim and Mahesh patted him on the back from the back bench, recognizing the significance of Pushkar's habit of reading the newspaper, earning him everyone's respect in class.

Pushkar was a diligent and intelligent student, often a subject of discussion among teachers inside and outside the classroom. His sharp mind retained information long after it had been assimilated, leaving a lasting imprint in his memory.

During breaks and holidays, Pushkar frequented the local *'shudh desi Babba's chaat'* shop near the school, enjoying the delicacies with Atin, Sujit and other classmates. He often requested his mother, Bishna Devi, for two rupees twice a week to indulge in this treat. Apart from academic studies, the school encouraged children to take part in various extracurricular activities. Pushkar became interested in hockey when he learned about the legendary Major Dhyan Chand's disciple Tekchand Yadav's prowess in the field from his classmate Sujit Chouksey.

Sujit informed Pushkar that the hockey legend Tekchand Yadav frequented the place, offering guidance to hockey enthusiasts. In the evenings, numerous players from different clubs engaged in matches with school students across the city. Pushkar's bond with fellow student Harvansh Singh Rathore gradually strengthened; he often visited Rathore's house with other classmates. Amid discussions about current events, Pushkar outlined his future aspirations. Rathore suggested he must pursue a career as a lecturer, while Mahesh and the Chouksey brothers proposed to him to choose a career path either as a journalist or a politician. Pushkar merely gave a broad smile at their suggestions.

Within a few days, some of Pushkar's new classmates became his fans, while others became jealous of him due to his rapidly growing popularity. Time was passing at its own pace, signifying the transition from childhood to a more serious phase for Pushkar. Even his hairstyle had changed. Previously groomed by his dear sister Indra, he now disliked that old style. With the assistance of pure aromatic amla oil from the army canteen, provided by his father Sher Singh, Pushkar groomed his hair himself. He adjusted his sleeves, occasionally wore glasses, and ventured into the world of mimicking actors like Mithun Chakraborty.

The widespread influence of the film industry lead many to aspire for an attractive image, yet not every cinematic style fit seamlessly into everyday life. Sometimes, attempts to imitate such styles resulted in comical scenes, akin to a joker. It's often said that imitating requires wisdom! One of the teachers, Karan sir, known for entertaining students with various renditions of songs, frequently sang the famous tune:

> *Dam-dam diga-diga, mausam bhiga-bhiga,*
> *Bin piye main to gira, main to gira, main to gira...*
> *Haaye allah! Soorat aapkee subhanallah...*

The rainy weather is absolutely wonderful and filled with joy. Seeing the beauty of this season, I feel so intoxicated that I start swaying without even drinking. Oh God, the creator of such a breathtaking atmosphere, you must truly be magnificent!

In response, mischievous students playfully dubbed him as 'Dum Dum Diga Sir'!

Therefore, with the passage of time, the child from the hills developed an interest in the world of love and music, and it kept on increasing. The new year was just days away, and most boys and girls were busy crafting new year greetings cards for their dear teachers and friends using colourful pens.

However, Pushkar was seen lost in thoughts. He had found some money in his pocket and decided to buy a greeting card for the principal. School students and common folk had already filled the streets, which were bustling. He took his bicycle and sped it up to reach home early after school. As he was cycling home, his backpack was suddenly pulled backwards. The bag's strap had gotten caught in the bicycle wheel! Before he could comprehend the situation, the bicycle toppled uncontrollably. Further ahead, school children were caught in the traffic and were trying to manoeuvre their way through the mess. And here was Pushkar, fallen to the ground near an under-construction road, with stones and bricks severely injuring his elbows, knees and hands. He tried to stand up but struggled due to excruciating pain. Some school students who were passing by helped him get up and assemble his bicycle and belongings. The grimace on his face showed that his injuries were serious and painful, because he was a resolute young man who would hardly be affected by small wounds. Eventually, with the help of his friends, he was safely seated on the side of the road, and his father, Sher Singh, was contacted, who arrived within 15-20 minutes.

Sher Singh was shocked to find his barely conscious son and rushed him to the Army Hospital in the cantonment. The doctors diagnosed Pushkar with a fractured hand and applied a plaster cast. When Pushkar reached home with his injuries, his mother's and his sisters' eyes welled up with tears. The next morning, Bishna Devi said that her son must rest for a week, but Pushkar insisted on attending his important science and mathematics classes. Accepting his son's determination, Sher Singh accompanied him to school for many days, managing his time from official duty and personal life to ensure Pushkar didn't miss his classes.

Sher Singh always embraced his father's mantra to face life's challenges fearlessly, with patience and respect, never giving up despite difficulties.

After dedicating 28 years to the Indian Army with the Mahar Regiment, Subedar Sher Singh was set to retire on 30 April. The same year, Pushkar was to face the first significant challenge of his life—the board exams. Pushkar now sported a beard, which covered a significant part of his face. The day of the first exam had arrived. The table was adorned with a new clipboard, pen and ruler, which were kept ready since the previous night. Looking into his son's eyes, Sher Singh asked, 'Are you alright, son? What's the matter?'

After a bit of thought, Pushkar stood up from the bench after tying his shoelaces; he sighed deeply and reassured himself, 'Absolutely, I've got this! I'll excel just like I did last year, and I didn't even need to cheat!'

Bishna Devi handed him a glass of milk infused with turmeric, gently advising him, 'Son, remember this is your board exam. Make sure you read each question with care and think it through before answering.'

Then his elder sister Pushpa came with her advice so that her brother would avoid repeating the mistake that she had committed. She recounted: 'In my Class X geography exam, I mistakenly wrote about tides (*jwaar*) and ebbs (*bhata*) instead of cyclones and anti-cyclones. When asked again, I confused the teacher by explaining jwaar as a digestive grain and bhata as soybeans for curry. This led to a funny situation where Master ji, in frustration, pulled my hair and jokingly threatened to "fix my bone and digestive system", reminding me of his week-long class on the topic. In the assembly, I was disciplined to "become a cock" by squatting and holding my ears in front of everyone. It was so because

I had learned the topic that day in the morning, and it was stuck in my mind.'

Nandi and Indra laughed, teasing her, 'You must have made a hen, you silly, instead of a cock.' Everyone laughed.

Meanwhile, Sher Singh gently reminded his child about the importance of the upcoming board exam, saying, 'Overconfidence isn't always good, son. You're grown up now; it's time to think wisely and define your own life goals. Your future is right in front of you, and the days of just playing are nearly over.'

The child confidently replied, 'Don't worry, father, I'll do well. I promise to get better marks than my sister!'

Pushkar had been endowed with a great memory by the Almighty. Once something was told in class, he did not forget it even if he did not want to remember it; no matter in whichever way his teacher taught or how complex a subject was, and whether it happened to be out of his scope. His learning antennae were always active and his memory ever ready to store all sorts of information. Something similar happened in the examination hall. Even if he didn't know the direct answer to any question, he would devise ways to answer it by circling his answer around some relevant information. If he wasn't sure, he didn't hesitate to leave that question. After his father's retirement, he prepared and appeared for the remaining examinations in the quarter of his father's batchmate, Subedar Nanda Ballabh Bhatt (Kaladhungi, Nainital origin).

The exams were conducted smoothly, followed by holidays till the results were out. During the holidays, Pushkar tried his hand at creative writing, kabaddi, hockey and cricket. Also, under the guidance of the RSS, he learnt the know-hows of politics and understood the scenario then prevailing in the country.

Where there is hard work, success surely follows, given the hard work is applied with complete honesty and courage. It was the peak of the summer. Though the monsoon had descended in some parts of the country, half of India was simmering in the scorching sun. According to the forecast by the meteorological department, this year was to be no exception. As usual, Sher Singh was busy in a tea stall debate among his elderly mates about the events in the country and society. His attention was suddenly caught by the day's newspaper which had carried the result of the high school examination with the serial number of students on the newspaper's first and seventh pages. Subedar Sher Singh quickly gulped the last sip of the tea, got up from his bench, and tried to get closer to the group. As he took a closer look at the newspaper, he was now convinced that the results were out. He got up and rushed towards the house to note down the roll number of his son Pushkar. On his way, he told everyone that the result of the high school examination was out. Oblivious to his father's excitement, Dhami was busy composing his first lines in verse. The first lines evocatively read like this:

Door jaana, door jaana, mat puchho kitni door jaana!
Mat roko, mat roko bahut door hai mera thikaana!

The news of the high school result being out started spreading like a forest fire. As soon as the house was in sight, Sher Singh suddenly heard Sundar's grandfather saying, 'My grandson has tripped this time.'

Startled, Sher Singh asked with sympathy, 'Has he been rushed to the hospital or not?'

Sundar's grandfather chuckled and said, 'Dear, he has only tripped through his high school exam.'

Sher Singh took a sigh of relief and comforted him. 'Oh! It doesn't matter much. Not all the children who sit for the exam pass it as well! There is nothing to worry about, if he works hard, he will pass the exam next time.'

Going a little further, Manoj's mother was returning with fodder for cattle. She also greeted him and informed him in a calm voice that Manoj and Harish too had 'tripped' for the second year.

Sher Singh's heartbeat intensified a little now. After entering the long and wide iron-gate, he noticed there was silence in the house. He looked towards the courtyard. At nine o'clock, the sun was desperate to spew fire. Taking a little breath on the cot in the verandah, Subedar Sher Singh said in a sharp voice, '*Kaan khin gaya hoo nantino sabaka sab oooh...* Pushkar! (Where have you all gone, children? O Pushkar!).

After a few moments, Indra walked in with a glass of lemonade and said that Brother Pushkar had gone to Chandar's uncle's house. Desperate, Sher Singh also started putting on his shoes properly to leave for Chander Chacha's house. Suddenly, Pushkar's five to seven friends began to open the gate of the house; they had the newspaper in their hands! Pushkar also appeared all of a sudden and put his hand on Manoj's shoulder from behind. As he saw his father in the verandah, he removed his hand from Manoj's shoulder and asked his friends to enter the house respectfully. He closed the door behind him and rushed to touch his father's feet. He then broke the good news that Sher Singh had been so eager to hear. Pushkar had passed the high school exam! His friends were carrying the grief of having failed themselves, but they all clapped for Pushkar's success. Sher Singh folded his lips inwards and patted his son on his back with two to four heavy thuds. 'Well done, my son! Wonderful! That's why I rushed from the tea-stall.' Next, he turned towards Manoj and said, 'And what happened to you all?'

Manoj replied, 'Uncle ji, the roll numbers of Thapa and both his sisters are not on the list as well!'

'Oh! But what happened to Bhatia, Narendra, Jagdish and Amit?' Subedar asked with sadness and curiosity.

Manoj replied, 'Uncle ji, Chaurahewali Pushpa Tai's daughter has also failed!'

Subedar Sahib looked at Pushkar angrily, 'Hey! I am asking for your result, son; you are telling everyone's result but yours! First, tell me your story individually; let's check with Pushkar! Give your details.'

Bhatia turned to him and said, 'Uncle, when so many children have failed, we are not specially blessed, are we? See, Pushkar is advanced in his studies. He used to go to school by preparing lessons before the teacher, and we could never do so even after our teacher had taught a lesson and asked us to learn it by practice.'

After this, Pushkar returned from Sagar, Madhya Pradesh, to his hometown Khatima and enrolled at Tharu Government Inter College. Like most students, he would cycle to school and return home in groups in the evening. As soon as he would reach home, he would turn his back, put the bag on his table and search for his Eeja.

When she was nearby, he would change his clothes and freshen up. But if she was away, busy in the farm or the barn for work, he would rush to her side, take a bundle of fodder and move towards the house, saying, 'I am starving. First make some arrangements for food and then think about work!'

After coming back from school, Pushkar would often see food covered in different tiffin boxes for the four siblings in the kitchen. As soon as he had food, he would go the playground and the barrage and play with friends. It would be a fest of fun and frolic in cricket, kabaddi, fishing and swimming in the barrage throughout the summer! Whenever his mother could not keep food due to her busy work, Pushkar, who would be starving, would insist that she leaves for him leftover food from the night before, so that he may at least not be late to join friends at the playground.

Nandan Singh Kharayat used to often be in competition with everyone to reach the field first! Even in the school, Pushkar continued to improve his image in front of other students and teachers by participating in every activity. This is why other children, of whichever age, looked up to Pushkar with great respect, sometimes seeking his advice to solve their problems, at other times through his help in schoolwork.

One day, a parent-teacher meeting was called in the school, where prominent people of the area had come. Regional social worker and owner of the fibre factory, Dr Chandra Rastogi, had also come for the meeting. He knew Pushkar very well. A stage was set and the principal welcomed all the visitors and thanked them for accepting the invitation. Senior boys like Pushkar, Amit, Indra and Dewan arranged chairs and water for parents. During the parent-teacher dialogue, everyone was sharing their problems. Meanwhile, a woman got up and said, 'I am grateful to Tharu Government Inter College and the boy who helped my poor child get a book and dress.'

Hearing the woman's words, most parents and teachers started looking right and left. Then Rastogi ji got up from his chair and said that the child was none other than Subedar Sahib's son Pushkar, which had inspired them to help her child!

Hearing this, the headmaster asked Pushkar to hand over the water tray to one of his classmates and come to the stage.

Everyone praised him for being prompt for such a noble act and being an active participant in other curricular activities. Seeing his child being praised directly in front of him and the dignitaries, Sher Singh was overwhelmed.

Everyone present wished Pushkar a bright future and congratulated him. His teacher, B.C. Mehta, said that Pushkar differed from the students of Tharu Inter College in many ways. He recounted fondly: 'He is someone who keeps an eye outside and also maintains social co-existence with his classmates and others in the college. He has a good mix of leadership traits and diligence. Despite being a disciple, he is even ahead of his teachers in some ways. Even in the classroom, if he is asked a question, he tries to explore all possibilities through his own perspective, and that too in economical words. With an impeccable image, Pushkar is popular among teachers and students. On any activity or function of the school, Pushkar is entrusted with essential responsibilities, which he performs well with the help of his classmates and junior students. In this way, the children of junior classes are included and made aware of their responsibilities, while also developing leadership abilities in their classmates!'

This time, as exam-time rolled around, the school began actively working for better results. On the notice board, the watchman pinned up a piece of information, stating: 'On Monday, the examiner team will come to take the practical examinations of Chemistry and Physics.'

All students were supposed to prepare well and be present in the science room at 10 a.m. with chart paper. In this first step of the board examination, everyone could get good marks quickly. Hence, everyone's endeavour was to make as much effort as possible. Pushkar decided to prepare his practical on the theory of Archimedes in Physics and the method of making ammonia gas in Chemistry.

The examiner first asked the children their names and favourite topics so their scope could be better assessed! First came Pushkar's turn. Standing upright, this good-looking and confident boy charmed the examiner at the first sight.

The examiner asked the first question, 'Explain the Haber method of making ammonia gas in simple terms.'

Pushkar replied, 'Sir! First, we must mix the pure form of nitrogen and hydrogen in a ratio of 1:3 and then combine this mixture to 200 atmospheric pressure and 500 degrees Celsius temperature. After that, the iron powder will be mixed with molybdenum as a catalyst for catalyst enhancement. Then, leave this mixture in another beaker for some time to cool. When this mixture cools down, the impurities in front of us will be found in pure form in the liquid, along with ammonia gas. But it is an exothermal reversible reaction so that we will feel a decrease in volume. Sir, the equation of this reaction is $N_2 + 3H_2 = 2NH_3$.'

After the practical examinations, students were given some time for self-study for the board examination to be held in March. Pushkar studied school notes as well as some critical external sources. He also took coaching in physics, chemistry and mathematics with the help of nearby teachers. He would sit on the terrace under the lukewarm sun all day and keep himself busy in preparation.

The first paper was Hindi. Seeing the papers, the brightness of the faces of the students remained intact, which meant that the examination paper was within the scope of their preparation. Pushkar gave the exam with a happy heart. But when he was writing the conclusion of the essay, the school bell rang and it meant the time was up. All of them submitted their answer sheets to the invigilator. They came out of the examination hall and fiercely debated on unread passages and short answer questions, including *rasa*s, verses and figures of speeches.

The following exam was to be English, whose very name gave everyone jitters. Pushkar quickly reached the main gate, went inside, and started racing through copies, books and refreshers related to the English subject. He couldn't prepare that well, but was confident that he would be able to pass the exam. Mathematics was Pushkar's favourite subject, and he had always outperformed his classmates in the subject.

Now, only the results were awaited, before Pushkar had to prepare for a long-term plan in life. While waiting for the examination results, he worked to understand the Sangh politics and ideology closely.

Also, as per order of his father, Sher Singh, he began preparation for medical examination and army recruitment. He would get up every morning and start running, practise balancing, push-ups, long jumps, etc., for physical efficiency tests for joining the army. He was also, at the same time, preparing for bachelor's medical programme so that his father's dream of his son becoming a doctor or surgeon could be fulfilled.

But amid the thoughts of all these career options, Pushkar often remembered the oath of the adjuration of the Sangh, which he not only pledged because of personal resolve, but it had also seeped into his heart. It was about the all-round progress of the Hindu nation, i.e. *Sarve bhavantu sukhinah* (May all be happy)'. Overwhelmed by the spirit of the Almighty, and remembering his ancestors, the holy Hindu religion, Hindu culture and Hindu society, he realized his dream was to become a part of the RSS! His dream was to do the work of the Sangh, lifelong, with authenticity and selfless intelligence!

Meanwhile, his elder sister Nandi's marriage was fixed, and preparations began at his home. According to Hindu customs, Subedar Sher Singh and Bishna Devi, with moist eyes, blessed the newly-married couple to always be bestowed with good fortune by handing over their sweetheart to the care of their son-in-law who was working in a well-known company in Mumbai. Pushkar, along with his cousins, picked up the palanquin and bid farewell with a heavy heart to his dear sister, with the resolve that:

> *Even in a fast-paced life,*
> *I'll never forget you, dear.*
> *Wait for me in every difficulty,*
> *I promise to meet on Rakhi every year.*

And thus, the sister's palanquin departed. The house was full of familiar people, relatives, merriment, decoration; but despite that, the daughter's departure had left tears in everyone's eyes.

7

UNIVERSITY: A NURSERY OF PERSONALITY DEVELOPMENT

Unless your shoulders are strong enough to carry your own burden, you cannot be ready to carry the burden of life.

Almost five months have passed since the Sun entered Uttarayan (northern). Therefore, the doldrums, also known as the inter-tropical convergence zone, is also eager to touch Kanyakumari, which is positioned away from the equator. The ocean breeze, which flows from east to west in the Indian ocean, has attracted—like a lover's warm breath—the hot winds (or loo) blowing in North India, creating monsoon winds of love. However, the entirety of North India would have to wait a little longer to be drenched in the spray of water from the southern sea waves.

Chugging through such a humid night and breaking the prevailing silence, the Mailani Express arrived with the first ray of morning sun at platform number one of the Lucknow railway station. The train ran from Khatima and, passing through Pilibhit and Sitapur, it reached Lucknow. The passengers alighted with dreary faces, laziness having accumulated during the overnight journey.

As they got down on the platform, an army of coolies and rickshaw and auto drivers descended on them with offers of their services. They named famous places of the city and assured their prospective customers that they would take them to their destinations safely. Even if passengers refused their offers, these coolies and autowallahs walked with them till outside the station, persuading them with their offers, even making concessions. When they couldn't strike a deal, many of them walked back inside the railway station, in search of other arriving passengers.

From this Mailani Express, a slim young man with a bright face also got down. Removing a pair of goggles from his eyes and carefully avoiding the onslaught of coolies and autowallahs, he came out of the station with his suitcase and bag.

Many porters tried to lift the young man's luggage, but he refused. His military-man father's words began to echo in his mind: **'Unless your shoulders are strong enough to carry your own burden, you cannot be ready to carry the burden of life.'** As soon as he left the station, the young man found that the grey clouds of Shravan or Sawan (July) were lurking in the horizon in the sky. Removing them with their red fingers, the sun's rays were trying to make way for itself. Seeing this wizardry of nature, the young man was filled with energy, fire and hope, like the rising sun's blazing brightness.

To him, Lucknow seemed immersed in a golden aura. His heart bowed to the holiness of this city, which was to be his workplace for the following years. Lucknow has been known by several epithets—'the city of Nawabs', 'city with the Ganga-Yamuna *tehzeeb* (etiquettes)', 'city of finesse and elegance', 'the golden city', 'Shiraz-e-Hind', 'the city of gardens' and 'city of *adab* (respect)'.

People in this city express themselves with a certain finesse and elegance in their dialect, irrespective of being in a situation of agreement or dispute. Even in anger, their language doesn't turn coarse. Pushkar himself shared his own experience of Lucknow days and recalled that even in heated disputes, people addressed each other with honourable and self-respectful pronouns like *aap* (you) and *hum* (I, or the royal we). It is as if Lucknow follows the essence of writer A.G. Gardner's essay, 'On Saying Please'! As Dhami grew acquainted with this magnificent city, he became more and more besotted. He was in awe of expressions of its people, the grandeur of its buildings, etiquette of its gentry and the commoners alike, and its friendly ambience. He found the ancient buildings majestic and a fine specimen of medieval architecture. They made him wonder how hard must have the nawabs and their maestros worked; so hard that their palms must have ached to build such structures.

Mashakkat se utha hua, mashakkat ka dard bhaanmpta hai, Ambudh, ambar se jyaada vasudha ki kadr aankata hai.

Only the needy value the benevolent, as only those who toil understand the pain of labour.

When it comes to Lucknow, we all must have heard a saying: 'Smile sir, now you are in Lucknow.' Indeed, from pavement to palaces, every alley and corner of this city boasts of its own unique story that can bewitch with its multicultural elegance and panoramic description. Such narration works like a talisman and casts its spell on listeners as the narrator assumes as many facial expressions as there are curves in the story. A pure verbal magic!

The mode of life, food, dialect, buildings and dressing in Lucknow bear a sharp stamp of its majestic past and inform that the city was under a long rule of Nawabs. It is said that Nawab Asaf-ud-Daula founded the modern and prevailing form of this magnificent city. Looking back, we find that this city has an extremely interesting history. Many Nawabs of Awadh have spent their entire life in its construction. These include Saadat Ali Khan, Safdar Jang, Nawab Shuja-ud-Daula, Asaf-ud-Daula, Wazir Ali, Saadat Ali Khan, Ghazi-ud-Din Haider Shah, Nasir-ud-Din Haider Shah, Muhammad Ali Shah and Wajid Ali Shah.

'Brother, will you take the auto? Where do you have to go?' an autowallah pestered Pushkar again.

Pushkar took out a folded slip from his pocket and read the address, 'Dollygunj.' Sharing the friend's name and address, he was in a dilemma whether this driver, who was looking at him strangely, would be able to take him to the destination or not! Overcome with doubts, he moved past this autowallah and proceeded towards others. There were five or six autos waiting there. He stopped by one whose driver seemed to be of his age and, after telling him the address, he boarded the auto.

After 10 minutes of ride through the bustling road full of vehicles, the autowallah finally signalled him to get off. Pushkar was lost in day-dreaming and didn't seem to hear the driver. The driver roared to awaken him, 'Hey, get down, you *hoshiyar* (Mr Alert).'

When his heavy voice hit his ears, Pushkar handed over a new five-rupee note and sent him away. Soon, this young man standing on the roadside was bedazzled by the sight of high-rise buildings. He was also puzzled regarding which one he must walk up to? Fortunately, in no time, his friend appeared with two plastic buckets tied to both ends of one stick placed on his shoulders in a scene that was reminiscent of Shravan

Kumar's *kanwar*. As soon as Pushkar came out of his thoughts, he rushed towards his friend. Both of them shook hands with unspeakable warmth. He put the buckets on the stairs and first helped him with his two bags. Only after that did the friend bring the buckets full of hand pump water inside as well.

On reaching his friend's room that looked like a cell, he found that there were other people living there as well. Whenever someone from their village came, everyone anticipated that he must have brought something for them. Every time when someone from the group would go back home in the village, the rest of them would keep waiting for his return, hoping that he would bring homemade edibles, even if it might turn out to be merely coriander or hemp salt. Pushkar took out from his bag two one litre bottles, filled with milk and buttermilk, respectively. And there was his mother's love, neatly arranged in the rest of the small bags! Pushkar was stunned to see his mother's selfless love and affection, even though it would happen often. He paused for a while, sitting on the floor, leaning against the corner of the table, and kept staring at the symbols of his mother's affection.

He resolved that he would not let his mother's dreams be shattered, that he would face all the challenges to make his way forward through hard work. *If a man like Dashrath Manjhi can sear through a mountain in order to do justice with his emotions, why can't I rise from among brothers and sisters like me and do something different and better*, he thought to himself.

About a week later on a Friday evening, when Pushkar sat down to discuss with his friends about his future education, a unique picture of the university started appearing in his mind. All the companions, on their behalf, apprised him of what the regional colleges had to offer. Pushkar thought of his parents at this crucial time. His father Sher Singh had retired from his duty of protecting the motherland, keeping fear at the tip of his gun with his life at stake amid terrorists and enemies. For Pushkar, it was crucial at this time for him to decide which subject would suit him to build his future, and thus he had to make a careful choice. Had his mother been around, she would have said that she was not able to complete even her primary education, that having been married at a tender age had rendered her like a kite tethered to one hand, continuously navigating the struggles of life. So she would want her son to make the best of his education that he had been blessed to have. Sher Singh wouldn't have been able to give him more information due to his own social busyness. Therefore, Pushkar was confident that he must have to choose between science and arts streams, according to his true capacity. One minute he was sure about what he wanted, and the next, he was caught up in a vortex of confusion about what to do and what not to do!

He was ruminating on his future prospects when suddenly someone knocked at the door. He stood up quickly, hastily arranged the room a little and headed towards the doorway where his worn-out slippers were lying on top of each other. He was putting on his slippers when he heard a knock again, a little more loudly this time. Pushkar was frightened as to who could it have been. All the companions had already marched towards their respective destinations. Wearing only one chappal, he opened the latch of the door, saying, 'Who is it?'

'Postman!', said a voice, softly, from the outside.

The tone was very light, yet Pushkar understood; and with joy, he quickly opened the door. When he saw thin Chhoturam, the postman, in khaki uniform in front of him, with a letter in his hand and satchel on his waist, he understood that his father must have remembered him and sent some of his suggestions.

The postman turned the page of his old register, held out a Reynolds pen, and said, 'Sign here.'

In his unique style, Pushkar dragged the pen on paper, signing against his name, and asked the postman to have some water, but he refused, saying he was not thirsty. Pushkar swiftly opened the envelope and began to read the letter. On sky-coloured paper were the words of his father's love and suggestions to live in discipline. It was expected of a father as a routine. But as he proceeded reading it, a smile on his lips and tears in his eyes arrived simultaneously. Father was empathetic with his son and encouraging him:

'Good luck, son! Work hard like this, move forward. You do not lack anything. Take up science, for you must become a doctor, do not forget! The rest, you yourself are wiser now! You've grown up! You have passed matriculation! A good doctor is like God embodied on this earth, and is free from any malice towards any being. He is always friendly and kind-hearted. He is balanced in happiness and misery, forgiving by nature, always satisfied and mentally united with the people. Having such a person between us is like God taking incarnation himself.

Adveshta sarva-bhootanam maitraha karuna evcha,
Nirmamo nirhankarah sama-dukh-sukhah kshami,
Santushta satatam yogi yatatma dridha-nishchayah,
Mayyarpita-manobuddhiryo mad-bhaktah sa me priyah.

Last lines of the letter first stirred a fresh wave of patience, determination and courage in Pushkar. Then, as though wearing the white coat of doctors, with stethoscope hanging from his neck, a scene from his childhood when he had been vaccinated and the injection had given a sharp pain flashed in front of his eyes as an exciting memory. He had vowed to take revenge from that doctor who had vaccinated him despite his protest. But that was childhood! Now, he was imagining about an operation theatre, operation tools arranged on the table, bandages and cotton kept ready for use by doctors. After receiving a loving letter from his father, filled with words of guidance, Pushkar decided to go to his village, Nagla, Khatima, to sort out the confusion and avoid the conflict between selection of science or arts for his further studies.

There were still 10 minutes left for the train to depart from Lucknow. So Pushkar stepped out of his coach and looked around. He found that some passengers were looking at the seat list pasted at the coach gate. On the busy platform, a man and a woman got into an argument, which quickly escalated when the man turned to out to be a male chauvinist and started misbehaving. Other passengers around complained that they were also in queue to check their seats, but that man was not ready to listen. As Pushkar noticed that his voice was wavering and his steps were stuttering, the former guessed that he was intoxicated with either *laal pari* or *8PM*. Pushkar murmured to himself, 'She is also someone's sister or daughter. If I cannot discharge my duties like other passengers, tomorrow I may see my own mother and sisters at her place. So I will have to act.' Pushkar adjusted his silver-glazed steel-frame watch that was coiled around his wrist next to the red and yellow holy threads. The watch showed that there was still five minutes for the train to depart. So, Pushkar made his way through the passengers to confront that drunkard who was continuously using abusive language like he was chanting some mantra.

Hearing such expletives enraged Pushkar, and he moved towards the drunkard.

'What's the matter, uncle?' Pushkar raised his eyebrows and said in an indignant tone.

But the drunkard was unmoved! On the other hand, after getting Pushkar's support, the woman's lost courage returned. She thought Pushkar had come forward like a saviour from between the disappointing crowd of passengers. She pulled the dupatta that was on her shoulders onto her head and came closer to him with folded hands, and said, 'Son, see what has he been uttering? Look at his insolence! He is neither checking his seat nor is he allowing others to do so.'

Suddenly the drunkard roared, 'If slippers adorn heads, where would turbans go!'

At this, other passengers also started shouting because everyone was fed up of his antics by now, but no passenger wanted to waste their precious time on an argument with him. As a result, most of the passengers were forced to tolerate his humiliation even if they did not want to. But Pushkar responded to the woman who was still standing with folded hands.

Pushkar: Don't worry, sister! Have a little more patience. I'll see what I can do. I'll put him straight.

Drunkard: Who sister? Whose sister? Who the hell are you?

Pushkar (angrily): What are you saying... Should I put you straight? You will immediately come to your senses. Stay in your limits! If she is not saying anything... Do you think this is an anarchy? Keep in mind this is a public place, not the courtyard of your home!

Drunkard (in a staggering voice): Who are you, trying to be a leader here...!

Pushkar: Don't forget this, the dupatta of a mother or a sister is the turban of a man's head, and men who treat women as garbage have no right to adorn turbans on their heads! Being such an older man, all this does not suit you, uncle. Either you behave yourself, or I can set you straight right now!

Drunkard (in a subdued voice): 'Wh... what?'

Hearing the young Pushkar's words, the man fell onto a platform bench and finally sat in a quiet manner.

Lady: 'I also wanted to see my seat, but I don't know how to check... I have two small daughters. Had their father been alive, I would probably not have been pounced upon by such vultures and crows at every turn, nor would I be considered so helpless...'

The woman burst into tears.

Pushkar remembered the lines of Sant Kabir Das taught by teachers in sixth or seventh grade. All the students like Pushkar were obsessed with those couplets, even if they were unaware of the meaning then!

Durbal ko na sataiye, jaakee motee haay.
Maree khaal kee saans se, lauh bhasm ho jaye.

In this verse, Kabir Das says that a powerful person intoxicated by his ego should not do any atrocity on a weak person, because his pain and curse are very harmful. Just as the blacksmith's hearth has the power to consume iron even though it is lifeless, in the same way, it is possible that the whole clan can be destroyed with the curse of a grieving person.

The passengers, including Pushkar, carefully heard the woman's poignant lament, which moved all of them. Pushkar lifted her two children who were curiously running here and there on the platform, and he then took all of them to their seats inside the coach. The woman showered her blessings and gratitude on him. She prayed that he passes his exams with good marks and wished that every mother should beget a son like him. She said that all mothers must raise their children like him. Her wishes and prayers caught the attention of other passengers as well.

Pushkar humbly acknowledged all her blessings and came out of the train coach feeling proud of what he had done. Immediately, the train gave off a high-pitched long whistle, which was the last warning for its passengers. Pushkar ran towards his coach as the train started moving! In that rush, he just latched onto a coach that he could manage to catch. It was an unknown compartment, but he kept walking through it. The train slowly sped up and left for its destination.

Almost the entire station was about to be crossed, but there was still so much hustle and bustle in the train. Finally, Pushkar reached his coach and berth. A young man of his age and a young woman were already there. Pushkar sat on the window seat and got lost in the scenic panoramic view which was rolling past him as the train sprinted ahead. Fields full of swaying multicoloured crops appeared and disappeared swiftly just as a desert mirage does.

Along with the sight of fields, dense forests and small huts exhibited the quintessential diversity of India in its full view for the travellers. Pushkar felt besotted with the magnetic charm of such natural beauty for quite long. Soon it was past midnight. Sleep lay heavily on his eyes and soon he drifted off. When the train reached the scheduled destination, all the passengers began pulling out their luggage lying under their seats. The sound of screeching bags entered Pushkar's unconscious body and killed the innocent sleep within a moment. As a result, he suddenly woke up, rubbed his eyes, and tied up his bundle of stuff, which he had not only enjoyed using as a pillow throughout the journey, but was his preferred way of travel, the traditional Indian style of travelling. So now it was the bundle's turn to be respectfully carried on the back or shoulders of its owner.

As soon as he stepped onto the platform, a coolie tried to grab the bundle from Pushkar's shoulder. But Pushkar stopped him endearingly and said, 'Oh no, brother, sorry! I am the son of a soldier.' In a gesture of grabbing one end of his moustache and twirling it, which is a mark of Kshatriya sublimity and self-respect, he said with pride and humour: 'In this youth, I can carry even you along with the bag.'

After hearing the young boy, a lean, thin coolie, wearing colourful underwear and vest, said something to him in a lisp and patted his back with a wide smile. He walked a few steps alongside him. The train's arrival was announced just then. Pushkar noticed a man passing by, carrying a large, shiny tea kettle in one hand and a basket filled with samosas on his head.

The man was trying to attract passengers by loudly calling out, 'Samosa... Tea... Tea... Hot Tea...' He was trying to persuade people to buy his items.

Pushkar evaded his screams and reached the road, which was a short distance from his house. Upon reaching closer to home and seeing his mother sweeping the courtyard, he sped up! Dropping his bag on the ground, he excitedly shouted 'Eeja! Eeja! Eeja!', calling out to his mother in his local dialect.

His mother, turning around, was surprised to see her son and warmly embraced him. Pushkar asked about her well-being and volunteered to clean the remaining part of the courtyard. Afterwards, they sat on the cot, engaging in lively conversation. Pushkar fondly remembered swimming in the Sharda Barrage during his childhood, doing so in styles like the backstroke and butterfly. A discussion ensued about the superstitions regarding broom placement. His mother believed keeping it upside down invited disease and enemies, while Pushkar recalled his uncle's opposite belief—that downward placement attracted wealth. They debated the topic before concluding that such superstitions shouldn't cloud their judgment and befool them. Everyone must do their work according to their convenience and must make sure that it doesn't cause inconvenience to others. 'We must know the fundamental principle that our rights end where others' begin,' one of them said.

His elder sister soon arrived and, seeing her brother, playfully greeted him as *Chhote Sarkar ji* (Little Sire). Her face lit up with joy and affection as she caressed his hair. Pushkar respectfully touched her feet, seeking her blessings. In a teasing manner, she loudly demanded sweets and playfully insisted that he bring her jalebi from a nearby shop. Unaware of the joke, their mother attempted to calm her, not realizing that siblings were ecstatic on uniting after a somewhat long period and were just having fun. Familial warmth and playful banter ensued, as often happens when there is a get-together after a long time. Their mother began explaining, 'Your brother is tired right now; in the evening, your father will finish his work. Just wait. He will bring it... We must divide it in the neighbourhood too...! Chandra Chacha and Paru have also been asking for it every day.' Thus, a peaceful agreement was reached between mother and sister.

Nandi burst out in laughter at the innocence of her mother. She then, beaming with happiness, told her rather seriously, 'Our brother has passed his exam with good marks. This is no less than a jalebi and kaju katli for us.'

His other sister Pushpa fetched water for her brother in an earthen jar and gave it to him in a traditional *lota* (small rounded vessel). After a heartfelt exchange of greetings with his sister, he gulped it in one go. Suddenly some neighbourhood boys passed by the house and as soon as they spotted Puskar, they came in excitedly to meet him.

'Brother, you have done wonders!' they all exclaimed in unison.

'You have scored a century, brother, a century,' Indra, sitting at the window, announced proudly.

The other friend seconded Indra: 'Our brother is no less than Kapildev Ramlal Nikhanj. As our cricket team had won world cup under his leadership, we too one day will pass intermediate in the leadership of our brother Pushkar.' Although, there was a tinge of sadness in his voice as well.

Another chimed in, 'Yes, brother, we might have failed today, but there's no regret. We'll at least receive participation certificates. And if we pass next time, we'll have two certificates to show for our efforts.'

'True, absolutely! Why not?' Pushkar agreed, with a smile.

Finding himself lagging behind in his enthusiasm, his loving friend Bhatia ji leaned forward 45 degrees, 'Brother, passing intermediate is no less than climbing Mount Everest. And when someone like our brother Pushkar ascends it in his first climb, it becomes even more special.'

Pushkar embraced all of them with warmth and thanked them for their wishes and compliments. And then, a friendly session commenced among the youth brigade. After some time, Deewan told him that all the friends in the village missed him and that they should all meet in the evening.

Pushkar bid them bye, locked the iron gate of his house, and when he turned, he found that his sister Nandi was waiting for him by the cot. She had come to her parents' house from her in-laws' house only a day before. After marriage, she had been living with her husband in Mumbai. As she cast a look at Pushkar, she asked worriedly, 'Don't you have proper meals? Look at your face, it's so gaunt!' She then called out her mother.

'Behold! How weak is he become, Eeja? This time, he's not recognizable at all!'

Mother affectionately stroked Pushkar's hair, highlighting the stark contrast between the comfort of home and the outside world. She noted that at home, one could eat as they wished, unlike outside, where laziness or a lack of options might force one to go to sleep even on a hungry stomach. She pondered if living in a hostel had been good for him or not, as there, unlike at home, no one would lovingly prepare and serve food according to personal preferences.

The Dhami family had always been disciplined and devoted, a trait ingrained through the efficient leadership and traditional teachings of their grandparents and parents. This family's ethos ensured that all tasks were completed promptly. Each family member began their day early, diligently fulfilling their responsibilities. Subedar Sher Singh Dhami, in particular, had been instrumental in applying the strict rules and regulations of the Indian Army in their household, ensuring a well-ordered domestic environment.

Believing in the importance of a healthy, disciplined home environment, Subedar Sher Singh Dhami has always emphasized the need for everyone to be actively involved in worldly tasks. He advocated that good health was crucial for a happy life and a progressive society. He instilled the habit of practicing yoga early in the morning and maintaining a regular bedtime routine in his children. He taught that waking up in *Brahmamuhurta,* roughly an hour before sunrise, and adhering to yogic principles would lead to a day filled with freshness and confidence. Missing this crucial time zone, he believed, resulted in missing the rejuvenating effects of the morning, leading to laziness and poor health. Thus, one's success could be delayed or remain unachieved. Pushkar had always valued the efficient use of time since childhood, maintaining a systematic approach to life with the occasional childhood mischief.

In the joy of having her son home, Bishna Devi headed to the kitchen to prepare his favourite meal.

She handed fresh cucumbers to her youngest daughter Indra so she could grate them. It was to be mixed with a paste of aromatic spices, prepared by grinding mustard seeds, green chillies and fresh coriander leaves on the grindstone, and mixed with home-made curd. Whenever women use *silbatta* or *okhli* (smaller and larger mortar-pestle) in villages or homes, the jingle of their bangles heralds a sense of joy through their presence and their love for their household. It has been a common scene in Indian houses since ancient times. Often, innocent young ones easily find their mothers by following the jingle of their ornaments and curl up in their laps.

His mother offered roti, *sabzi* with *raita* to her son Pushkar; for this, she had picked fresh vegetables from the garden herself. Pushkar took a bath and left the bathroom, drying his wet hair with the help of a towel. His glistening skin, smelling of soap and shampoo, was exuding freshness. Pushkar peeped inside to ask his sister Pushpa to hand him a pair of pyjamas, shirt or whatever was lying on the bed.

Pushpa walked towards the black painted aluminium trunks stacked in the northeast corner of the room. On each of these trunks, the name of Subedar Sher Singh Dhami, the number of his unit, etc., had been painted. Some of the letters had faded over time and were now illegible. One of these trunks had been set aside for Pushkar's clothes during their division among the siblings. The sister opened one of them and took out a sky-blue shirt and black trousers and handed them to her brother. Having dressed up in fresh clothes, Pushkar walked over to the kitchen and peeked inside. The delicious fragrance of dough, coriander and chillies being roasted and fried in ghee increased his appetite. Pushkar went closer to the stove and poured another spoonful of ghee on the paratha to wake it up from a slumber that it seemed to be enjoying, gently sizzling on the hot pan. As soon as the ghee melted over and slid under the paratha, it got puffed up with anger, and seemed to be giving Pushkar some sort of look. In retaliation, Pushkar pressed it down with a tong to remove all the air inside and flipped it over with the help of a tong. He then slid it onto a plate, eagerly waiting to teach it a lesson...!

Pushkar, looking at the balls of dough resting on a platter of shining brass next to his mother, pleaded, 'Oh my god, why so many parathas? One more is enough... Hurry up a little, Eeja. I am very hungry!'

Leaning on the door, Indra said, '*Wah*! You alone will eat, or what? Everyone else will do *bhajan-kirtan* here...'

Pushkar smiled, made her sit beside him, and urged her to wait until he was done eating.

Hearing their conversation, Bishna Devi said, 'Yes, in just two minutes. Sit down comfortably.'

Pushkar said, 'Let me tell you one thing, Eeja, a lot can happen in two minutes. I will tell you a story till then...'

'Yes, by then, more parathas will be ready.' Bishna Devi said, 'Maybe your father will come too. Then you have to make more for him.'

To this, Pushkar said, 'Okay, listen! There was a king named Napoleon of France; you know how he succeeded in defeating his enemy country Austria?'

'No, Babu, tell me, because I am illiterate. Or Indra must be knowing,' their mother wiped sweat off her forehead and said.

Pushkar said with a long sigh, 'So listen! The Austrian soldiers were late to the war site by two to four minutes, and due to this delay, they had to face defeat. On 18 June 1815, Napoleon was captured by the Russian coalition in the Battle of Waterloo because his commander came just three minutes late due to heavy rain.'

Meanwhile, the elder sister asked, 'What happened then, brother?'

'What was to happen? Napoleon was defeated in the Battle of Waterloo only because of a little delay and his name was merely printed in pages of history as having suffered a loss. That is why time has been the pillar of the greatness of great men,' said Pushkar.

Hearing this Bishna Devi said, 'Don't worry, my dear! I won't let you lose! My son, you will always win even if you suffer a loss somewhere! May this blessing always be with you regardless of whether I live in this world tomorrow!'

'What are you saying, Eeja?' Pushkar lovingly raised his voice a little. 'What is going to happen to you? My mother is still young and no one can match her beauty!'

Indra nodded in agreement. 'True, she ends up saying anything...'

Bishna Devi noticed her children's love and said, 'I'm

only joking, Babu. You eat properly. I will make more! Eat until your stomach is full; I don't know for how long you haven't eaten well!'

His sister interrupted their mother and said, 'He must be having chowmein and all. Who would feed him such delicious raita and vegetables there. I was studying inside but its aroma pulled me here. That's why I closed the book and ran here!'

Hearing this, Pushkar immediately put his next morsel in his sister's mouth. She protested a little, but she swallowed it.

'Son, you only concentrate on your studies.' Bishna Devi said suddenly, as if remembering something. 'There is no shortage of food and drink here. We are already working so hard. Make sure that you don't entertain any bad company and develop bad habits. Like watching cinema and loitering. Otherwise, your father won't let you come home. He doesn't like wastage of time and sauntering purposelessly.'

Pushkar was relishing the food his mother had made. Pushing a warm morsel into his mouth, he said, 'Father had sent a letter only yesterday.'

In a frightened voice, Indra asked, 'What subject will you take next?'

'Hmm...' Pushkar seemed to be taking his time responding. 'Well...'

That's when Bishna Devi interrupted his thought. 'Yes, he did not have time to suggest any subject on the day of your departure. You know that we have to maintain societal relations and give time to people in the village as well. We have to share in both their celebrations and sorrow. This is necessary for the smooth functioning of the community as a well-knit unit.'

'Don't worry, Eeja, he's very happy. But he's asking me to take up science!'

'So, take it, Babu, see if something good happens, it will be good; we all have a lot of hopes and expectations from you. You must strive to make a name for yourself. We're investing so much effort for your education. Otherwise, we might have suggested you to work in the fields with us,' his mother explained.

His sister probed him further, 'What do boys of your group say? What do your teachers suggest? And what do you yourself want to study?'

'I don't know what others are planning or have in their minds. But I want to take up the arts stream. However, Papa is insisting that I should take up science and prepare to become a doctor... So, I am in a fix...'

Pausing for a few moments and taking a long breath, Pushkar assured his mother and sister, 'Don't worry, I will find some solution.'

Bishna Devi was now clearing the cooking utensils and taking them to wash. Taking care of this chore, she said, 'Yes, think carefully and do what is right. Carefully seek opinion of educated people and also discuss this issue with your teachers. If you make a wrong decision now, tomorrow you will regret it and then it will be meaningless. Keep in mind that one day your classmates will be enjoying a successful life and you will be left with nothing but regret, so be careful in making all decisions.

Pushkar remained silent for a few moments, took another deep breath, and said, 'No, no... It will never happen, don't worry. I will fix everything.'

Amidst the conversation, the sister picked up Pushkar's plate and took it for washing.

After a few moments of silence Pushkar continued, 'I have come only for today. I will leave tomorrow by the morning train... If Papa arrives on time, then I will consult him and will be able to take a decision and follow it.'

'Ok, son, then tell me, what will you take with you from here? I will pack some essentials, pulses, rice, etc. Now it is not possible to come and go from such a distance every day.' Bishna Devi began to care for her son just at the thought of his departure.

'Yes, yes. Pack whatever you have. But only a little,' Pushkar responded. And then he slipped out to meet friends in the neighbourhood.

After coming back, Pushkar saw that Eeja had cooked beautiful *sail* (a local sweet dish) for dinner, which was Pushkar's favourite. 'Eeja, just give me the sail. My stomach is already full. I have already eaten at a friend's house.'

'Okay, son. Eat as much as you want,' his mother said.

In the meantime, the sound of Sher Singh coughing could be heard outside, announcing his arrival.

Pushkar rushed towards him, and after touching his father's feet, he took his bag from his hand and opened the gate to help him enter. Father and son immediately got to discussing the most important matter in the guest room along with the family. Ultimately, it was concluded that the subject in which Pushkar felt he had a good grip and which was also future-oriented must be chosen.

Pushkar felt relieved after solving this dilemma over subject selection. A vital hurdle had been removed and he was happy. But his mother was emotional as he was leaving.

She said in a choked voice, 'It is essential to sleep on time; if you want to leave in the morning, you have to get up early. So go to bed now.'

After helping her children prepare their beds, Bishna Devi gave her husband medicine and warm milk. Everyone went to bed after meals and milk. Pushkar's mother, however, kept tossing and turning in bed until late in the night.

In the morning, Pushkar woke up even before his mother. He poured Dabur Lal Dant Manjan tooth-cleaning powder on his palm, and taking some on his index finger, began rubbing his teeth with it. As he turned on the bathroom tap, it woke up his mother. Soon, his sisters also left their beds.

Bishna Devi approached her son and said, 'Got up so early, son? There is enough time for your train. Why did you wake up so early?'

'Nothing, Eeja,' Pushkar said. 'I just woke up... And see, it will soon be time to leave! I have bathed comfortably and done yoga, too. You all too are up now... Let me know what all is to be done. I can help you with something.'

Mother started going to milk the buffalo with a steel bucket in one hand. Pushkar followed her. He sat near his mother and while she milked the buffalo, they gossiped a lot, and helped feed the buffalo and calf. When the little calf had drunk enough milk, he helped his mother tie it back on the peg, which was a struggle. It is said that when a mother is around, the house looks like a temple; otherwise, even a temple feels deserted.

Bishna Devi walked ahead and behind her walked Pushkar with the milk bucket in one hand. He followed her into the kitchen. She found some empty bottles and filled them with milk and buttermilk for her son to carry with himself. Pushkar kept refusing, but a mother's heart is a mother's heart!

Time was short, and thus Pushkar asked his elder sister to pack his bag. Meanwhile, he got ready to leave. In the kitchen, Bishna Devi cooked *cheela* for Pushkar (rice flour crepes) and put it on the table with hot milk. She turned to secretly wipe the tears dripping from her eyes with the loose end of her saree, so that he did not have to see his mother crying.

A mother's affection has been considered selfless in this world. A mother is a beautiful masterpiece of the Almighty. She is not only a well-wisher, who always seeks worldly welfare of her children, but is also affectionate, compassionate, kind-hearted and full of virtues. All colours of love are imbued in her for the benefit of her offspring. Whether the period has been Satyuga, Tretayug, Dwaparyug or Kalyuga, she has been considered as being equal to the Almighty. She is above everyone else, and it is no exaggeration to say that heaven lies at the feet of the mother. If one tries to look a little more deeply, one would find that even the Almighty, i.e., *Vidhata* himself, needs the mother's womb to descend on this earth. This is the reason that *jagat janani maa* (mother, a creator of the universe) has a limitless sea of emotional characteristics along with the maturity to understand the child. No praise will be sufficient enough to befit the large-heartedness of a mother's heart. Whether it is Bishna Devi in the form of mother herself, or Yashoda, a symbol of magnanimity or Panna Dhai in the form of sacrifice! **Without the love of a mother, a child is incomplete, and a society is crippled!** Every day, we are getting alienated from our culture and civilization; it's our foolishness to think of the Western civilization as cutting edge. Let me tell you however hard we may try to fit into the fabric of western civilization, it will bedazzle and befool our young generation for a while, but it will never snatch from our children the natural essence of their own culture and civilization.

The sisters packed up the things that their mother had kept for their brother in parcels to be kept in his bag. Bishna Devi picked up the *tilakthal* from the temple. As per tradition,

Pushkar kept his right palm on his head as his mother applied *teeka* on his forehead. He said, 'Mother, please keep it small. The big one mixes with sweat and drips down the neck.'

Sher Singh smiled and said, 'Yes, son, it is quite small; why do you worry? Your mother has mastered this work by now; she who has brought you into this world and nurtured you till today has anointed your forehead with soot, or curd-rice, and sometimes *roli-chandan*... But remember never say no to a chandan tika, it is considered pious in our Hindu tradition... You got it!'

Accepting his father's words in great spirit, Pushkar greeted his parents and sisters by touching their feet. With a lot of blessings from all of them, he was ready to leave to pursue higher goals with his higher education.

Seeing the tears flowing from his mother's eyes, Pushkar's heart was also filled with emotions; he tried to search for his handkerchief in his pockets and recalled that he must have left it on the back of the chair. Indra swiftly rushed back inside and fetched the white handkerchief. His mother was still unaware that her son was making arrangements to wipe her tears and thus she was still convulsing inside with the pain of separation and yet was bidding farewell to her only son.

Pushkar understood his mother's emotions and explained with great affection that he was merely going away to study, to become educated. This would not only bring laurels to the family and society, it would also prepare him to serve the country responsibly and with a great sense of accountability. Therefore, this was not the time to cry but to happily bid him adieu. Tears were about to well in his eyes too, but he held himself back with all his might so that he could maintain a courageous face before his mother. He wiped tears from his mother's face and kept the handkerchief in the side pocket of his pants.

Hearing such mature words, Bishna Devi's face suddenly lit up like a lamp in deep darkness.

Seeing his mother a little happy, Pushkar gave a slight smile and said loudly, 'Mother, I am lucky. I am moving in the shadow of parents like you. Otherwise, everyone does not get a chance at school and college; how many boys like me are still not able to study in the village. I only hope that poverty should not become a mountain in front of us. Father is already sick. If I also start loitering in the streets purposelessly, I will become a burden for my elder sisters and you. So be happy, it's a happy moment, Eeja! I'm not a daughter going to my in-laws. You are getting me educated in a good college and most importantly, despite being uneducated, you have ensured that I am well-educated. I'm proud not only of this, but it's also my privilege that God has sent me to such a house where I have parents like you... What could be a more unique thing than this, for all of us.' He turned to his sisters and said, 'Right, sister?'

After listening carefully to their brother, the elder sisters shook their heads in agreement; they also explained the essence of their brother's words to their mother. This way, Pushkar left his house and boarded the train at the railway station.

Late in the evening, the train reached Pushkar's destination—the land of the Nawabs.

This is a day from where Pushkar never looked back as he sowed the seed of a strange dream and then set out caring for it, nourishing it, towards what at that time was a destination, invisible, far away in the distance.

Realization of a Realistic World

University life is very different from school life, when we gradually come to terms with the reality of the world, step by step. Almost every student in the school is a king in himself. Even new students are looked at with more respect. Students tend to make friends promptly in school. Will it be the same in university?

Pushkar was curious to know the answers to these questions; but those were hidden in the womb of the future. The sun, with its fading rays, had plunged into the horizon by imparting a golden colour to the sky.

Embracing the dreams in his eyes, deciding to go to college at 9.30 a.m., Pushkar set the alarm on his table clock for 4 a.m. He checked whether the trousers and shirts for the college were clean or not. He found that the shirt needed ironing. He was so particular with everything because the first day of college was memorable for every student. After all, to make a good impression on friends, teachers or even any future love interest, it was important to look good.

Pushkar started gliding the hot iron over the crease on his shirt while humming an old *pahadi* (highlander) song. On the one hand, there was enthusiasm of going to college, and on the other, there was a sense of obligation to carry forward or maintain his school image in college too. All in all, he felt a strong urge to sing a specific song, but he was unable to recall the exact lyrics. Even that began to occupy his mind.

This momentary clash of thoughts led him to metaphorically row two boats at the same time; thus making him forget all about the shirt that had the hot iron over it. Suddenly, he smelled something burning. He quickly lifted the iron. However, as soon as the iron was lifted, he found that it had swallowed the whole upper pocket of the shirt like a hungry jackal. The iron was plugged out, and the shirt was scrutinized back and forth, right and left.

After gathering his wits, he realized that no doctor would be able to cure the wounded animal. So he searched for another shirt in his bag with despair. Suddenly, his friend called out to him. As soon as he peeked through the door, he took a deep breath. He immediately gestured towards Pushkar by pressing his nose between the thumb and the index finger, suggesting to him that there was indeed a very bad smell that was coming from his room.

Pushkar, however, feigned ignorance, and raised his eyebrows. 'What's the matter, brother?'

'What is this smell you have dispersed here, brother?' his friend said.

'Oh, brother! I intended to go to college in a neatly ironed shirt, but then I got carried away dancing to the tune of 'Bedu Pako Baramasa' in Raga Durga. Look what happened to my new shirt! Where can I get it stitched now, eh?'

The friend felt sorry for Pushkar. 'That is very much possible, my brother.'

Next moment, barely concealing a smile, the friend was examining the shirt affectionately. 'Not only is the pocket torn, but the back is ripped as well. If we were girls, we could drape our hair over it.' He then seemed to intently think over the matter. 'But we're Indians, brother; we don't give up so easily! Let's do something. A tailor could fix it enough to be worn in the room, if not outside. Besides, don't worry, isn't there another shirt you can wear tomorrow?'

'Oh yeah... Yes... I'm just looking for that. Although, I hope I have not left that at home. I had gone home only last week.'

'Hey! Bring this bag here. Let me check,' the friend said, pulling his bag towards him.

One by one, the friend freed all five-seven clothes from the bag as if he was freeing birds from a cage. And out of the recently uncaged clothes, he threw one towards Pushkar.

Pushkar caught the shirt and began kissing it. 'Thank you, Brother, you are awesome! Not only will I wear this today but also I will be out comfortably for two to three days, then I will think about it further! Yes!' He seemed elated. 'But now I will not iron it; I will just fold it a little... Like this.'

'Don't be afraid, brother. The same doesn't need to happen every time. If you find a rotten apple in a pile, will you take all of them to be rotten?'

'That's right. Many problems will continue in my life! If I get scared this way, how will I overcome them. For how long will I be afraid of them?'

Finally, the cloth stuck on the iron was removed. And this time, Pushkar was very vigilant in the process, as if all his five senses were alert.

Soon, it was nearly 11.30 at night. Pushkar prepared his outfit and bag, and got into bed to wake up early morning. He kept tossing and turning on his bed restlessly. Even before the alarm rang, he was up and about. After his bath, an enthusiastic Pushkar donned his trousers and shirt. He reverently bowed before the idols on the table and lit the lamp to honour Ma Saraswati, feeling a surge of positive energy in his body and mind. The room was fragrant with the scent of mogra incense, which uplifted his spirits and brightened his face. Pushkar spent time in front of the mirror, adjusting his hair in various styles. Finally, ready for college, filled with aspirations and dreams, he picked up his bag and left.

Pushkar was not just any student; his eyes sparkled with thousands of dreams, one of which was to imbue his college life with the same reverence and respect he had for his school life. He aimed to fulfil his parents' dreams and lay a solid foundation for a bright future. Pushkar aspired to be a model son and citizen, and he was driven by a desire to make a significant impact on the contemporary world. His soul and mind were abuzz with ideas of becoming a national hero, a literary creator, a scientist, a social worker, a sportsperson, a successful lawyer and even a sports commentator. He meticulously planned his path and persevered with determination. Pushkar's mental focus was unwavering as he knocked on the door of a future where success would greet him.

Stepping out of the building where he lived, he encountered an auto driver and inquired about the fare, only to be interrupted by the driver's enthusiastic response about his new auto.

'I just bought this new auto yesterday after selling my land. I'm offering the ride to you today as a gift! Ha!'

The young lad responded, 'No, brother, I only need to go to Lucknow University. How much will you charge?'

The auto-driver's fare was steep, reflective of its lofty status. The boy, mindful of his family's financial constraints, opted for the large shared three-wheeler, the Vikram tempo, instead. He dusted off a seat and soon found himself en route to the university, passing the historic Rifa-e-Aam Club, a legacy of the Nawabs and a hub of literary activity. The tempo, filled with the melodies of Kishore Kumar, stopped right at the University's gates. After paying the fare, the students dispersed to their departments.

Upon entering the campus, the young man encountered

new faces, exchanged greetings with seniors and teachers, and navigated the common freshman confusion of finding a suitable seat. Most students were eager to acquaint themselves with their peers. Spotting an empty seat in the front, Pushkar took it, sitting next to a silent neighbour. Eventually, they exchanged names and details, beginning their acquaintanceship.

Acharya Narendra Dev Hostel was also a short distance from there and was known as ND Hostel. It was natural for the youth to be overwhelmed by the 132-room building, which sang songs of historical grandeur. After entering the hostel, the first thing he encountered was the caretaker of the hostel, who looked at him and asked in a serious tone, 'What is your name?'

He took off the bag from his shoulder and held it in his hand, then took off his glasses, cleaned it with the edge of his shirt, and said, 'My name is Pushkar Singh Dhami.'

All the formalities related to the allotment of the hostel were completed at the time of admission to the university. Therefore, the caretaker found his name in the allotment list present with him and matched the name, address, etc., in the hostel register. After this, pointing to a room on the first floor of the hostel, he said to Pushkar that a room had been allotted to him. He went to the office and brought the key and handed it over to Pushkar.

As soon as Pushkar grabbed the key, he read 'Room no. 119' written on it. He remembered the Almighty at that time and pressed the key to his chest. *This room no. 119 is going to be my address starting today*, he thought to himself.

Pushkar set his bag on a table in the corner, his gaze going over the state of the room. As the ceiling fan whirred overhead, memories from before his arrival here flooded his mind. He recalled the pivotal day he had expressed to his father, Sher Singh, a desire to study at Lucknow University, a dream his father eventually supported despite financial challenges.

◆

Confrontation with Circumstances

As the sun dipped below the horizon, casting a vermilion glow, Sher Singh and his wife Bishna Devi were sitting in their verandah, discussing a potential match for their daughter Pushpa. Pushkar, fresh from passing his intermediate exams, interrupted their talk. Ever since the results had been out, his routine was revolving around spending more time with friends. Sher Singh, having served in the army, harboured same aspirations for Pushkar, but his dwindling eyesight had marred this planning. He was feeling sad that his son would not be able to learn valuing the discipline and pride instilled by military service. He worried that without this experience, Pushkar might miss out on these vital life lessons, which had shaped his own character. Sher Singh's dreams for his son, steeped in a tradition of bravery and service, reflected his deep-seated beliefs about the values learnt in the army.

In fact, in the eyes of this soldier, every person with a non-military background was an ordinary person whom he saw as a 'common' man. In such a situation, the inability of his son to join the army disturbed Sher Singh. He worried about his son's future because, in the rural environment in which they lived, finding the right way for a young lad's progress seemed full of challenges.

With all this on his mind, when he saw his young son enter the house, the soldier inside him woke up. He said in a severe tone, 'Whenever I check on you, I find you are practically living outside the house. It seems you have started thinking of yourself as a *teesmarkha*! How often do I have to tell you to keep your hair short, but you have to become Vinod Khanna...' He gave his son a hard stare and continued, 'Have you thought about what you will do next? Or do you think that passing intermediate is enough!'

Hearing all this, Pushkar's self-esteem started to crumble. Seeking support, he turned to his mother, Bishna Devi, whose maternal love overflowed in defence of her child. She gently reminded her husband, 'He's still young; let him have his moment. Then you can ask him whatever you wish, but remember not everything is about military discipline.'

Sher Singh's tone softened upon hearing his wife's words, and he invited his son to sit beside him, asking about his future plans. Pushkar, feeling a wave of relief seeing his father's milder demeanour, shared the thoughts he had been mulling over with friends and classmates. He announced, 'Father, I want to enrol in Lucknow University.' This revelation took both parents by surprise, with Bishna Devi expressing her shock aloud at her son's choice.

Sher Singh questioned his son's desire to study in Lucknow, wondering what special advantage it offered. 'If it's about graduating, why not consider colleges in Kumaon-Garhwal? You could go to Guru Nanak Degree College in Rudrapur, Motiram Baburam or Lal Bahadur Shastri Degree College in Haldwani. Or even strive for admission in a reputable course at Pantnagar University. And if you're keen on studying away from home, why not choose Ruhelkhand University in Bareilly? How did Lucknow come into the picture?' he asked, perplexed by his son's choice.

Mother Bishna Devi, too, was taken aback by her son's

decision. Not only did she express her disagreement, but she also strongly opposed the idea of sending her only son so far away from home all the way to Lucknow. Her maternal concern was evident as the thought of her son leaving the safety and familiarity of their home for a distant city was unbearable for her. The family's discussion about Pushkar's educational future revealed the deep bond and care they shared, each member wanting the best for him while also considering practical and emotional aspects.

Observing her son's quiet demeanour, Bishna Devi gently addressed him, 'Why do you need to go to Lucknow, dear? Choose a college closer to home where travel is convenient. Like the other local children, you can attend college and return the same day. How will you manage living away from home? What about your meals? The outside environment might not suit you. It's better to enrol in a nearby college, get good grades through tutoring and then secure a job. Don't be swayed by what your friends say.' Her words reflected both concern and practicality, emphasizing the importance of staying close to home while pursuing education and future opportunities.

Understanding his mother's worries, Pushkar decided to clarify things with his father. Utilizing knowledge from friends and seniors, he approached his father with a persuasive argument. 'Papa, Lucknow University, being in our state's capital, offers a superior educational environment than local colleges. It promises holistic development and a conducive learning atmosphere. Alumni like Shankar Dayal ji, Dr Zakir Hussain, Harish Rawat, Anup Jalota and Surjit Barnala have all emerged from there, excelling in diverse fields. It offers guidance for further studies too. While I may not fulfil your dream of me joining the army, I am committed to making you proud. People will recognize you by my achievements.

So, please trust me and let me go to Lucknow; I won't let you down.'

Sher Singh, who had previously seen his son as a child, was rendered speechless by Pushkar's confident and determined demeanour, recognizing him as the future of India. He reminisced about Pushkar's birth, his features hinting at a strong personality.

Bishna Devi, observing her husband's bewilderment, firmly stated, 'You don't need to go to Lucknow-*wakhnau* for your studies. Stay around here. After your studies, find a job that provides well. I won't send you alone to the capital.' Pushkar, hearing his mother's words, blinked in surprise, taken aback by her decisive stance.

'How much is the fee? And your food and lodging? Have you figured all this out?' Sher Singh asked.

In the meantime, his daughter Indra offered him a glass of sherbet and mysteriously smiled and went inside, saying, 'An act of Mahabharat is being staged.'

The mother and son could not digest the incredible statement coming from the head of the family Sher Singh! Pushkar's eyes began to paint a grand picture of Lucknow University seen in papers. So he replied in a few words, 'Dad, the fees isn't too high! I came to know from friends that the cost of staying in the hostel and the cost of food and college will be around 1,500 rupees a month.'

After hearing from his son, Sher Singh quickly calculated his pension and household expenses. With assurance, he said, 'I can provide you with 2,000 rupees monthly. This should cover your fees, hostel meals, and the rest 500 for travel and notebooks. Son, that's the best I can do for now. If it's alright with you, you have my permission. Don't worry about your mother; she'll come around.' His pragmatic approach balanced his desire to support his son's education with the family's financial realities.

Hearing his father's words, Pushkar touched his father's feet and said, 'Okay, Father, this is enough, I will manage everything else.'

Not finding any place in the conversation between father and son and thinking of sending her son miles away from home, tears started dripping from Bishna Devi's eyes. Choking back tears, she got up from there, wiping her eyes, and went inside, while outside, the father-son duo became absorbed in further discussions about living in Lucknow and the process of admission in the university.

After dinner, Pushpa called out to her brother. They had chosen to dine on the verandah to escape the heat, setting up their meal on a plank. In a reflective moment, their father shared a profound verse, encapsulating his thoughts: 'The cord of the universe is connected to the stomach; for the stomach is the ultimate truth.'

> There's the matter of the stomach here,
> There's the matter of the stomach there.
> In the matter of here and there,
> It's the stomach that is everywhere.

The next few days were spent completing the admission process at Lucknow University. Based on the suggestions by the University students, Pushkar prepared for the entrance exam and appeared for it on the scheduled date. Looking at the glorious campus of the University during the examination strengthened his resolve to study there even more.

On a humid afternoon in the midst of the onset of the 1994 southwest monsoon, his mother, tired of taking fodder from the fields, was resting in the atrium; Pushkar was eagerly waiting for a glass of cold water before sharing with her some good news. Seeing her son's gestures, Bishna Devi sensed that it was something special. An excited Pushkar immediately touched her feet and said, 'The examination result has come, Eeja, and yes, I have got admission in Lucknow University!'

Bishna Devi was struggling to not let her fears dampen the happiness of her son. Eventually, she swallowed her feelings for the sake of her son's dreams and bright future. Sher Singh also made every possible effort to resolve the challenges faced by his son with this good news and started discussing future strategy.

◆

Handling the Hassles

Pushkar's thoughts were shattered by a noise outside the door of his room. He could hear a few boarders discussing various things about university life and campus. They were all standing outside in the hallway in a group, some of them resting their backs against the railing overlooking the greenery and colourful flowers of the courtyard. Pushkar urged the boys standing outside to come inside. A Nigerian boy sat on the wooden bed with his feet down, legs hanging over the side, a Poorvanchali boy sat in the armchair, while a Lucknavi climbed onto the table. At first, there was a discussion on their names, states, districts, etc., which gradually shifted to various neighbouring hostels and university activities.

A few neighbouring students who were seniors apprised Pushkar of the rules and regulations of the hostel, the living conditions and daily routines. Due to limited time in the morning, it was decided that the shower had to be quick, along with meditation. The food was prepared in the mess, where they were to have breakfast after which they would have to run to college. They were expected to adopt the same routine almost daily. The next day, when Pushkar got ready to leave for breakfast according to the time they had suggested, other classmates reached there, and all walked to the mess together.

After coming out from the hostel, Pushkar saw that several students from nearby hostels like Birbal Sahni, Chandra Shekhar Azad (Butler), Habibullah, Balrampur, Mahmudabad, Kailash, Golden Jubilee, etc., were going towards the university premises by talking amongst themselves and laughing in the crowd. It seemed as if a crowd of young students was going out to participate in an assembly organized in a school assembly hall.

Pushkar had become familiar with the university auditorium during the admission process, but today, for the first time as a college student, walking into that space felt thrilling to him. Other fellow students, who were accompanying him from the hostel, left for their respective departments after entering through gate number 1. Pushkar noticed that these buildings had departments of other subjects and specialities, taking cognizance of the names inscribed on them; so he looked around and finally reached his destination.

Young students were feeling proud from the bottom of their hearts about the joy of starting a new session. The students who already knew other people or had older friends present with them were full of confidence. But those who had left their villages and towns for the first time to study or were alone, were in a state of despair, seated in isolated chairs. The inner turmoil is something different. Pushkar too found himself in a similar state. But somewhere, an optimism at the bottom of his heart encouraged him to remain patient. He reminded himself that despite all odds, he had finally reached his dream university.

Pushkar curiously looked around from the door at the room full of students, but did not find any student suitable for company; he consoled himself and sat in the middle of other newly-admitted students in the front seat. There were still a few minutes left for the class to start.

'What a fish market! You are here in university classrooms; don't think that you are in little school cells here! Have you been forcibly caught and herded here from the village?'

This single attack made the whole class come to an incredible moment of silence! Suddenly, a large group of students—dozen or so—entered the classroom one after the other and terrorized all the newly-admitted students with their loud, aggressive demeanour. Some of the newly-admitted students present there realized that those were the senior students who had come for 'ragging'—a word they had only heard about so far. Many others were, however, completely unaware of this unknown ritual.

'Stand up everyone in your places and, one by one, let us know your names, district and state. Tell us what are you looking for here. Yes, sit down—one by one—in a line! We shouldn't have to repeat it!' A senior student, looking like a heavy gym trainer, flaunted his biceps on the pretext of brushing his long hair. He ordered a girl in the front row to stand up and then gazed deeply into her eyes and said in an angry tone, 'If I come into my element, your entire education will be over right here. So, better open your mouth and start answering the questions.'

The girl was frightened. She remembered the folk singer

University: A Nursery of Personality Development

Malini Awasthi, whom the students had asked to sing many times in the name of ragging; then in a trembling tone, she said, 'M...my...my... name is Meeeeenaaaakshi.'

'Where are you from?'

'Biiii...bihaa...from Bihar... Purnia.'

Every attempt was made to embarrass Meenakshi in a fully-packed classroom. One student even called her 'Biharan' to humiliate her till she sat down, crying bitterly.

Unwillingly, everyone was forced to tell their names and addresses one after the other. At which, the senior students' raggers group would make sarcastic comments and make fun of them.

Soon, it was Pushkar's turn to fold his hands in a prayer posture, giving hint of both fear and respect. He said, 'My name is Pushkar Singh Dhami! I am a resident of Khatima district, Udham Singh Nagar,' he said in a single voice.

After hearing this sentence, a senior mischievously said, 'Have you come to become a hero here by wearing photochromic frame glasses? Can't you find plain glasses in your Khatima?'

The senior burst into laughter at this too, and said, 'Everyone should open their eyes and ears and listen. Boys will come in shirts, and close all the buttons up to the collar. Girls will come in two braids and their entry would be completely prohibited if they are wearing jeans or are without a stole or scarf. That is, no one will come to the class undisciplined.'

With this order the seniors left. All freshers shivered like dried leaves! Everyone started discussing this incident with each other and talking about not coming to college.

For a long time, Pushkar listened in silence. But at the end, he said confidently, 'No brothers and sisters, we need not be afraid; we have to study here. That is why we have come here from afar. If we start thinking about other's opinion or what they say about us, we will never be able to move forward. Many such elements are prevalent in our society; these are also some of those social elements. Just take note of yourself, correct your shortcomings and move ahead... Today we may be scared or nervous in this new place, but remember that tomorrow, we will also be called seniors here. But our point of view and manners will be different.'

All students listened to Pushkar with great attention, and their lost confidence returned. Some patted him on the back, while others applauded him. Sooner or later, the professor entered the class, and the first class of the session commenced with the attendance on register. On the first day, due to many disturbances, only two lectures could be held smoothly. After that, all the students left for their respective destinations.

Upon reaching his room, Pushkar threw his bag on the chair and fell on the bed. Due to fatigue/stress, he complained of a headache. He immediately fell asleep after eating leftovers in the mess in a hurry.

The first year of college is always a different experience for newly-admitted students. They come out of the disciplined environment of the school, and suddenly feel the open atmosphere of the graduate-level college, and find that there is no one to stop them. A student has to decide his future, whether he wants to fly in the sky or improve his ability of staying on the ground. While studying in school, students are afraid of the pressure of preparing for tests and exams every month with proper books and copies. They have to dress in a common uniform, and endure teachers' punishments. But, in a university, they have to prepare only for the annual exams and can wear colourful, fashionable clothes, with only a pen in the pocket and a register in hand. And there is no particular pressure from the teachers, no one to spoon-feed them.

Pushkar had made many friends in the hostels and university campus within a few days due to his kindness and willingness to help everyone. One of them was Pradeep Pandey. He lived in the same hostel as him. This boy, a resident of Basti district, was very fond of Pushkar and realized that he could talk openly with him. Pushkar loved to meet new people while taking care of his studies and sports. He learnt new things from them. He had soon formed a unique group of friends who maintained honest friendships while having the same thinking and competitiveness to move forward.

Pushkar treated everyone with respect and pursued his studies along with his group of friends; this also made him stand out in the eyes of his professors and senior students. In the early days of ragging, he obeyed his seniors and followed their orders without hesitation and anger, which made him a subject of affection for senior students. Due to this, he became popular in the university in a short time.

Soon the academic session was about to end. But from the beginning, this session had been crucial in turning the face of student politics in the region. New young faces in the state started riding on the wave of student power and increasing their political power. The days of March 1994 are also reminiscent of these golden pages when a 21-year-old *sant* named Yogi Adityanath, originally from the hills, but later based in Gorakhpur district of Purvanchal, was arrested after the police raided the hostels of innocent students despite knowing that the shopkeeper was guilty in a clash between the students of the intermediate college run by the Gorakhnath Temple and the owner of a shop in Golghar. There was a fierce protest in Gorakhpur. Finally, impressed by his eloquence and perseverance, the young students, who until then had considered the mafia and bahubalis their role models, declared the young saint to be their role model!

At Lucknow University, student leaders like Dhananjay Singh, Abhay Singh, Arvind Singh Gope and Pawan Pandey were gaining recognition at the state level. The University, being prominent in the capital, had become a breeding ground for political activism. Students from remote areas now viewed the campus as an entry point into politics. However, this activism often overshadowed the commitment to improving the learning environment, with some student leaders prioritizing personal gain over genuine issues. This pursuit of power and involvement in violent activities had begun to affect the University's atmosphere, overshadowing the primary goal of providing quality education.

Strong student leaders started to dominate the scene with the help of new slogans, such as, **'The era is moving towards the direction where the youth marches to' and 'There should be a collar in a young man's hand, not merely a sleeve.'** Issues such as fee hikes, discrepancies in education policies and lack of government jobs triggered violent protests among students! Aggressive groups of influential student leaders had also started dominating the life of the city. Under the guise of political parties, students had started using the campus as a training institute for political ambition. Seeing hundreds of strongmen coming and going around in unity, the administration had also caved in before them. The youth power, which is called the future capital of the country, seemed ready to commit any heinous crime to serve the interests of political parties. They would sometimes intimidate or threaten politicians of Opposition parties, and at other times spread anarchy along with the Opposition and use their large, young-student force as a weapon of demonstration.

Most political parties were also eager to use such forces to serve the selfishness of their interests. When student leaders associated with such parties dressed in black starchy kurta pyjamas, sporting heavy gold chains and fingers full of rings, entering the campus in a convoy of four-wheelers, the newly admitted students would be attracted to their powerful, dominant look and would start belauding them to receive their protection!

Clearly, this was the time for the decline of the prestige of exclusive student politics. Evidently, contrary to the political principles of Kautilya and Machiavelli, this perception has started to grow in the general public, that being rowdy, being a bully and a criminal, instead of intellectually superior, morally courteous, diplomatically clever, practically gentle and spiritually determined, was the primary criterion for becoming a student leader.

The dominance of student union presidents was not only a challenge to local MLAs but also MPs and ministers. The university administration had started feeling helpless in controlling their anarchy and violent activities, because they thrived under the patronage of strong political parties. Even national-level leaders would come to participate in their regional programs. Such an atmosphere of chaos all around began to provoke Dhami, who was determined to establish the esoteric principles of politics.

Pushkar considered himself an advocate of integrity, modesty, transparency, accountability, dutifulness and political reform. For clean student politics, he believed, that there was no need for bullying or intimidation, but a humanitarian concern was absolutely necessary. He kept himself updated with the day-to-day national and international developments and inspired other fellow students accordingly. With his logical and frank eloquence in the political discussions over evening tea in small groups, he had also tried to make students aware of issues of national interest! Due to political leanings, he had already started participating continuously in an RSS *shakha* or branch alongside his school life. Physical and mental maturity through participation, meetings and practice in the branch's collective discussions had forced him to take up the goal of selfless service to the motherland.

Therefore, the pride and respect of being a former RSS volunteer was ingrained in his heart. This was the reason that, despite his simple personality, he was able to easily attract university students. He had now gained enough experience through university activities. He was not only influencing hundreds of students with his disciplined routine and positive ideology but was also trying his best to mould their personalities. Many such students were Pushkar's classmates and friends, but they still did not have enough mental capacity to think of something extraordinary or were incapable of independent thought. In order to make their state of mind better and make them socially useful, Pushkar decided to start a shaakha in the lawn near the gate leading to ND Hostel in front of the Faculty of Commerce with collective consent.

Pushkar's tireless efforts started the first phase of the shaakha, which was first supported by his fellow boarders; but within a few days, students from neighbouring hostels also started joining. Knowingly or unknowingly, it intensified the exercise of awakening the spirit of nationalism and Sanatan (Vedic) culture beyond anarchic and violent activities in the hearts of the students of the university. It proved to be the first successful means of bringing about a radical change in strong student politics. Addressing the morning shaakha, he said that anarchist student politics had ruled its golden throne for long enough, **but now the time had come for such abominable politics to end and the violent empire standing on the pillars of oppression to collapse.**

Pushkar started connecting with some senior students and experienced dignitaries of the regional branches. Most of the students on campus became strong supporters of his ideology. Not only juniors but senior students also started becoming part of the shaakha drills on the lawn. While focusing on his studies, Pushkar also started encouraging young people towards leadership to become the future pride of the society and the country. His understanding extended beyond academic and political books, keenly observing student politics in the state capital.

Meanwhile, a significant movement erupted in Pushkar's home district. The residents of the hilly region, long demanding a separate state of Uttaranchal, grew frustrated with the limited impact of local protests and agitations. Despite repeatedly petitioning the government, they decided to organize a larger mass movement to achieve their collective goal.

Pushkar started collecting strategic information about regional agitators from his local friends and family. One day, while talking to a friend over the phone from a phone booth, he expressed frustration, questioning why governments in the state and national capitals couldn't understand that the culture, livelihood and issues of hill residents were vastly different from those in the plains. He noted that the development of hilly regions was significantly behind that of Uttar Pradesh's plains districts. He believed that forming a separate state of Uttaranchal was crucial for the area's welfare and development. Eager to participate in this significant movement for *Uttarakhandiyat* or the identity of Uttarakhand, Pushkar was constrained by his family's financial situation and the trust his parents and sisters had placed in him. He maintained that financial challenges shouldn't lead one to abandon education, as it was often addictions and bad habits that disrupt schooling.

Therefore, for the time being, Pushkar continued to gather the right intellectual, political and spiritual support in the university by arguing in favour of a smaller state. Pushkar, along with friends from the hostel and the university, sat at the famous Basanti chachi's tea stall and sometimes on the soft green grass of Tagore Lawn to support the state of Uttarakhand and convince his friends with the reasoning behind the same.

In the first week of August 1994, a regional leader, Indramani Barauni, announced an indefinite hunger strike to protest against the recommendations of the 1978 Mandal Commission. In this, the demand for a separate state was also merged. The dictatorial regime adopted every possible violent tactic to crush this peaceful movement, as a result of which bullets were fired on protestors. Atrocities were committed on women and children and the revolutionaries were forcibly pushed behind penitentiary.

Among these revolutionary activities, Khatima Kand, which happened on 1 September 1994, was among the first ones. It turned out to be very tragic. The government forces opened fire on thousands of unarmed protesters who came out on the streets; people of every age group were hurt. But the hillmen did not give up. The next day, shots were again fired on the protesters protesting against Khatima Kand in Mussoorie. But despite all this, about 10 lakh affidavits were filed there in favour of the formation of the state. Somewhere the protesters protested with the slogan of 'No state, no elections', somewhere singing songs like *'Le mashalein chal pade hain log mere gaaon ke* (People of my village have started walking with torches)', and other songs.

On 1 October of the same year, protesters gathered in 24 buses and were on their way to New Delhi for demanding the formation of Uttaranchal as a new state. Based on intelligence inputs from security agencies, every effort was made by the administrative machinery of the Uttar Pradesh government to stop these revolutionaries at Narsan border in Roorkee as per the instructions of the central government in Delhi. But the revolutionaries, full of enthusiasm and energy, defied every government tactic. They kept moving forward, the sky echoing with slogans like *'Madua baadi khaenge, Uttarakhand banayenge* (We will eat Madua Baadi and build Uttarakhand)'.

But as soon as dark clouds started to cover the golden rays coming from west to east, the protesters were stopped by a heavy police force at Rampur Tiraha in Muzaffarnagar. As the police personnel stopped the protestors from marching ahead, the protestors hurled stones at them in which even the district magistrate was injured. The police then resorted to lathi charge. This sudden baton charge caused chaos all around. Before the revolutionaries could understand the whole situation, about 250 people were detained. The police did not show any laxity in excesses not only with young revolutionaries but also with children, the elderly and women. There were even allegations of rape. When the information reached other revolutionaries, more protesters left for Rampur Tiraha in about 40 buses overnight. Even before the sun rose, thousands of protesters had surrounded Rampur Tiraha.

On 2 October 1994, the birth anniversary of Mahatma Gandhi, the symbol of non-violence, the sun rose with the sacred blood of the revolutionaries. This fierce struggle between the revolutionaries and the police administration was a black chapter on the revolutionary land of Muzaffarnagar and came to be known as the Rampur Tiraha firing case. This incident left seven hill people gone forever, with many agitators left injured.

The Rampur Tiraha incident brought national attention to the demands of the mountainous region and the government's authoritarian tactics. News of the incident reached the Parliament, sparking widespread protests against the Samajwadi Party (SP) government's dictatorship, which significantly destabilized the state government. Motivated by these events, hundreds of youths from the mountainous regions, including those in the capital, organized processions to demand a separate state.

Pushkar also published the story of governmental atrocities on the people of the mountains under his young leadership in regional newspapers and magazines, in which the demand for a separate state on the basis of the adverse geographical conditions of the mountainous region was also described. He started seeking support from people studying and teaching in the university campus as well as living in Lucknow for the demand for a separate state. In this way, he also expanded the scope of the movement by introducing himself to it as a leader. Through various discussions, he resolved to extend full cooperation to the Uttarakhand Kranti Dal, which had been formed much earlier, in July 1979, with the aim of forming a separate state under the chairmanship of Devi Dutt Pant. Pushkar once again drew the attention of the hill people to the public announcement of 1988, in which the government itself had announced the formation of Uttaranchal as a separate state, which it was now turning away from.

He also made ordinary citizens aware of the importance of the Uttaranchal state movement and the need to make Uttaranchal an independent state. He became a source of inspiration for students from the hill region. His speeches and public addresses reflected the dedication of all hill students towards the state. Pushkar encouraged the students, who were busy in their nascent romantic liaisons, and motivated them towards the state movement. The fervour of the agitation caused many romances to be extinguished even before they could ignite, while many others to collapse even after taking shape.

One day, Pushkar had just returned after addressing a meeting when suddenly Pradeep Pandey came to the door of room number 119 and said in a low voice, 'Let's go, Pushkar bhai, to Birbal Sahni hostel. Let's introduce you to my elder brother today! I often visit him, but today you also come. Seeing your inclination towards student politics and growing popularity, I am sure that if you meet him, it will open new avenues for you.'

Pushkar, after listening carefully to his friend, thought that he would go after resting a little, but respecting his friend's request, he quickly got up and both of them left for the nearby Birbal Sahni hostel!

Pradeep's elder brother, Jaishankar Pandey, lived in room number 31. Pradeep knocked at the door and waited for his elder brother to open the door. Introducing his friend to his elder brother, Pradeep pointed to Pushkar and said, 'Bhaiya, this is Pushkar Singh Dhami! He lives in ND hostel and is a very good friend of mine. He is also a first-year undergraduate student at the university.'

Jaishankar Pandey carefully heard his younger brother's words and asked Pushkar with respect, 'Come, come! Sit here! Pradeep has talked about you many times. So I told him, "Brother, introduce your friend to me too." I thought let us also understand how such a promising child from the mountainous region reached here!'

Then he said, 'Look! My name is Jaishankar Pandey, and I am doing MSW [Master of Social Work] from this university!'

Pushkar replied politely, 'Yes, Brother, I was told by Pradeep many times that you also study here, but I finally had the privilege of meeting you today!'

Pradeep had already told his elder brother a lot about Pushkar's activities and his popularity. Jaishankar was particularly happy to hear about Pushkar's dedication to the Sangh shakha. That even after coming from miles away, far from his home and family, the young man had worked to set up an RSS shakha in the university. And that too in such an adverse time when the government did not have a positive attitude towards the nationalist activities of the shakha and Sangh (RSS). After enough discussion about his well-being and family, Jaishankar further said, 'I am not interested in the political activities of the campus despite being very close to student politics! The main reason for this is that my goal is to establish myself in the field of education and to take the Sangh's ideology and dedication to the nation and to the coming generations on a large scale. I am currently holding the post of district general secretary of Akhil Bharatiya Vidyarthi Parishad (ABVP). At the same time, I am committed to bringing the basic spirit of the organization's slogan, "Knowledge, Modesty and Unity", and to conveying the purpose of the organization to the students in the same spirit!'

Jaishankar Pandey's brief statement had a profound effect on Pushkar's soul and mind. Although he had heard and read about ABVP even in his school life, he got to know about the basic objectives of the organization in such a precise way that he got a spiritual feeling from it. After all, its purpose was also to convert student power into national power. After discussing student life, future goals and strategies for a long time, Jaishankar encouraged Pushkar to join ABVP. He said, 'I think you can expand your positive energy and creative thinking by connecting with this organization! And the strongly conceptualized organizational power hidden within you can prove useful for all of us as well.'

After having such a detailed and positive discussion with someone in whom Pushkar could see an elder brother, he did not need to think any further. This is why he gave his approval after only a moment's thought, 'Brother, if you think that by joining, my personality will develop and I will be able to do something more for this organization to the best of my ability, then I will be very happy!'

Jaishankar Pandey shook his head in affirmative and said seriously, 'Okay Pushkar, I am appointing you a member of ABVP today! I wish you all the best for your bright future but keep paying as much attention to your studies as you are paying to student politics.'

After joining ABVP, Pushkar started visiting the student council office of Navin Market in Kaiserbagh and gradually started getting acquainted with the office-bearers. At the time, Nagendra Singh was adorning the post of regional organization minister of ABVP. By frequently visiting the student's council office, Pushkar started getting closer to him. Nagendra Singh also became famous across the state for his gentle behaviour, dedication to the organization and organizational skills. He eventually recognized Pushkar's leadership ability and his decent image among the students.

One day in 1995, when Nagendra Singh was discussing organizational expansion in the regional office of the Parishad with Jaishankar Pandey, he also called Pushkar to the office and said, 'Pushkar, I've observed that your style of functioning and ethical conduct is compatible with the principles of the student council. I want you to be an office-bearer of the council! For this, you have our good wishes!'

On hearing the open invitation of the organization's general secretary, Pushkar felt proud and said, 'Your wish is my command, brother!'

'I am appointing you as the secretary of the Lucknow University unit of ABVP! The organization has high expectations from you, and we all have a heartfelt desire that you expand the organization in the university and other colleges as a diligent young person, we are confident that you will live up to this!'

Thus, Pushkar achieved his first official position in student life, leading his friends to seize the opportunity and insist on celebrating with a party.

After gaining office in ABVP, the direction of Pushkar's thinking, his approach to student politics and the outline of his working style changed radically. His politics took a very different path than the corrupt and undefeated politics going on in the University. Under the banner of ABVP, he started organizing debate seminars among the students to develop a logical attitude among them. Highlighting the historical background of the Parishad, he reminded the students that, formed on 9 July 1949, under the leadership of Balraj Madhok ji and Professor Yashwantrao Kelkar ji, ABVP was the largest student organization not only in India but also in the world; that this was a reflection of the power of all students, like them. According to ABVP, student power *was* national power, the purpose of which was national reconstruction. He told them that thousands of students like them had so far led nation-wide movements by highlighting issues of students and of national interest. Whether it was the issue of Bangladeshi infiltrators and the Tin Bigha Corridor, Article 370 in Kashmir, the commercialization of education, separatism, minority appeasement, corruption, terrorism or anti-national activities, the organization had always raised its voice and provided all possible solutions. The organization had held the record for maintaining the highest number of blood donation camps so far. Therefore, it was not only an apt but a sacred platform to come together for national reconstruction. He added that they constantly needed young colleagues like them. 'So come and encourage your colleagues to join this organization,' he said.

Pushkar's address brought smiles on each face, a glow in their eyes and a shine of confidence on the foreheads. Seated amongst a group of students at Basanti chachi's tea stall, Pushkar tried to resolve their grievances and the irregularities prevailing in the university over a cup of tea. The university soon started preparing a planned strategy to increase the facilities required for the study and teaching of the students in the campus. Rational speeches against the rapidly rising unemployment soon made him famous in the eyes of the campus students. Dozens of students started joining the organization every day under his skilled leadership, influenced by the policies and principles of ABVP.

The organizational position of ABVP could not be considered relatively good until 1995. The number of its members was limited due to a lack of publicity in Lucknow University and its colleges. As a result, in student union elections, the official vote count of the ABVP candidate for the post of president of the student council was about 300 votes, and the candidate for the post of vice-president/general secretary was reduced to 200 votes.

The year 1995 proved to be the year of a dark chapter in Uttar Pradesh politics when the 'state guest house' incident on Meera Bai Marg in Lucknow took place on the night of 2 June.[1] Due to the differences between the SP and the BSP, Mayawati withdrew her support to the coalition government, which her party had initially given to the SP to oust the BJP from power in the 1993 Uttar Pradesh Legislative Assembly elections. At that time, out of 422 seats in the state, BJP had won the most seats (177), while SP had 109 and BSP 67 seats. However, as a result of the support of the BSP, SP supremo Mulayam Singh Yadav had become the chief minister and had formed the government.

However, due to mutual differences, Mayawati, also known as Behenji, on 2 June 1995, publicly announced the withdrawal of support. After this, a frenzied crowd of SP MLAs barged into the state guest house in the scorching afternoon sun with the intent of causing harm to the strongly-emerging female political leader in the political scene of Uttar Pradesh. The SP workers allegedly vandalized her room, thrashed and abused her, pulled Behenji's clothes, and scuffled with her supporters. Somehow, Behenji tried to save herself by bolting

---

[1]Loreng, Abhijeet Christopher, 'The 1995 Attack on Mayawati by SP Activists that Turned Her Against Mulayam Singh Yadav', *Times Now*, 10 October 2022, https://tinyurl.com/3jepxpep/. Accessed on 7 March 2025.

one of the doors inside her room unit and locking herself in, but the crowd became so angry that they started kicking at the door in attempts to break it.

Suddenly, BJP MLA Brahm Dutt Dwivedi came to know about this, and without caring for his own life, he pushed the frenzied crowd behind him, went ahead to protect Behenji, reached near the gate and clashed with the armed thugs of SP with the help of only a stick. Brahm Dutt Dwivedi had inherited something else from the Swayam Sewak Sangh as well, but he had also got the training to use a lathi. He single-handedly faced the crowd of hundreds and escorted BSP leader Mayawati Behenji to safety. This is the reason that Mayawati declared him as her brother on the same day and decided never to pitch a BSP candidate against him; she also started campaigning in his favour in the Farrukhabad constituency.

The very next day after this shameful episode, BJP gave full support to Behenji, allowing her to take the oath of chief minister, fulfilling the promise of the empowerment of women made to the Uttar Pradesh public! This commendable step taken by the BJP was considered to be a well-known strategy to pave the political way for the overall Hindutva equation in the RSS. But this unforgettable experiment could not last even six months.

However, again, ideological differences started to crop up between the two parties of the new alliance, and on 18 October 1995, BJP was forced to withdraw its support from the government. Taking advantage of this opportunity, Congress imposed President's rule in the state at the hands of President Shankar Dayal Sharma.

Away from all political viciousness, Pushkar was engaged in giving a new dimension to the membership campaign by participating in university delegations to the regional colleges, along with other ABVP colleagues, to share with the students the policies of the organization and the objectives of national reconstruction. Students started getting excited to know about the struggles and movements of the organization on issues of national to international interest. Thus, under the skilled leadership of Pushkar, several members of ABVP continued its enhancement. Pushkar established ABVP units in most of the localities by making inroads through delegating leadership to students living in different localities of Lucknow.

The year 1996 proved to be a year of great political instability for the politics of Uttar Pradesh. In the Assembly elections, BJP emerged as the largest party by getting 174 seats but it could not end the President's rule! Unfortunately, the turmoil for BJP continued in the Centre as well. It emerged as the largest party in the country in the general elections of the 11th Lok Sabha, but the government formed under the leadership of Atal Bihari Vajpayee collapsed in a very short period of just 13 days after not being able to prove its majority in the Lok Sabha. As a result, a new coalition, United Front, came into existence, led by Janata Dal leader H.D. Deve Gowda, who took oath as the prime minister in place of Atal Bihari Vajpayee. This election also was the second worst election result for the Congress after Independence, since this was the first time that the BJP, with 161 seats, became the largest party in the country after winning more seats than the Congress.

Takaleephon ka dhuaan udaakar, hum aage badhe hai.
Nhin rooye aabalon ko dekhakar, hum paravat chadhe hai.

We have progressed by setting aside troubles and hardships because, despite a thousand wounds, those who are laborious have the strength to conquer mountains.

Keeping a keen eye on all these political developments, Pushkar was engaged in fulfilling his goal. He continued to prove his usefulness in the student organization. Regional organization head Nagendra Singh also encouraged him by seeing his readiness and dedication. In the same year, Nagendra Singh ji formed a new team of ABVP. Among them were Vishwavidyalaya Mantri Pushkar Singh Dhami, Shivaji Chandramouli as organization head, Jaishankar Pandey as university head and Somesh Vardhan Singh as Vice-organization head. Ram Prasad Singh, Prabhatkant ji, Udaykant, Sandeep Shahi, Bajrangi Singh Bajju, Santosh Singh, Dayashankar Singh, Pradeep Chandra, etc., were appointed to other key positions in the organization. This team was actively involved in the expansion of the student organization under the leadership of Nagendra Singh ji. Two rupees membership fee per new member's appointment was levied. There was a competition among all teams to get more and more student as members; there was also a competition among them about who could enlist the most members in which month; and often, the number of members brought into the fold by Pushkar were the highest.

Amidst all these duties, Pushkar did not forget his own hill area. He kept meeting prominent leaders of the prospective Uttaranchal state. Prominent leader and RSS veteran Bhagat Singh Koshyari lived in a flat in OCR Building, Lucknow. Because of Pushkar's activeness and brilliance, he soon became Bhagat Singh's favourite student leader. At the same time, he met other prominent leaders of the hill, Trivendra Singh Rawat and Prakash Pant, who he soon became dear to. Pushkar's agility, perseverance and dedication to the organization were very much liked by all state leaders. Despite all these arrangements, Pushkar did not show any negligence in studying and attending classes.

Meanwhile a new song '*Sandese Aate Hain*' from the upcoming film *Border* was rising the charts of popularity. The film was yet to be released, but this song had gripped everyone's attention, and people could be seen humming it everywhere. In the month of May, the scorching heat of Lucknow usually forced a curfew, practically locking people indoors. Pushkar, in a vest and half pants, was sitting in the backyard of his hostel and got distraught as he heard the song on his Walkman. Suddenly, his gaze fell on the south-facing table, where he saw a letter peeking out from between the stack of books sent by his mother. He saw the handwriting and discerned that Eeja must have got it written by his sister Indra. Eeja's words on paper transported him to his home, and scenes of being with his family began to flash in his mind. He was overwhelmed with love and affection that Eeja had showered upon him, with concern for him and his well-being. In this letter, she had advised him to take care during the hot weather, avoid unnecessary outings and visit home if possible. She mentioned preparing fresh ghee for him and offered to send money if needed. These words highlighted her caring nature and efficient management of household finances. Meanwhile, Pushkar, like other hostel students, eagerly awaited the end of exams, longing for a return to the familiarity of home.

◆

Dilemma of Diversion

Seeing his brother suddenly moving towards the house under the scorching sun, Indra shouted, 'Bhaiya has come, Eejaaa.!'

When both his parents came out to receive him, Pushkar greeted them. While talking to him about his examinations, his father, Sher Singh, asked, 'How long is the holiday this time?'

Pushkar took a sip of water and said, 'One and a half months, till the results are out!'

The summer of May–June ended in the company of his family as well as with friends in Khatima, Rudrapur and Haldwani. Days went so fast that he only realized it was already July when the monsoon shower arrived and it started raining in the courtyard.

'I have to go to Lucknow tomorrow. I have received a call from there that the result is going to be out in a day or two!' Pushkar said while sipping morning tea with his father.

His father, glancing up from the newspaper, turned to his son and remarked, 'Yes, I was just thinking that the university must be reopening soon, and the results should also be coming out!'

Sher Singh noticed his son shaking his head in acceptance of his point; he further added, 'So son, this time you will graduate; what will you do after that? Politics has no future! Come home, we will look for some job here.'

'I have had a lot of discussions on this with my seniors in the past months...about what to do next so that I can stand on my own feet. Most of my senior classmates are of the opinion that along with membership of the ABVP, you should also enrol yourself in a professional course. So, I have decided to ask Vinita Kachchar ma'am for admission to get a master's degree in human resource management and industrial relations [MHRM&IR]!'

The name of the course sounded strange to Sher Singh who did not understand anything, yet expressing his consent, he said, 'Well, son, what you must have thought and consulted with the seniors must be right...We will definitely do whatever we can for your studies. Pay attention to your studies and fill all job-related forms now. You don't even know how quickly age slips from between one's fingers.'

Subedar Sher Singh, without informing anyone, directly visited his close friend Dr Rastogi, a renowned fibre industrialist in Khatima. Dr Rastogi, busy scrutinizing papers on a bamboo bench in his compound, warmly greeted Sher Singh with a 'Ram Ram!' He invited him to sit and inquired about his absence, noting it had been weeks since they had last met. Sher Singh, stroking his moustache and smiling gently, explained that his time was mostly spent at home due to his son Pushkar's visit.

Dr Rastogi, pleased about Sher Singh spending quality time with Pushkar, remarked how sons often become friends. He mentioned meeting Pushkar at the dam, who said he'd be leaving in a few days. Sher Singh, nodding, shared that Pushkar was considering higher education courses like MHRM&IR. He had come to seek Dr Rastogi's advice about whether these courses were suitable for Pushkar's future. He expressed uncertainty about modern education and its relevance to career prospects.

Taking off the glasses from the tip of the nose and placing them on the table, Dr Rastogi said, 'Look Subedar Sahib, your boy is very bright and serious about his future. He is also aware of his family responsibilities and knows very well that he has to be your support in the future! And as for this course, I know about it; it will be very good for him. Let him study this happily and rest assured that everything will be good!'

After discussing his son's studies with Dr Rastogi and other local events, Sher Singh returned.

Back in Lucknow, Pushkar was again absorbed in the activities of the student organization. Fortunately, the graduation exam result had also been satisfactory. Therefore, by enrolling in MHRM&IR, he was looking into new future chapters from the same room number 119 of the ND hostel.

Making inroads into student politics even further, while pursuing university activities and studies, was Pushkar's next stop. Whether it was Basanti Chachi's tea stall or Parag Milk Bar canteen, every evening a crowd of students gathered there. Along with educational activities, issues such as the ongoing President's rule in the state, which lasted two years, political instability and its impact in the field of education and employment were debated in detail. Some were hardcore supporters of their ideology, others preferred to be moderate, but the debate kept raging.

Pushkar's attempt at lobbying as much as possible with the concerned university administration for all the tasks related to new students, such as admission of freshmen, change of subjects, etc., continued to make him popular among them. While other political party-sponsored student leaders had the audacity to underscore their influence by pressuring professors, disrupting their classes or boycotting them, burning their effigies, Pushkar had never resorted to pressuring the university administration, behaving unfairly with professors or showing unnecessary strength in student council politics.

In view of the increasing trend in social cultural programs, pahadi leader Bhagat Singh Koshyari also drew his attention towards the Parvatiya Chhatra Parishad (Hill Student's

Council). Seeing Pushkar's love for the mountains, Prof. C.P. Barthwal invited him to attend the executive expansion programme of the organization to be held during the third weekend of February. So the founder of the Parvatiya Chhatra Parishad, Harish Chandra Tiwari, declared him the chief administrator of the program.

Pushkar finally began to understand the subtlety of life—that human life was like that stream of the Ganges which was flowing in time, where Gomukh was his birthplace and he ultimately merged into the ocean with the ritual of death.

Behaviour greatly impacts an individual, their family, society, and ultimately, the nation. Pushkar, known for his moral ethics, embodied this belief. His character, shaped by lessons of discipline learned from his father, demonstrated that disciplined behaviour leads to a society that contributed positively to the country. Pushkar's life showcased the importance of morality and disciplined conduct in fostering societal and national well-being.

Generally, there is a perception that politics is a corrupt and unethical field, leading many to suggest that morally upright youth should avoid active political engagement. This view is further reinforced by the prevalence of dynastic politics, where political power is often inherited within families. In such a scenario, the common person could easily feel marginalized in the absence of a robust democratic system. Since colonial times, dynastic rule has dominated politics in some democracies.

The presence of a single family in positions of power and influence in politics raises questions about the appropriateness and impact of democracy. Dynastic politics meant that a political leader, by dint of his inheritance, could rise to political power without struggle or a merit-based elevation process. Here, a ruler departed for his cremation and there the descendant eagerly got ready to take his place. This cynical display of hunger for power was the sine qua non of dynastic politics.

What do we see in the Mughal period? The story of Shah Jahan's illness and its aftermath is widely known. The intense struggle for power within families ensued as the old ruler was removed from daily monarchical duties because of his illness. His sons, led by Aurangzeb, engaged in a brutal succession war. Aurangzeb, known for his staunch Islamic beliefs, went as far as to kill his brother Dara Shikoh and other siblings, ultimately imprisoning his father in Agra Fort. This historical episode is used metaphorically to reflect the current situation in Opposition parties, highlighting the relentless pursuit of power and internal conflicts.

Pushkar deeply reflected on the entirety of political history, contemplating the sacrifices made for India's freedom. Envisioning a nation breathing freely, he pondered how, after a prolonged struggle, India had achieved liberation. However, his contemplation turned to disappointment, when he realized how, post-Independence, Nehru's ascent to the post of the prime minister led not to the anticipated liberation from years of oppression but rather took Indian politics towards a family-centric power politics.

This reflection brought a mix of respect for the freedom struggle and a critique of the post-Independence political landscape.

Pushkar contemplated the trend of dynastic politics in India, focusing on examples like Lalu Prasad Yadav in Bihar, who was then found involved in the fodder scam. This led to his wife becoming the party president and Bihar's chief minister. Similarly, in Uttar Pradesh, families like Mulayam

Singh Yadav's illustrated the same dynastic approach.

Pushkar concluded that in these instances, politics had shifted from being a service to becoming personal property.

> *Khwaabon ke dhundhale shahar nahin balki,*
> *Majeed manzil ko hee kooch karoonga.*
> *Takaleephon, sangharshon ka ho manzar bhale,*
> *Mazloomon ke liye jiwant huqooq banoonga.*

Truth is not found by chasing daydreams; it is achieved by walking the difficult path of reality. No matter how many obstacles arise, I will fight for the rights of those who are suffering.

Pushkar, the vibrant heat of the Himalayas, took a deep breath and blurted out: 'This will not work. Ours is a clarion call for democracy. India is a country of diversities; it talks about *Vasudhaiva Kutumbakam, Yato Dharmastato, Satyamev Jayate*! The world is one family; where there is dharma, there is victory; truth alone triumphs! He was talking to himself in an empty room. According to him, it is not only difficult but impossible to maintain personal dominance in such a situation! From the Indus Valley Civilization to the present, we have always been victorious. This has led us, and our society to remain intact even in the midst of infinite continuous storms that have lashed at our nation. Thousands of young people like me will not allow the disease that is being forcibly spread in our country.

'From a profound insight, the whole world seems to be beating the drums of democracy or claims to be championing its cause. But democracy is masked; no one can know how clean or how dirty the real face is. Therefore such a democracy is bound by illusion, contradiction and paradox; it does not appear consistent to me in itself. Each of us, whether it is an ant or an elephant, seeks freedom! The truth is that we just want to find the freedom that is actually beyond our reach, rather than liking the freedom that we already have.

'Consider carefully, Voltaire also believed that equality in democracy is just a myth; unity among human beings is as impossible as it is impossible for two Vedantic scholars to not be jealous of each other. Although it is the duty of all of us because we are the children of an awakened world; we have to come out of the pothole of these contradictions; in a true democracy, there can be no lion or cheetah more powerful than the people.'

Pushkar, in this turmoil, resolved not to let it weaken his confidence or deter him from his path. He believed he must uphold the legacy of being born in an Indian Rajput family, comparing his determination to Winston Churchill's resolve. He vowed to advocate for adaptability and tolerance in political alliances, emphasizing the need for new leaders to represent India's multicultural society. Questioning the centralized approach in a democracy that valued decentralization, he wondered why politicians followed a hierarchical progression from local to national leadership.

Pushkar reflected on historical rulers from Vedic texts, including the Aitreya Brahmin of the *Rigveda* and the Shatapatha Brahmin of the *Yajurveda*, as well as Buddhist *Jataka* tales, citing examples of unpopular and misguided kings like Nahus, Subhas and Sumukh. He realized that merely reading about these figures wasn't enough; the youth must actively embody the ideals championed by leaders like Swami Vivekananda. It was a call for the youth to be proactive and live up to the expectations of great thinkers and visionaries.

After a long spell of intellectual churning in the ocean of deep thoughts, Pushkar sailed to the island of rest. He felt for a moment that he had travelled too far and that it had become too late. It appeared to him that the world has stopped. But he knew that it was not possible. The next moment he laughed loudly at himself and reminded himself, 'With its ever-flowing rivers, birds and mountains, this world remains indifferent to the comings and goings of even the most extraordinary individuals; it neither gets overjoyed by arrivals nor excessively saddened by departures. In this grand scheme, I am but a fledgling scholar, fresh and inexperienced, akin to a newborn. However, my potential should not be underestimated. Given the chance, I, too, can devise strategies, implement policies and emerge as a social reformer. I harbour aspirations to walk in the footsteps of illustrious figures like Chanakya, Vivekananda, Ram Mohan Roy, Bhagat Singh and Subhash Chandra Bose.

'Do I lack courage? No. Just as the Indian Army is deployed in the security of our nation, I can also form an army with the help of the youth and student council members of the country; I can motivate every soldier for the upliftment of society! It is foolish to give up by being afraid of personal deprivations. I am physically and mentally healthy; is this less than any wealth? *Vivek* or prudence is the best quality of a brave man, in the absence of which, we are like a jar of juice or a bottle of honey that remains unaware of its taste all its life.'

Pushkar made up his mind that he had to work for the society and national interest by coordinating with the politics of the country by all means. It was his firm belief that even the stumbling blocks in his path were making him experienced. The quality of humanity was gradually being absorbed in his behaviour. Narrowness of jealousy, malice and self-defeat were being replaced by 'Vasudhaiva Kutumbakam'.

It is not that he happened to have an extraordinary class; his class had students with different types of ideologies, who had different ways of thinking. But by nature, every individual has the same desire—to represent humanity, to lead a decent life and move forward with happiness, but it is not possible to think like this here, because student life is a life full of stress. At this age, a person displays the path of the present, past and future and gets a signal of what his tomorrow will be!

Therefore, Pushkar understood that it is natural to have obstacles in the way! One who will fight these obstacles and weather all storms firmly and patiently will often enjoy the pleasures of this world. But at the same time, whoever runs away from obstacles and does not shun laziness, frustration and despair at this crucial stage, these stubborn obstacles will not leave him for the rest of his life. Pushkar seemed to be moving forward with the resolve that in this life that lasts only a few days, he had to make essential goals and have a unique journey. And to achieve those goals, it was necessary to walk on the right path. Otherwise, he would forever consider himself a burden on the planet.

In the meeting of the hill students council held at Tagore Lawn, he was awarded the title of president of the council, and Shankar Singh, the title of vice president. The news was also covered by newspapers like the *The Times of India*. Also, a cultural program was organized in the premises of the famous Indian Sugarcane Research Institute to celebrate hill culture and civilization and encourage hill students towards identity. Sohanlal Thapliyal was the chief guest and his presence made the stage proud, and encouraged the students.[2]

Thus, given Pushkar's efficiency and his influence among the youth, in 1997, he was made the head of the Hill Student Council. As a result of his increased responsibilities and the unwavering affection of senior officials, he had started getting inspired to expand the organization with double enthusiasm and hundreds of supporters.

ABVP organization minister Nagendra Tripathi held a meeting to extend the membership of ABVP in which the number of members for organization expansion was unanimously set with the target of increasing the number of members from 2,500 to 11,000; and Pushkar was entrusted with the responsibility of its leadership. In the discharge of his duty, he got the membership fee reduced by ₹2 per person and gave

---

[2]Sohanlal Thapliyal, a resident of Dhaund village in Garhwal, was born into a poor family. His mother passed away because of complications during childbirth. He mentioned that when he was merely six years old, his father also passed away. He considered his widowed aunt as his mother and often said, 'I am unique. I have no brother, no sister, no uncles.' When he went to Dehradun for his primary education, his aunt registered his name as Sohanlal instead of Urmil. Since then, he became accustomed to changing his name. After 1964, he moved to Lucknow. A few years later, he became associated with Lucknow University, where he guided the students of the Parvatiya Chhatra Parishad (Hill Students' Council) like a guardian, making them aware of their rights. He was also a newsreader for Akashvani (All India Radio). Sohanlal contributed to Garhwali folk music and theatre. In 1972, he established the Darpan theatre group, which connected students from the hills, not only from Uttarakhand but also from neighbouring Himachal Pradesh, and dedicated himself to theatre. Ultimately, he passed away from liver cancer on 20 July 2021 in Lucknow.

membership to hundreds of students at regional colleges. Also, senior colleagues Dayashankar Singh, Prabhatkant Tripathi, Shivaji Chandramouli, Somesh Vardhan Singh, Bajrangi Singh Bajju, Santosh Singh, Pawan Upadhyay, Anoop Verma, Manoj Jaiswal, Ram Prasad Singh, Uday Veer Singh, Manoj Singh, Udaykant, Pradeep Chandra, and others, went to various universities, business establishments, localities, colleges, etc., every day and interacted with the youth, trying to bind them in the strong spirit of patriotism under ABVP's banner.

Every evening, meetings were held at different venues, alternating between Pushkar's ND Hostel, Shivaji's Birbal Sahni Hostel, Prabhat Tripathi's Golden Jubilee Hostel and Dayashankar Singh's Butler Hostel. Often, enjoying the daal-rice and egg curry made by Pushkar, everyone was happy to get first, second and third place for the maximum number of new membership receipts. Due to the tireless efforts of the student council of ABVP, this year, the number of members had crossed the prescribed target of 11,000, reaching up to 15,000, which was beyond the expected number.

With increasing public relations and leadership skills, the number of Pushkar supporters was also increasing. Daily, hundreds of students were convinced of his simple, gentle and benevolent behaviour, and did not feel tired of telling the stories of his working style. In the university students' union elections, young men began to be influenced by the ideology of his speeches and addresses at various meetings. Encouraged by the progressive increase in its membership strength, the ABVP also campaigned vigorously by fielding hard-working candidates in all the colleges affiliated with Lucknow University. In the role of a star campaigner, Pushkar appealed for votes for ABVP candidates through various public functions and meetings. As a result, for the first time in the student union elections, this year, i.e., in 1997, ABVP not only got Santosh Singh as the president of the Lucknow University Students' Union, Dr Dayashankar Singh and Dr Rajesh Mishra as vice-presidents, but also succeeded in making a one-sided claim on the student union building. Also, Manoj Rai in DAV Degree College, Nitin Tiwari in Shri Jai Narain Misra Post Graduate (KKC) College and Diwakar Chauhan in Christian College won the posts of president with sound majority. These victories led to other candidates contesting on the main posts of other degree colleges who had been endorsed by the council also winning one after the other.

These victories started attracting everyone's attention, and the workers dedicated to the council, especially Pushkar, could bring in a fresh influx of new members. As a result, the organization never looked back. All this when there were constant ups and downs in the state's politics!

Chief Minister Mayawati's government had collapsed within 184 days. After the political turmoil, Kalyan Singh finally managed to form his government with the support of allies. Bhagat Singh Koshyari, a son of the hills, was appointed a state legislative council member for the first time. The political gurus of thousands of youths resided in the OCR building in Lucknow.

Around the same time, Pushkar fell sick because of a tough routine and improper meals in lieu of post-victory celebrations. When the news of his poor health spread in the hostel, a crowd of his well-wishers flocked the ND Hostel.

Somesh Vardhan Singh looked at his face and said, 'What has happened, Pushkar bhai... You need to take care of yourself too! What will you do with the supporters when your own body will not support you?'

'I know there has been a bit of negligence, but dozens of

candidates had invested their hopes in me and I couldn't let their trust fumble. I tell you, Somesh ji, I have spent many sleepless nights or went to bed on a hungry stomach. But now my body feels so weak; I cannot possibly get up and go out to the lawn...!'

Somesh showed Pradeep Pandey the empty wrapper of paracetamol lying on Pushkar's desk and pointed to the yellowness in his eyes! Pradeep put his hand on Pushkar's forehead and said, 'Brother, you might be afflicted with jaundice... Your eyes are yellow... Come on! Let's get a check-up done at the clinic at Babuganj intersection!'

Sensing the gravity of the situation, Pushkar agreed to ride on Abhinav's scooter. Somesh and Pradeep were also behind them.

Charging them with a fee of ₹100, the doctor in the white coat slapped them with a note, asking them to get some blood tests done. The pathology report proved that Pushkar had jaundice, after drawing blood through a long syringe and charging ₹220. The doctor of Babuganj intersection insisted on them buying medicines from his familiar medical store and only then handed over the prescription! Along with the advice of drinking boiled water, he warned him to be careful about eating and taking complete rest.

The young man recovered completely by giving business to three healthcare establishments. Now the disease that was afflicting him was the worry of the month's financial expenses. Somesh and some of his friends again came to Pushkar's room to see him. A close scrutiny of the recent developments was made.

In the meantime, another friend, Harsh, left for Lalbagh with a colleague of his, who was going to submit his job application form near Novelty Cinema. When his partner started submitting the form, Harsh slowly slipped inside the cinema, following the film posters on the wall. Harsh's self-esteem was awakened when the cinema staff asked him to leave the auditorium as he was without a ticket, saying that the film had already started! The conversation soon ensued into a scuffle and the staff of the cinema hall started beating Harsh brutally. When the colleague, who was done submitting the form, saw Harsh being beaten black and blue, he was shocked. He tried hard to protect his friend but failed. On the contrary he too was punched badly, but somehow escaped and reached ND Hostel room number 119.

Like a deer escaping from lion's mouth, he gasped, 'Listen! Brother Pushkar, Harsh is being beaten up by Novelty employees who are not letting him leave the theatre. If we don't do anything, they will finish him like wild jackals!'

On hearing this, all the students, along with Somesh Vardhan Singh, sprinted towards Novelty. Pushkar set aside his illness and jumped to save his brother. Fellow students stopped him, but he was the first to reach Novelty Cinema.

The news spread like wildfire among all students. *A university student has been assaulted...* So it was natural that angry youth from other hostels also started moving in groups towards Novelty Cinema.

On reaching, Pushkar introduced himself to the staff and requested them to release the friend immediately. But the manager was not ready to accept it; he said that Harsh had abused his staff and misbehaved with them, and thus he would not let him leave. Pushkar was talking to the manager when the angry mob of university students suddenly started vandalizing the cinema hall. The cinema employees also attacked them with stick and belts. A belt hit Pushkar right on the forehead. The attack proved to be so heavy that blood came out like a stream from a pitcher, due to which he fell unconscious! As soon as the news of both the angry parties reached the Lucknow Police, the police officers tried to disperse the students. Taking advantage of the situation, the cinema staff dragged Harsh and Pushkar and some other students inside the hall and pulled down the shutter of the premises.

After chasing away the students on the spot, the police brought an injured Pushkar and other students to the Kaiserbagh police station. When the students got the news that an injured Pushkar Singh Dhami was locked in Kaiserbagh police station along with other students, hundreds of Lucknow University students started gathering in Kaiserbagh.

The Local Intelligence Unit (LIU) informed the police officials that hundreds of students were seething over the assault on the students of the university and were planning to set Novelty Cinema on fire. Shocked by this information, Lucknow Police deployed heavy police force at Novelty Cinema, Kaiserbagh and Hazratganj overnight. Despite the tireless efforts of the student leaders, the police administration did not release Pushkar and others from the police station, citing deterioration of law and order.

The following day, the university students' group, using a political tactic, surrounded the sangathan mantri of BJP Jai Prakash Chaturvedi, and forced him to confront the station house officer (SHO). District Magistrate Navneet Sehgal had been invited to the residence of BJP's influential urban development minister, Lalji Tandon, at Sondhi Tola Chowk for personal reasons. Sensing the students' anger, Lalji Tandon put pressure on the DM and on the SP City West Lucknow over the phone and ordered the immediate release of the students from the kotwali.

Thus, the case was solved by hundreds of students

With Mrs Droupadi Murmu, president of India

Presenting a statue of Lord Shiva to Mr Narendra Modi, prime minister of India, at Jageshwar Dham, Almora

With Mr Narendra Modi at the launch of the 'Sankalp Se Siddhi Tak' campaign

With Mr Amit Shah, union minister of home affairs

With Mr Rajnath Singh, defence minister of India

With Mr Nitin Gadkari, union minister of road transport and highways

With Mr J.P. Nadda, union minister of health and family welfare as well as chemicals and fertilisers and president of Bharatiya Janata Party (BJP), the world's largest political party

Welcoming Mr Ramnath Kovind (third from left), former president of India, and his wife Mrs Savita Kovind (second from left) at the chief minister's residence in Dehradun with his wife Mrs Geeta Dhami (extreme left)

Presenting a basket of regional produce to Mrs Nirmala Sitharaman, union minister of finance and corporate affairs

Presenting a crystal memento of the divine Neem Karoli Baba to Mr Narendra Modi

At the Uttarakhand Global Investors Summit

With Mr Yogi Adityanath, chief minister of Uttar Pradesh, at Lucknow

Receiving a bouquet at Lucknow University auditorium from his favourite professor, Dr Nishi Pandey, as Mr Brijesh Pathak, deputy chief minister of Uttar Pradesh, looks on

With Mr Mohan Bhagwat (extreme left),
chief of Rashtriya Swayamsevak Sangh (RSS), who is inaugurating
Madhav Seva Vishram Sadan in Rishikesh

With Mr Shivraj Singh Chouhan, union minister of agriculture and
farmers' welfare as well as rural development

Receiving blessings from the divine Jagadguru Ramanandacharya Swami Rambhadracharya, founder and head of Tulsi Peeth

Inaugurating Yuva Dharma Sansad along with Indian yoga guru Swami Ramdev (second from left); Champat Rai, leader and vice president of Vishva Hindu Parishad (VHP; extreme right); and Acharya Mithilesh Nandani Sharan (extreme left) at Patanjali University, Haridwar

With the newly formed cabinet in the presence of Mr Narendra Modi (fifth from left) and Lieutenant General Gurmit Singh (Retd; fourth from left), governor of Uttarakhand, at Dehradun

With Mr Murli Manohar Joshi, one of the founding members and former President of BJP

With Mr Satpal Maharaj, who is serving as the tourism, cultural and irrigation minister in the cabinet of the government of Uttarakhand

With Mr Ramesh Pokhriyal 'Nishank', an author and former chief minister of Uttarakhand

Presenting Mr Trivendra Singh Rawat, former chief minister of Uttarakhand, with a shawl

With Mr Tirath Singh Rawat, former chief minister of Uttarakhand and present national secretary of BJP

With Mr Ajay Bhatt, member of parliament (MP) from the constituency of Nainital–Udham Singh Nagar

With Mr Ajay Tamta, MP from the Almora constituency

With Mrs Mala Rajya Laxmi Shah, political and social worker as well as MP from the Tehri Garhwal constituency

With Mrs Ritu Khanduri Bhushan, speaker of the Uttarakhand Legislative Assembly

With Pujya Swami Chidanand Saraswatiji Maharaj, president and spiritual head of Parmarth Niketan

Welcoming Mr Dhirendra Krishna Shastri (extreme left), leader of Bageshwar Dham, to Dehradun, along with Mr Ajay Bhatt (extreme right)

With Mr Harish Rawat, former chief minister of Uttarakhand and a senior leader of the Indian National Congress

With our Sikh brethren, celebrating the 400th birth anniversary of Guru Tegh Bahadur, the ninth of ten gurus who founded the Sikh religion

With Pritam Singh, former leader of opposition in the Uttarakhand Legislative Assembly, at the chief minister's residence in Dehradun

With Mr Sakshi Maharaj, Lok Sabha MP from Unnao, Uttar Pradesh

With Major General Bhuwan Chandra Khanduri (Retd), former chief minister of Uttarakhand and a senior member of BJP, on the occasion of his birthday

With the late Mr Kailash Chandra Gahtori, former MLA from the Champawat constituency, during the Champawat by-election

With Mr Mahendra Bhatt (extreme left), BJP Uttarakhand state president, and Madan Kaushik (extreme right), MLA from Haridwar constituency

With Mr Dharmapuri Arvind, MP in the Lok Sabha from Nizamabad, Telangana, at the chief minister's residence in Dehradun

Receiving blessings from elders of the state

Taking oath as a young student leader of Akhil Bharatiya Vidyarthi Parishad (ABVP), an all-India student organization affiliated to RSS, while studying at Lucknow University

Standing behind Mr Rajnath Singh (third from left), who was the then chief minister of Uttar Pradesh

Unforgettable moments with batchmates as a young college graduate (top: extreme left and bottom: extreme right) at Lucknow University

With classmates and friends from Lucknow University during the Mumbai session of ABVP (sitting: second from left)

With his parents, Mrs Bishna Devi and Mr Sher Singh, and his three sisters, Nandi, Pushpa and Indra, during his childhood days

With Mrs Geeta Dhami as a newly-wed couple on 28 January 2011

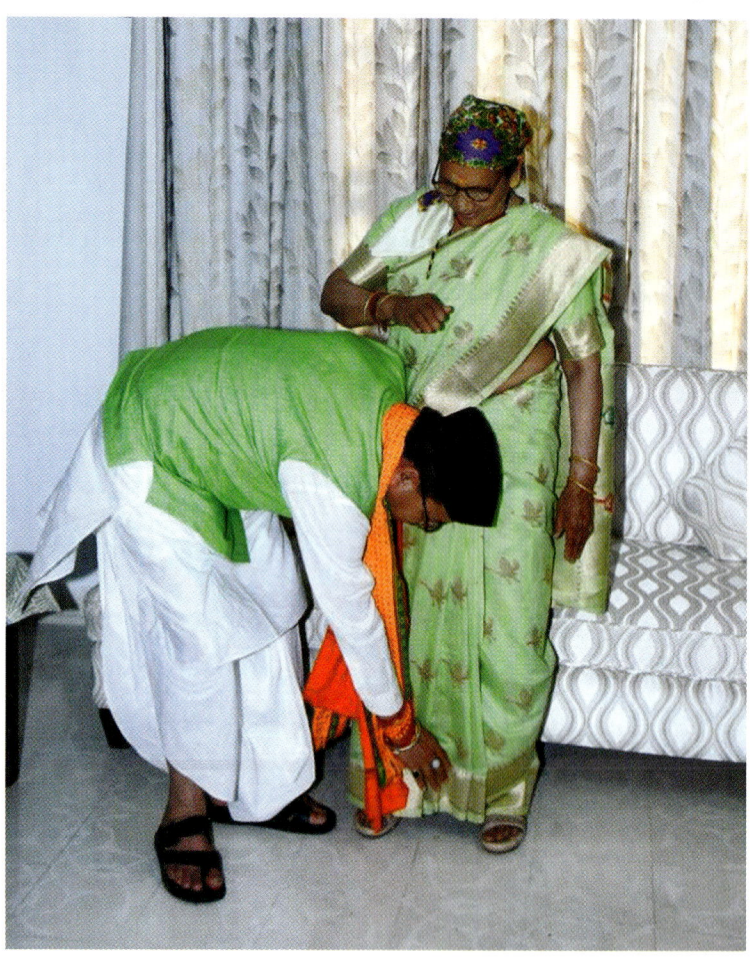

Receiving his mother's blessings after taking oath as the chief minister of Uttarakhand for the first time

Receiving his mother's blessings after winning in the by-elections

With his elder sisters Nandi and Pushpa now

Planting saplings with his mother as a part of the Prime Minister's 'Ek Ped Maa Ke Naam' campaign

Celebrating the birthday of Prime Minister Narendra Modi with young kids, who are the future of our nation

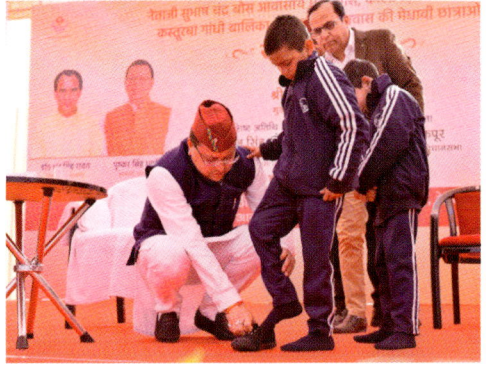

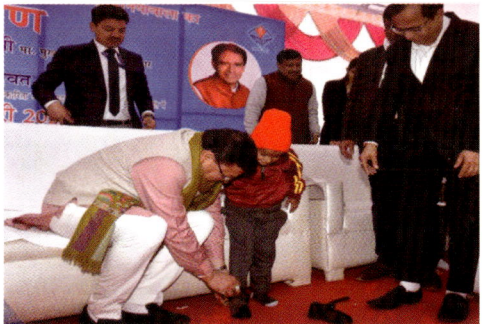

Special moments of love and affection with the future of our country

During the yajnopavit or thread ceremony of his elder son Diwakar

Spending time with Gaumata (his cows) at the chief minister's residence in Dehradun

Praying to Goddess Laxmi along with his family

In pure Indian attire during his youth

shouting slogans against Novelty triumphantly and bringing their dearest and innocent Pushkar and others back to the hostel!

By now, Pushkar had carved his unique identity in the eyes of every student; slowly, he had re-engaged in his studies and student council work.

In December the year before (1996), ABVP had compiled an overview of various commissions brought in for comprehensive reform of higher education in the country and their efforts in this regard. The worldwide organization ABVP, active for twelve months of the year, was entering the field this time with a new campaign, *Sanatan Dharma Pravesh*. The exclusive purpose of this campaign was to awaken the feelings of unity, integrity, security and social harmony and celebrate the glorious Vedic past of the country. Diversity was also necessary in a diverse nation, but the youthful zeal of the modern generation was beginning to push national diversity into a different horizon. Therefore, Pushkar was appointed as this campaign's administrator under Laxmanananda Saraswati's leadership. Barely five to seven people took part in its meeting in front of the Tagore Library.

The biggest reason for this was that Christianity was being propagated in every corner of the country through sporadic lure of temptations. The victims of such conversion drives were innocent people and people with low incomes. To prevent this, Pushkar asked for a list to be prepared with the council's help of those who return to sanatana dharma. When the list reached him, he was shocked to see only five names mentioned in it; they had never got such a weak result. But with patience, he expressed gratitude from the bottom of his heart. 'We are enough, brothers. It is not necessary that one and one is always two! We will show the power of the eleven!

So, remember Swami Vivekananda ji's words, "Arise, awake, and stop not till the goal is reached."

It is another matter entirely, and a strange one at that, that out of those five names four were from Christian community. Through the organization, Pushkar had continuously worked towards accelerating the collective efforts of people, with the goal of essential, accessible and quality education, structural improvement in existing resources, protection of cultural heritage, and curing the youth suffering from various social diseases. As a result, the organization had also gained popularity through his creativity, sense of responsibility, nationalist spirit and appealing policies. That is why, many peaceful, hardworking activists of the organization were standing up against the anarchist elements of the university.

'Pushkar bhai, I have faced great humiliation today,' Shivaji Chandramouli said, entering Pushkar's room. The postgraduate second-year examination was near. Pushkar was somehow taking time from the university's classes and council programs to prepare for it, and here had arrived Shri Shivaji Chandarmouli!

Pushkar was peeved with this sudden arrival of a problem. With reluctance he looked at the guest standing near the desk and noticed that his face was crimson red. Pushkar asked, 'You seem outraged, brother. Where are you coming from? Having your honour tarnished?' He thought his light comment would lessen the atmosphere's severity.

'What does he think of himself, this Bhasin? Just because I'm a student, does he think that he can say anything to me? Did I go there to be ridiculed by him?' Shivaji was not ready to calm down; his anger was like that of an erupting volcano.

Sensing his friend's inner turmoil, Pushkar sat beside

him, gently patting his shoulder, and said, 'Brother, who can strip you of your honour?' He added, 'If this happens, we'll protest by shutting down the Hazratganj market; just say the word! Dhami made the mistake of considering himself a satirist like Harishankar Parsai and said, 'Can you tell me what happened to you?'

After drinking a glass of water, Shivaji Chandramouli broke his silence. 'Ahead of the ABVP's Mumbai convention, our organization has been tasked to print a souvenir magazine. We've already received receipts for advertisement publications in the office, and we're also planning to raise more advertisements...'

Pushkar learned that Chandramouli Sahib had visited Bhasin & Sons, a clothing showroom in Hazratganj, to procure advertisements for the magazine. There, during the negotiation, he had clashed with Adarsh Bhasin, the owner of Bhasin & Sons. Adarsh was willing to provide a small advertisement, but Shivaji insisted on a full-page ad, befitting his business's stature. Adarsh, annoyed by Shivaji's persistence, asked him to leave the showroom immediately. This deeply offended Shivaji, affecting his self-esteem and leaving him frustrated. Finally, he came out by warning him. 'We'll see you tomorrow!' he had said. And that is why here he was breaking down in front of Pushkar.

Pushkar calmed Shivaji down, citing the dignity of his organization, and suggested he talk to Adarsh Bhasin calmly.

Shivaji left Pushkar's room, and Pushkar started studying again. Even in the real world, Mauli Sahib is counted among those who have a 'do or die' attitude for the organization.

One day, Shivaji, Somesh Vardhan Singh and Dr Anoop Verma reached the ND Hostel, room number 119 with the first rays of the sun! Dr Anoop had been appointed as a doctor for a public hospital a month ago while being an ABVP office-bearer. But he was displeased because his first appointment was far from Lucknow. Therefore, he had come to discuss the possibilities of an appointment in Lucknow or the adjoining areas. Friends suggested him to consult the health minister at the time, Shri Ramapati Shastri! Fortunately, Shastriji assured him of a transfer to Barabanki, which is in the vicinity of Lucknow.

Shivaji Chandramouli, who had been agitated for the last several days, said, 'Let's go from here to Bhasin & Sons too. He has been making excuses about the advertisement; we'll be back with an agreement for a full-page ad today.'

'Okay. But please don't get angry, Mouli Sahib,' everyone asked for his assurance, and suppressing their laughter headed towards the showroom to meet Adarsh Bhasin.

As they reached the showroom, the staff and owner immediately recognized Shivaji. The entire group stood firm on their demand for a full-page ad in unison.

Bhasin Sahib had already suspected, that by arguing with the young students at the university, it was possible that they would return in large numbers and create disruption at the showroom. Therefore, in the face of the stubborn attitude of the students, they called officials of the trade board at the showroom. Not only this, when the matter was exacerbated, the police also reached the spot.

Now there were the young firebrand student leaders on one side, and there were rich, pot-bellied traders on the other end. One side was physically strong and the other had the might of money. Sensing the organizational strength of both of them and the potential of some eventuality, inspector-in-charge Ram Singh from Hazratganj reached the spot. And when he found that the weight tilted towards the traders, he intelligently put student leaders in his jeep and rushed towards the police station.

Shivaji stared into the eyes of the police inspector and was almost about to say something when the inspector smiled mysteriously and said, '*Abeey*... Keep quiet, or else...' with tobacco in his mouth.

Every effort was made by the inspector-in-charge to convince the traders and find a way to reconcile, but their intentions were thwarted in the face of pressure from the board of traders. Suddenly, the crowd of students also started moving towards the police station from behind.

Given the possibility of breach of peace, Section 151 of the Code of Criminal Procedure (CrPC) was announced in a hurry, and all students, including Pushkar and Shivaji, were fined. On hearing of the challan, an astonished Pushkar in a gesture of searching his empty pocket looked at Shivaji and others.

Shivaji tried to call his fellow student leaders to the police station. But Inspector Ram Singh explained to them that it would prove to be a childish strategy and would result in contrary consequences for them. He told them that by appearing before the magistrate they would get the bail on the day itself. Therefore, accepting his advice, the accused students appeared in the court of the deputy DM.

In the court, Somesh Vardhan Singh saw a well-known lawyer, a university senior, who looked at him and took off his glasses and leaned in towards them. 'What's the matter? What are you guys doing here?'

Somesh placed his hand on a friend's shoulder and whispered with great affection in his ear, 'It is not possible to arrange the lawyer's humongous fee for which he is approaching us and so when he asks us, just say that it's nothing serious. I will testify on your behalf before the magistrate and get you released on a personal bond.'

All the friends agreed, knowing that they would be released. So, when their turn came, they said whatever came in their mind and laughed.

The inspector looked at them with angry eyes and roared, 'It seems that you still haven't matured past puberty; two thwacks with this lathi and you will come to your senses. Keep it in mind!'

The policeman's strong words sent shivers down their spine—including that of Pushkar. They immediately agreed to surrender. But Shivaji did not want to give up his self-respect and come to his knees.

The lawyer told the magistrate that the students had to go to Bhasin to demand donations under their student council obligations. He cited student interest and requested for the release of the innocent youths.

Hearing the statement of the lawyer, the magistrate assumed that the group of students must have entered the showroom of Bhasin & Sons for extortion, who then brought the matter before him.

'Have these students come to the university from remote areas to study or to collect donations? How justified do you think it is to threaten and argue with traders by asking for donations in this manner? These are criminals, and I cannot let go of this gang who are involved in a crime like this. So let them go to Lucknow jail as per the due act.' Saying this, the magistrate dragged his pen on the paper and went away.

'Perhaps if the lawyer had talked about the advertisement for the magazine, the magistrate would have understood the matter today,' said newly-appointed Dr Anoop Verma.

Shivaji Chandramouli exclaimed, 'What nonsense are

you talking about? You just lost your nerve. Before achieving success in ventures of life, one often garners a few so-called criminal accolades! You'll understand this gradually; you're still naive!'

Shivaji Chandramouli was prepared to face any challenge. But upon hearing that they were being sentenced to jail, Dr Anoop Verma, Pushkar and their colleagues realized the seriousness of the situation. They started praying for a peaceful resolution, hoping their families wouldn't find out. Unaware of where to find a lawyer, they were distraught. Meanwhile, the police took all the accused to the district jail in Lucknow. Dr Anoop Verma was particularly distressed, not due to jail time but because his marriage had been fixed for the next month. He feared that the bride's family would discover his involvement in a crime and break the arrangement.

Pushkar, seeing this as a life experience, tried to calm Dr Anoop and the others, asking them to treat this challenge as a part of life.

Somehow, the first night was spent in the prison cell. Being students, all were kept in separate barracks from other prisoners. In the early hours of the morning after, when this news spread in the hostel and university, the council made tireless efforts to get them out on bail. But unfortunately, due to it being a second Saturday, the offices were closed. And the next day was a Sunday.

On the first night, honouring his public-serving spirit, Pushkar started to sing the song 'Raghupati Raghav Raja Ram'. After that, he announced that he would like to sing 'Vande Mataram' too. Honouring his wishes, all the prisoners present there also decided to sing 'Vande Mataram' every day.

When the court opened on Monday morning, a day

dedicated to Lord Shiva, so much time had already passed since their bail release paperwork had been on the table that their expiry was cited as a reason to defer the bail even further.

Fortunately, Bajrangbali Pawanputra, Lord Hanuman, the god of strength, heard their request. On Tuesday, after having experienced imprisonment, thanks to Shivaji, Dr Anoop, Pushkar and Somesh Vardhan were released. They had spent three days and three nights in the district jail. At the same time, Adarsh Bhasin too realized his mistake in treating students engaged in pursuits of national interest under the banner of the council as bullies or gang-members, like other student leaders; so he apologized to the students and dismissed the matter.

Only a month was left for the university's student union elections in November. Therefore, most student leaders had started their preparations and were busy in devising election strategies. In the last few years, the election for essential posts in the university had begun to be so elaborate and influential that it had been competing with the Assembly elections in the state. Money power and muscle power were being displayed openly to strengthen their wings. Samajwadi Party's Samajwadi Chhatra Sabha, Congress' National Students' Union of India (NSUI), Left's Students' Federation of India (SFI) and Right-wing ABVP were seen marching into battleground to test their powers. The ABVP had decided to field Gopal, a young man committed to the organization, but the nomination was cancelled due to some irregularities.

Unlike other student organizations, ABVP always tried to declare its candidates by giving importance to decent and famous faces. Therefore, Dayashankar Singh was unanimously selected by the student council as the candidate for the post of president. Dayashankar Singh was also Pushkar's senior and a good friend. Therefore, in favour of this diligent candidate, all well-wishers like Nagendra Tripathi ji, Jai Shankar Pandey ji, Prabhatkant Tripathi, Shiv Bhushan, Somesh Vardhan, Anubhav and Amarendra started campaigning, highlighting important issues.

Student leaders of student organizations of other parties were entering the university in a convoy of SUV vehicles like Scorpio, Pajero, Sumo and Gypsy, wearing white starched kurta pyjamas, creating a rowdy atmosphere among the students. With sloganeering, such as 'Zindabad–Murdabad', students carried their flags and strolled into classrooms, forcibly stopping lectures and trying to garner votes in their favour. They would sometimes boycott all classes and organize gatherings in the university campus. The situation had become such that the entire university seemed to be election-oriented. The teachers also understood that the student population had moved from the classrooms to the publicity grounds. So gradually they stopped their classes indefinitely. Whether it was in the university campus or the hostel, or the streets of Lucknow—especially in areas like University Road, Aliganj, Indira Nagar, Nishatganj, Daliganj and Hasanganj, where students lived in abundance—the walls, the electric poles were covered in banners, posters, hoardings of student leaders. Vehicles with groups of students would fly past crowds, throwing pamphlets at them.

After campaigning in hotels and eateries in Lucknow, many student leaders would eat with the staff and workers in those eateries till late at night; they would engage in discussions about the whole world. The 'election strategy programme' of student leaders at Durgamma Restaurant in Lal Bagh, Maa Durga Eatery in Burlington, Balaji Eatery and Bharat Restaurant in Charbagh, Sharma Restaurant in Aminabad had been going on continuously. As a result, there had been an unprecedented increment in the number of students who didn't eat in the hostel mess.

Every basic need from tea and snacks, and diesel and petrol, to pan-masala was being fulfilled by the student leaders with complete devotion. Throughout the day, students could be seen roaming around the university and distributing attractive pamphlets with folded hands to get votes in their candidates' favour. Not only this, as soon as the evening would descend, a crowd of student leaders and their supporters, arriving on scooters and motorcycles wearing garlands of fresh yellow-orange marigold flowers, would enter the rooms of students who were living in the locality and college hostels, They would appeal for votes throughout the day and would return to their own rooms only at midnight.

In every university, there is a troop of such oldies that hang around the university either because they missed out their degrees or they were expelled from the university. Some of them also happen to be former office-bearers of the university students' union. Most of these men turn out to be contract politicians; and whenever a university election commences, their services are sought by contesting candidates. Keeping complete information at their fingertips about where will a vote go are the unique selling points of these hired oldies.

In this election too, such elements were in demand; and like Sri Krishna, they were busy preparing an election strategy based on past experiences for their Arjunas (candidates). They would help them figure out things like, for example, how many student voters are there in which hostel or locality, which district's student leader has the most dominance, students of which caste and community will be influenced by whom. Since they possessed a practical political acumen and experience to orchestrate an election, they commanded both attention and respect. They sometimes got as much attraction as a film star who graces a wedding.

Various political parties were also helping their respective student organizations and chief candidates financially, because, after winning, the office-bearer had the power to unite many students in election rallies or demonstrations. In such an environment, when the entire student union was seen immersed in an election hue, it was natural for the enthusiasm and subsequent ruckus generated by the students to touch their peak. Aspiring student leaders would even clash with each other while conversing. In all these ways, the campus was buzzing with activity. It seemed that the police and the district administration would continue to have their heart rates ascend and descend till the end of the election! No office-bearer of the university wanted to take any risk for their lives by messing up with these ambitious youth. Thousands of supporters had been brought by student leaders from remote villages with the promise of the kebab-biryani of the Nawabi city of Lucknow. They were performing the task of adding to the crowd in various processions, roadshows and public campaigns.

If one were to look at issues in student politics, they seemed to be focused on moderate and logical issues. With few workers, ABVP candidates were going to the students who lived in hostels and were handing over their pamphlets while making appeals for their votes. Through cultural meetings on the university campus, one could see their priorities and plans. It is not that these ABVP student leaders were spending less money on posters, banners, billboards, pamphlets and public relations. But they had to stay away from an unethical way of functioning and stay within the limits of what Sanatan culture-based propaganda permitted.

Pushkar was also engaged in the campaign of council candidates with the help of student union workers. He, along with his colleagues, had been regularly appealing to the faculty members of various faculties of the university to permit them to read out the words of the manifesto with their permission. It had been almost four years since he had been working selflessly in the student council. So it was evident that, in these years, he had gathered around him an army of well-wishers and supporters. This was the reason that, due to the personality of all the ABVP candidates and the hard work of dedicated workers like Pushkar, Dayashankar Singh was declared the winner for the post of student union president, Shailesh Kumar 'Shylu' was elected as the general secretary and Prabhatkant Tripathi as the vice president, with full majority.

It was the month of December, and the cold had gained a foothold in Lucknow. After the massive success in the student union elections, the organization, which had settled into a relaxed routine, had now started preparations to participate in the upcoming meet of ABVP in Mumbai. Under the leadership of Nagendra, who was discharging the responsibility of regional organization minister, workers and office-bearers could participate voluntarily on behalf of the state.

Pushkar, in the role of administrator, made the list public, in which 150 members, including about 60 female students, were unanimously selected to represent Lucknow in the Mumbai meet. Among them were leaders such as Nagendra and Jai Shankar Pandey, along with Pushkar, Somesh Vardhan, Dayashankar, Anubhav, Amarendra, Rahul, Pawan, Shashank,

Smita Bahri, Ila Shukla, Arjita, Anshu and Anamika. Nagendra had prepared a road map to take four groups of ABVP from all four directions of Uttar Pradesh to Mumbai. The biggest tour took place from eastern Uttar Pradesh under the leadership of the council's state minister, Rajkumar. A well-dressed 150-member team from Lucknow finally reached Mumbai via train, sharing laughter and stories. Pushkar also remained the main centre of attraction among young colleagues with his playful looks, wearing his yellow Indonesian shirt and photochromatic glasses.

In this three-day convention, about 50,000 primary workers from all over the country had gathered, leaving aside the uncountable sub-chief workers and supporters. On all three days of this convention, ABVP National Organization Minister Dattatreya Hosabale and Pramod Mahajan ji had ensured that they were present among the students. Not only this, but to make the convention memorable, the dignitaries of the BJP and the RSS also participated in it and even shouldered some responsibilities. The convention's main focus was on creating a solid policy document on 'Education in Governance'. One of the most interesting things that happened was Jaishankar Pandey, general secretary of the student council, being selected to be one of the four speakers for the speech in Hindi medium. In his lecture on 'Brain Drain and Fellowship', he said that students studying in technical higher education institutions like IITs engage in various types of research and development programs with the help of government funds. However, after obtaining an engineering degree, they do not use that knowledge for research, discovery and inventions for their country's progress, but instead become administrative officers by preparing for civil services. He mentioned that they should cooperate in advancing new technology by becoming teacher–researchers or innovators. With his few minutes of speech, Jaishankar Pandey became cynosure of all eyes in the entire auditorium. Pushkar stood on his seat and cheered for him, with slogans such as 'ABVP Zindabad'! Soon the whole auditorium was flooded with slogans.

One should always do such deeds that they become the holy end in themselves instead of the means. One should aim to strengthen the arch of an egalitarian society and socialist democracy. While returning from the ABVP Mumbai meet, all students sat in Pushpak Express and went to their respective berths. When the train reached Bhopal, some objectionable elements entered among the students of the chemistry department. The group of miscreants started making rude comments on the council's students. Not only this, they started singing some parodies and teasing them. Seeing this, the girls started becoming angry. They conveyed this information to Pushkar's coach. The atmosphere became tense, although the classmates assured them that nothing would happen to them. When those boys started being excessively crass, Pushkar tried to convince them in every possible polite language. Giving priority to the honour of women, Pushkar stood at the door and took the responsibility of protecting them, although he couldn't have been physically stronger than a large group.

When the train stopped briefly, Pushkar looked out the window to get a sense of the view outside. What he saw shocked him. A large group of boys had gathered who started threatening to 'fix them' at the next junction. Seeing all this, Anubhav locked the door and windows of that coach so that no student became a victim of the attack.

The train's next stop was Jhansi, where angry groups entered the compartment. Anubhav and other colleagues stood at the door. Pushkar bolted the door from inside and held it. If there was any tension or fear on his face, it was for the safety of the co-passengers, especially the female students. Jhansi police were informed about this through some means. With the help of two police constables, Pushkar drove out the hoodlums and ensured that every girl student reached their destination safely.

Desires vs Destiny

As soon as Jaishankar Pandey was selected for the fellowship, he received the money from the university. Seeing the vehicles parked on the university campus, a flutter of ambition took birth in his mind. Many times, he had dreamt of buying a scooter, but financial constraints had always shattered those dreams. Small aspirations and firm actions mark the beginning of success, but it needs commitment and confidence to flourish. Sometimes, external support can make achieving goals easier. Jaishankar, with steadfast belief, asked Nagendra Tripathi for a loan from the organization's fund to buy a Bajaj Chetak, promising to repay it with his next fellowship instalment. Tripathi, trusting his friend, agreed to lend the money.

One day, sitting on the backseat of Jaishankar's new Bajaj Chetak, Pushkar raised a concern: 'Brother, I understand the MBA students' situation, but with university exams starting in the first week of May, how will they manage to take part in the PCS prelims?'

Jaishankar raced towards the vice-chancellor's office, saying, 'Let's see if the VC is available to discuss this matter. If the organization gets too busy with expansion, they might overlook this issue.'

Upon reaching the office, they were promptly invited

inside by the Vice-Chancellor D.P. Singh, who looked up from his papers with a surprised expression. 'Pushkar, it's unusual to see you with Jaishankar. Is everything alright?' asked D.P. Singh, removing his glasses and rubbing his eyes.

Both students respectfully touched the feet of the senior officer. Pushkar explained, 'Guru ji, we're facing a serious issue that affects the students' interests. We believe it can only be resolved with your understanding and help.'

The Vice-Chancellor, used to such visits from students, responded, 'Yes tell me about it. I had a hunch that you would come with a problem today.'

He then philosophized, 'Problems and solutions are like two sides of a coin; only a healthy and intelligent brain can generate both.'

Understanding this statement, Jaishankar said, 'Sir, the date of MBA semester examinations is out, but it is at the same time as PCS prelims. Both exams will clash and students will not be able to sit for one of them. We request you—if you think it's appropriate—to please order the examination date to be changed immediately, so that they are held after the PCS examination. It will be a blessing!'

The Vice-Chancellor thought for a few moments, scratching his head; he found the suggestion positive and did not see any significant problem in changing the date of the examinations. 'Okay, I'll consult the MBA head of department to get the new date announced; rest assured!'

Pushkar and Jaishankar bowed their heads, thanked the Vice-Chancellor, again touched his feet and came out of his office.

The Vice-Chancellor, D.P. Singh, knew that both the students consistently talked about students' interests. Unlike other student leaders, they had nothing to do with bullying and anarchy.

Soon, Pushkar received the last class of formal education, i.e., post-graduate degree. However, his informal education was to continue through various means.

Nasti vidyasamo bandhurnasti vidyasamah suhrita.
Naasti vidyasam vittam naasti vidyasam sukham.

The verse is often found in the Subhashitas—collections of Sanskrit wisdom verses—and resembles teachings from *Vidura Niti*—a part of the *Mahabharata*—and *Chanakyaniti*, emphasizing that there is no kin like knowledge, no friend like knowledge and no wealth or happiness greater than knowledge.

We should constantly engage in knowledge acquisition by making education a priority. The truth is that school or university education is just a formality; we should get lifelong knowledge through various means to create and improve a civilized society.

Pushkar was now shining like the sun on the vast sky of politics and, at the same time, understood the responsibility of fulfilling the dreams of his family. For both reasons, he found it inevitable to continue his journey at Lucknow University. Therefore, he set the Bachelor of Laws (LLB) as his next goal and enrolled in a one-year diploma course in personnel management.

His name was now being taken among the dignitaries in the Lucknow student council. He was committed and determined to increase the status of the organization.

Relation, Representation and Regulation

One day when Jaishankar Pandey reached the student council office in Kaiserbagh, he greeted Shri Swant Ranjan with great respect. Swant Ranjan, the state *pracharak* or functionary of the RSS, looked up and said, 'Hello! How are you, Jaishankar ji?' Swant Ranjan, with his melodious smile gestured Jaishankar to sit on the front bench. It is the culture of the Sangh and its affiliates to treat the guest as equivalent to god.

Jaishankar Pandey replied, 'I am well, brother, with your blessings. I wanted to see you for a long time and share some secrets with you.'

'I also feel overwhelmed in the company of an *anuj* (younger brother) like you,' Jaishankar said respectfully, sitting down with the chair in front of the table. 'It's good that you came.'

After getting information about the condition of the university and other student council-related activities, Swant said, 'An idea has been popping up in my mind for days, brother; I think you are the right person to implement it. That's why I look forward to discussing it with you. Many of our young versatile students who prepare for administrative services are not able to gain admission to any coaching centre and keep preparing on their own. Why not teach such students by opening coaching under the direction of talented senior students like you? And prepare such future captains for competitive exams by giving them proper guidelines and suggestions.'

Jaishankar found this innovative idea of academic pedagogy revolutionary and fascinating. The biggest reason for this was that he had taken steps towards teaching by getting a fellowship. Secondly, he also had a keen interest in teaching.

So, Jaishankar enthusiastically, giving his approval, said, 'Bhai Sahab, your idea is commendable. If our organization cooperates for the mental and economic well-being of the younger generation, then we can easily do this work.'

Pushkar also reached there, and the blueprint of the entire plan was put on the table. Everyone together held a rigorous strategic discussion to give this plan every possible effort to make it a reality. Within a few days, with the consent of the ABVP office bearers and those of the Sangh, a coaching centre was inaugurated at Saraswati Shishu Mandir in Nirala Nagar for hundreds of students preparing for civil services under the direction of Jaishankar.

Along with Swant Ranjan, Nagendra and Pushkar, many council workers also dedicated their souls and minds to the promotion of the coaching centre. Pushkar left no stone unturned in getting economically weaker and deserving students admitted to the centre.

One day during dinner at Moti Mahal restaurant in Hazratganj, biting into a piece of paneer with crisp tandoori roti, Jaishankar said, 'Pushkar, seeing the hard work of young students while teaching in coaching, I feel how many talents would have died without skilled guidance...'

Pushkar is friends with the owner. The staff here doesn't even charge us for the meal.

'Two days later, RSS's Rashtriya Sangathan Mantri Dattatreya ji is coming to Lucknow and has ordered that key office-bearers of the Vidyarthi Parishad should be present. There will be a meeting in the coaching centre, Saraswati Shishu Mandir... Take some time out; you must be present there.'

Jaishankar said thoughtfully to Pushkar, 'Yes, you have to stay there; Brother, we will go along...'

Pushkar had the final piece of roti and headed towards the wash basin.

Shriman Dattatreya Hosabale arrived as per schedule after finishing the formal meeting with the office-bearers of the RSS and interacting with the key office-bearers and activists of the student council. Many officials including Nagendra, Jaishankar, Pushkar and Somesh Vardhan were present. After presenting a detailed account of the work of ABVP state unit, Nagendra invited Dattatreya ji on the stage to address the packed auditorium. Dattatreya ji praised Pushkar, along with other office-bearers and activists, for the continuous success of the ABVP Uttar Pradesh membership campaign, which had broken all previous records. 'I want to organize a grand national-level event under ABVP. My plan is to hold the event in Chandigarh or Lucknow. And I would like to give the responsibility of successfully implementing its road map to the team of selected state workers,' he said.

On hearing this, the Lucknow ABVP team was overwhelmed.

'If you propose for this event to be held in Lucknow itself, we will be committed to its success here,' Pushkar got up from his seat and said.

All the dignitaries in the auditorium supported his point.

Dattatreya ji, with a sigh of relief, patting Pushkar's back, with a slight smile on his face, said, 'Son! If young workers like you are with us, then it is not a tough task for us to organize any event overnight; India is a young country, and you, the youth, are our identity. But I'd like to test your resolve! If you gather 200 workers here at lunch break after our meeting tomorrow, I will believe in the strength of your confidence! Then we can talk further.'

How easy or difficult it was for Lucknow ABVP office-bearers and Pushkar to gather 200 workers in 24 hours, was a matter to be seen.

However, accepting this challenge to save his self-respect, Pushkar's team, under the direction of senior officials like Nagendra and Jaishankar, delivered the news through PCO phone booths to the students in university hostels and every student representative living outside Uttar Pradesh by midnight. Also, students from Bihar, Madhya Pradesh and other states studying at Lucknow University were invited to visit Nirala Nagar Auditorium at the stipulated time. Not only this, but Pushkar also, along with all the colleagues of his hostel, was engaged in making arrangements for the program throughout the night. As a result, a crowd of Pushkar supporters started gathering in the courtyard of Saraswati Shishu Mandir from the morning itself.

By lunch break, more than 700 young activists had recorded their presence in the entry register. Seeing the enthusiasm of the educated youth and future leaders sitting in many queues, Dattatreya ji started addressing the workers with great enthusiasm. In the very first line of his address, he announced that the convention would be held in Lucknow itself! The Central Working Committee (CWC) soon informed Nagendra of the same over the weekend by fixing the date of the three-day program. Also, Pushkar's camp was entrusted with important responsibilities of the convention.

This was the first national three-day convention of the ABVP to be held in Lucknow in which selected workers from all over the country were invited to participate. Under the leadership of Nagendra, the Pushkar camp successfully hosted office-bearers and workers from all over the nation at the convention venue. On the last day of the convention, the volunteers under the leadership of Pushkar shared the importance of the religious and cultural heritage of Uttar Pradesh with all primary office-bearers by taking them on a tour of Ayodhya, Vrindavan, the Varanasi ghats, Lucknow city, etc.

At the convention venue, Pushkar had deployed his workers at designated locations to ensure that no one faced any problem in regard to guides, tea, snacks, food, etc. For a successful completion of the event, Rashtriya Sangathan Mantri Dattetreya ji wholeheartedly congratulated everyone present in the auditorium, including Nagendra, Pushkar and other ABVP workers, and expressed happiness for such a pleasantly surprising outcome, which further strengthened the morale of the young workers.

After this program, Pushkar's stature started growing among the workers. Many senior alums and office-bearers dedicated to the council cheered for Pushkar for his extraordinary organizational skills.

In the evening, many of his supporters gathered on the lawns of ND Hostel as usual. 'Brother, you said, if we worked hard with full dedication at the convention, you will make arrangements for our entertainment and food in the dhaba,' a guy from Poorvanchal said.

'I said it, brother! I remember. I don't forget a promise I made!' Raising his eyebrows and looking at the guy, Pushkar continued affectionately, 'Brother, you all have worked very hard to make this event a success. You don't know what you people have done... After honourable Dattatreya ji challenged the youth to show their strength... Wow. Tell me what to do, what should I do so that you are entertained?'

The boy mysteriously laughed and quipped, 'Brother, if you really want to entertain us, then take us to Goa beach. Take us to an opera house. Why are we sitting at dhabas here?'

'Brother, we want you to show us the film *Border*, which is running at Sahu cinema these days,' another guy said, adding that Akash Sahu, owner of Sahu Cinema Hall in Hazratganj, was a friend of Pushkar. Produced and directed by J.P. Dutta, *Border* was the story of the 1971 Indo-Pakistan war (Battle of Longewala). All the scenes had been filmed on the sandy soil of Bikaner and Jodhpur, with Indian cinema's stalwarts Sunny Deol, Suniel Shetty, Tabu, Pooja Bhatt, Akshaye Khanna and Jackie Shroff. How could a young man breathe a sigh of relief without watching such patriotic stories or emotions?

Pushkar immediately spoke to Akash Sahu from Somesh Vardhan's cell phone. 'Hello, Akash! How are you, dear?'

'Hello there, brother! What made you remember me today? You've become such a rare sight these days!'

'I can come over now if you like, but any decision will only be made with your approval...'

'Ah, my friend! We're not the ones to make big decisions. But mark my words, one day you'll be passing crucial resolutions, not just for the state but for the entire country. Don't worry about it now!'

'Listen up, brother!' Pushkar said with a seriousness. 'Some of our friends want to watch *Border*. Can you sort out tickets for tonight's show, if possible?'

'Ah, my brother, that movie's a total blockbuster, completely sold out. But I always keep your requests in mind. I'll tell you what... I'll arrange some extra chairs in the lower hall. Just let me know how many people will be coming.'

Hearing this, the students were divided; some insisted on sitting in the hall, while others were fine with even mats on the floor. They were determined to watch the film together, no matter what.

Pushkar helped them overcome this tricky situation. He said to them, 'Even the woodcutter who crafts the officer's chair never dreams of sitting on it. So, what right do we have to be so proud, friends?'

Later, they all agreed.

'Sahu ji, could you arrange 60 chairs? And let us know the cost for this.'

'Hey, listen! You'll just have to pay the chair rental to the tent house owner. As for the movie tickets, they'll be just ₹10 each at a discounted rate. Is there anything else I can do for you, brother?'

Pushkar grew concerned about the final headcount, prompting a recount. Fortunately, all 60 people were as ready as soldiers at the border. Pushkar announced that there would be no food or drinks, only the movie.

Once everyone agreed, he gathered ₹400 from his pockets and added ₹200 from the organization's funds, handing a total of ₹600 to Akash Sahu for the evening show.

Somesh Vardhan, imitating Sunny Deol's style, said enthusiastically, '*Ye dharti sher bhi paida karti hai, doosaron ko mitti mein milane wale sher* (This soil also gives birth to lions, lions that bury others in the soil)! Wow, what a powerful dialogue!'

When the film started, Pushkar's supporters filled the hall with joyful chants of 'Pushkar zindabad'. Some began singing a popular song of the movie, while others recited their favourite dialogues like '*Ham hi ham hain to kya ham hain, tum hi tum ho to kya tum ho* (What am I just being me, what are you just being you)!'

Everyone was engrossed in the movie. Somesh and Pushkar discussed their favourite parts. Eventually, Pushkar spoke up loudly: '*Ham to kise ki dharti par najar nahin dalte... lekin itne nalayak bachche bhee nahin hai ki koi hamaari dharati par najar dalen aur ham chup chap dekhate rahein* (We may overlook some misconduct, but we're not foolish enough to ignore threats to our motherland and remain silent).'

After attentively listening, everyone lavishly praised Pushkar, applauding the fearless heroism of Major Kuldeep Singh Chandpuri (portrayed by Sunny Deol) and his 120 braveheart soldiers.

Late at night, they dispersed into their respective accommodations. Pushkar, too, returned to his room, softly singing '*kisi dilvaali ne, kisi matvaali ne, hamein khat likkha hai...* (some sweetheart has written a letter for me...)' before drifting off to sleep. But he was soon awakened by a knock. Pushkar was surprised to see Nagendra ji. He quickly invited him in.

'I was passing by and thought I'd drop in. I hope I haven't disturbed your sleep.'

'No, brother, I've not been sleeping well for many days; it happens occasionally.'

'You've worked tirelessly with your team, brother. You're receiving a lot of praises today. Did you promise to show a film to your companions?'

Pushkar, adjusting the pillow on his bed, replied, 'Yes, brother. My team, meaning our supporters, has put in a great effort at the convention, so I promised them a movie screening. That's why we watched *Border*.'

'Well done, brother, but how did you manage to raise so much money for 56 students? If I'm not mistaken.'

'Nagendra ji, I contributed some, and for the rest, I had to withdraw from the organization's funds. The job is done, but it will take some time to replenish the organization's money,' Pushkar said proudly.

Upon hearing this, Nagendra gave Pushkar a serious look, toyed with the glass paperweight on the table, and then glanced at the walls. He said, 'Pushkar, society donates to us for organizational work and national service programmes, trusting that we'll advance societal progress. Using these funds for entertainment or personal needs sends the wrong message.'

Pushkar, feeling ashamed, realized he hadn't considered this perspective, despite intending to repay the money.

Nagendra continued, 'If the activists wanted to watch a film, we could have arranged a special screening. Spending organizational money on movies is inappropriate. As a responsible member, you need to replenish the funds quickly.'

Acknowledging his error, Pushkar reflected on Nagendra's dedication and sacrifices, a rare quality in today's materialistic politics. The next day, he borrowed ₹200 from friends, replenished the organization's fund, and vowed to avoid personal use of these funds in future.

In November 1999, the ABVP again organized a three-day national workshop at Lucknow University. Jaishankar Pandey, Satopanth, Amarendra, Anubhav, Ajay, Somesh, and all dignitaries of the council, alongside Pushkar, contributed to making the workshop memorable. They invested themselves day and night. Pushkar was appointed as the chief administrator. Esteemed academic personalities from across the country also graced the occasion with their presence. Additionally, their team felicitated approximately 200 meritorious students at the conclusion of the workshop.

Struggle for Stability

On the joyous evening of the new year (2000), as leaves blanketed the ground, signifying the end of the autumn season, the impending announcement of examination dates at Lucknow University intensified the pace of learning. Aside from the evenings, only a handful of students gathered in groups outside their classrooms. However, Anubhav, in his youthful zest, persuaded two or four of his friends to accompany him towards Kailash Girls' Hostel.

'Why are you taking us to the girls' hostel, brother? We're not keen on lurking around the gate,' protested one of his friends.

Amarendra, noticing the Kailash Hostel sign, grew anxious, as if he were seeing it for the first time.

Anubhav glanced back, sporting a mischievous smile. 'Come on, stick around for a bit. I've sent a note to your *bhabhi* (sister-in-law; referring to his own love interest), and today's the day for her reply. If she shows up, you can leave, and I won't hold you back!'

Annoyed, Amarendra retorted, 'Please, I don't indulge in these antics. Besides, Nishi Pandey ma'am is the provost here. If she catches sight of me, she'll take me to task. *You* wait; I'll leave, brother!'

Anubhav was aware that, like Pushkar, Amarendra preferred minimal interaction with students at the university. He instructed the other two students in the group to keep an eye on the provost. 'Just give me 10 minutes, then you can go,' he pressed, making Amarendra the reluctant scapegoat.

From behind, another companion interjected angrily, you know what will happen to us in 10 minutes! Your beloved will turn us all into uncles, and you'll become a father right here! So we have to bolt!'

Anubhav responded to them with an emotional tone, 'Hey, remember who's been burning fuel with you all these days, getting humiliated in front of everyone just for skipping classes. Consider that too...'

Moved by his friend's emotions, Amarendra stood by the gate as though he were an auto driver waiting for passengers on the roadside.

After a while, Anubhav's charming acquaintance emerged, her hair billowing in the air as she adjusted the scarf in her hands. Overwhelmed, Anubhav lost his composure, while Amarendra swiftly made his escape, akin to a parrot fleeing its cage.

On the flip side, Pushkar's popularity had soared within Lucknow University. He had earned a reputation as one of the most upright and adaptable student leaders, prompting both new and seasoned students to seek his counsel. Pushkar diligently strived to address their concerns through every possible means.

Months passed in the buzz of academic and extra-curricular activities. As the July heat began to wane, and with it started a fresh academic year, Pushkar spurred his fellow supporters to tackle issues faced by newly admitted students in their hostels, ensuring every individual in need received proper guidance within the university. With Independence Day approaching, the fervour of student union elections surged, entwined with patriotic zeal. Consequently, various parties and organizations intensified their claims by nominating eligible candidates for the impending student union elections.

Once again, Hanuman Setu Road leading to the university became adorned with an array of photographs, manifestos, posters and banners of candidates from opposing factions, vividly illustrating the youth's indispensable role in political dynamics and transparency. Prime Minister Atal Bihari

Vajpayee echoed the belief that a country enriched by the participation of its youth exuded a sense of vitality.

Hence, political parties spared no effort in planning and executing the university student union elections, recognizing the significance of charismatic young leaders, deeming these elections more pivotal than even the Lok Sabha elections. However, the current landscape of student union elections is far from what it used to be.

In 1970, Chaudhary Charan Singh, revered as the farmers' champion, introduced the Uttar Pradesh University and College Bill amid escalating chaos in the elections. He proposed that direct elections to the student unions be replaced with indirect elective methods, but the bill faced vehement opposition. The newly appointed CM Kamlapati Tripathi swiftly withdrew the bill within three days, maintaining the status quo.

Pushkar rallied his supporters and convened a seminar with senior council leaders, experienced mentors and progressive thinkers from the university. The gathering dissected the campus's shortcomings, fostering discussions centred on vital flaws.

When it was Pushkar's turn to speak, he proclaimed:

> Friends, whenever consciousness has to blossom in any nation or region, it's always spurred by its young men and women. While seasoned leaders often perceive us merely through the lens of emotional fervour and idealism, I can attest that the youth neither measures their values, beliefs, nor loyalties in the scales of profit and loss. They're unflinchingly dedicated to the welfare of the motherland, unswayed by business interests. Youth power surges like an evergreen river, overcoming

all impediments. It devises plans devoid of manipulation and chessboard strategies. We must align both passion and awareness to transform the campus's political landscape, an aspiration long anticipated by all. While seeking guidance and blessings from our elders, let us also ensure their strides are parallel to ours.

History stands testament to the fact that our nation's destiny has been written by courageous soldiers and immortal martyrs using the ink of their noble blood.

Upon hearing Pushkar's powerful words, independent thinker Pawan Upadhyay remarked, 'Brother, a young man like you is needed not only in this university but also in this country. Get ready for the field; we'll handle the rest!'

From different ends of the gathering, Somesh Vardhan and Pradeep, along with Anubhav from the middle, began chanting, '*Dhami tum maidan mein utro, isi mein haami hum sabki hai* (Dhami, you come to the political field, we all agree on your leadership).' This chant led to a significant surge in Pushkar's supporters, escalating from mere tens and hundreds to a resounding thousand.

Amidst this, Pushkar sought out his close friend, Jaishankar Pandey, and related the entire incident. Finding the timing opportune, Jaishankar advised him to meet Kshetriya Sangathan Mantri Nagendra.

Throughout the night, myriad questions swirled in Pushkar's mind, some finding their own resolutions, while others remained unanswered, lingering in contemplation.

Sangharsh ke us daur mein bhee jeevan chal raha tha.
Bhaav ko abhaav mein pratiphal raha tha jeevan.
Jab dost mile saathee mile tab main mila hoon.
Ab sangharsh se lakshya kee or chal raha hai jeevan.

This poem reflects the persistence of life amid struggles and deprivation. Despite hardships, life continued, though adversity often overshadowed aspirations. True friends and companions brought self-awareness. Now, life moves forward with determination, overcoming challenges and progressing towards its destined goal.

'Bhai Saheb, Sadar Namaskar,' Pushkar said respectfully as he sat in front of Shri Nagendra Nath Tripathi, the Kshetriya Sangathan Mantri of ABVP, at the organization's office early in the morning.

'You're a rare sight, Pushkar. What's going on? Where have you been lately?' gestured Nagendra, asking Pushkar to take a seat.

Pushkar explained, 'The first semester of LLB examinations was underway, and then I've been engrossed in the issues faced by the newly-admitted students. Now, with the elections approaching...'

While conversing with Pushkar, Nagendra sensed that there was something significant on his mind. It was evident that Pushkar wasn't someone who directly addressed the core issue but rather navigated around it. However, today was an exception—Pushkar and Nagendra were alone in the office, which was an unprecedented occasion.

'Would you like tea, coffee or something cold?' Nagendra asked.

'Oh, my apologies, forgive me, but let us have it some other time. Actually, brother, this time I intend to contest for the post of Lucknow University Students' Union's president, and I seek your guidance and blessings!'

Nagendra was taken aback, 'O Rajput! Claiming the presidency in the very first attempt. Remember, this is politics, this is akin to a chess match.' After a pause, he continued, 'Pushkar, I can't disregard your talent and courage, but my advice is that you gain experience by aiming for the positions of general secretary or vice-president first. A direct bid for the presidency might seem a bit unusual.'

Pushkar responded firmly, 'Brother, I belong to the land where even the mountains stand proudly. My forward-thinking vision gives me confidence. I aspire to rectify the flaws plaguing our university through collective action in the future. If the student council places their trust in me for the presidency this time, I'll forever be indebted to them.'

Nagendra found himself in a state of dilemma, witnessing Pushkar's unwavering dedication and confidence towards transformative student politics. Since the presidency often falls into the hands of those who have held previous union positions or contested elections, Nagendra couldn't give a direct yes or no.

The council boasted a long list of contenders for all positions, including president, vice-president and general secretary, with even more recommendations and endorsements.

'You must reconsider it, my brother. Politics isn't just about ability and skill. It demands tactics contradictory to morality—*saam, daam, dand, bhed*, or persuade, purchase, punish and exploit,' Nagendra cautioned, intending to discuss the matter with other state officials.

'I apologize, brother. I come to you with an offer for a position I deem myself eligible for. Just as it would be unfair to appoint a teacher for a watchman's role, I don't want criminals to hold honourable positions. I aim to promote truthful politics from within the university, steering our politics towards moral regeneration, embracing the ideologies of *Sarva Dharma Sama Bhav* or, all religions are equal, and Vasudhaiva Kutumbakam or, the world is one family. I seek blessings for the presidency,' asserted Pushkar.

'In the absence of moral politics, the distortions you've encountered stem from your tenacity. Remember, you need not be desperate; every night heralds a morning! Our cultured politics has deeper roots than we acknowledge. The need is to nurture these roots through individuals like you, but it's prudent to await the opportune moment! Hasty indulgence is always harmful, like haste is the devil's work,' cautioned Nagendra, emphasizing the importance of patience, and further added the famous sher of Dushyant Kumar:

Masalhat-e-aamej hotein hain siyaasat ke kadam,
Tu na samajhega siyasat, tu abhee naadaan hai.

Political moves are strategic and often driven by hidden interests. Understanding them is difficult, as an inexperienced person cannot grasp their depth.

Pushkar quietly exited the room with folded hands. Successive meetings of state-level office bearers took place in the council's office to finalize the ABVP-backed candidates for the student union elections. Various dignitaries, including Nagendra, extensively deliberated on Pushkar's candidacy. While Pushkar's name was on everyone's lips, senior student leaders like Prabhatkant Tripathi, Ashish Mishra, Rajesh Mishra, and others emerged as formidable contenders for the presidency. Notably, all of them had previously held positions within the students' union.

Pushkar hadn't held any official position. But his desire to run for presidency was aligned with six years of effort and dedication he had invested in its pursuit.

Satat sangharsh se hee jo apana naam kare.
Kaise tarakash mein apana teer kaman dhare.

A person recognized for their struggles cannot live without them, as a life of perseverance is their identity, success and foundation of existence.

Therefore, despite extensive deliberations, no definitive decision was reached. With time running short, approvals were granted for the names of vice-presidents, general secretaries, and other candidates based on caste and political equations. However, the name for position of president remained under consideration, akin to a bride waiting behind the curtains. Pushkar's tenacity insisted that compromising on his principles was not an option.

The following day, Sangh's state pracharak Swant Ranjan summoned Pushkar to the Sangh office, Bharati Bhawan. After the formalities, Swant Ranjan addressed Pushkar in a grave tone, 'Pushkar, your claim for the presidential candidacy cannot be overlooked. You've exhibited proficient leadership in numerous significant events, well recognized by us all. Your leadership and teamwork skills are commendable.

However, the council committee has unanimously decided to nominate a Brahmin candidate for the presidency this time, considering inclusive grounds. The organization regrets not supporting your claim. Nevertheless, acknowledging your determined will, we are willing to offer you the candidacy for the position of vice president or general secretary.' He took a breather and continued, 'Look! We cannot nominate Kshatriya candidates for all three positions due to constraints in the general secretary and vice-president roles. The Samajwadi Chhatra Sabha, our strong competitor, has also declared a Kshatriya candidate for the presidency. I've called you here to discuss this matter.'

Pondering over Swant Ranjan's words, Pushkar responded softly, 'Sir, I believe I am suitable for the president's role, unless the council expresses objections. If it causes any inconvenience, Parishad's decision will be final for me. I am devoted to putting an end to this era of anarchic politics; I have no personal agenda. I wouldn't stake claim to any other position. If conditions allow, perhaps reconsider next year. This time, I will wholeheartedly support the council candidates as usual on behalf of the student council. If I've pledged allegiance to the organization, I will abide by it. Therefore, under no circumstances, I can oppose your decision.'

Swant Ranjan patted Pushkar on the back and assured him, 'I pledge on behalf of the council that next time, our presidential candidate will be Pushkar Singh Dhami!'

Thus, Ashish Mishra was unanimously declared as its presidential candidate by the council. Pushkar, along with the council team, campaigned vigorously for all its candidates and also appealed to the students in the university to vote in favour of the ABVP candidates. Along with organizing voter awareness meetings every day, he went to all delegations and contacted the students extensively, and said that politics has to be moral, free from the pressure of caste and religion with fear, malice and prejudice!

But when the figures of the last phase were publicly announced from the vote-counting venue, it was found that Shailesh Singh 'Shylu' of Samajwadi Chhatra Sabha had been selected for president, while Abhishek Kumar Singh 'Ashu' and Bajrangi Singh 'Bajju' had won on behalf of the council for the positions of vice president and general secretary, respectively.

Often Pushkar and Shylu appeared to be opposing each

other in political ideology, which is why whenever there were mass debates, Shylu expressed his views strongly against the Vidyarthi Parishad while Pushkar passionately backed the Parishad. Sometimes this debate became as hot as hot tea or coffee. But Pushkar always won because of articulating his points with logic! Pushkar remembered Munawwar Rana Saheb's couplet after the defeat of the council's presidential candidate.

> *Shareef insaan aakhir kyon election haar jata hai.*
> *Kitaabon mein toh likkha tha ki raavan haar jaata hai.*

This couplet reveals the bitter truth of politics. It states that an honest person loses elections, whereas books always portray the defeat of evil or Ravana. In reality, ethics and honesty often fail in politics, while deception and cunning tactics lead to victory.

The process for the formation of a new state of Uttaranchal was at its peak in the State Assembly. With the BJP governing both at the Centre and in the State, public confidence in the realization of Uttaranchal as a separate state had strengthened. The combined efforts of the central and state governments hinted at the imminent fulfilment of the much-awaited dream of the Uttaranchal state.

Respecting public sentiment, after all the exercises, under the guidance of Prime Minister Shri Atal Bihari Vajpayee, with the help of the Rajnath Singh government of Uttar Pradesh, the proposal for the formation of Uttaranchal, a new state, was passed by both Houses—Lok Sabha and Rajya Sabha. Then, on 28 August 2000, President K.R. Narayan signed the resolution.

'Pushkar bhai, your Uttaranchal is going to become a new state, now you should be active in the politics there,' said Dr Anoop in room no. 119, in the presence of many well-wishers like Shiv Bhushan, Dayashankar, Somesh Vardhan, and Prabhakant, among others, while having a delicious meal of dal fry and aloo gobhi from Pappu Dhaba of Babuganj.

'Yes, brother, this is our dream. The regional people have worked very hard for the formation of the state, but I have learnt the art of student politics from Lucknow University. I have made my mark here and created a strong ground, not 10 or 20 but thousands of supporters. So leaving Lucknow is going to be very hard,' Pushkar said turning emotional.

Interrupting the ongoing conversations, Narendra Singh Deori, an office-bearer and member of the Uttarakhand Hill Council, entered the room, saying, 'Oh, younger brothers are having a dinner party here...'

'Hey, come, brother, you also join and have some fun,' Pushkar offered Narendra Singh a seat.

'No, no, you eat. I just ate before leaving home. I first had to go to the municipal corporation to finish an urgent work on time. After finishing there, I came to meet you.'

Narendra Singh Deori considered Pushkar as a younger brother. Pushkar had helped a lot in amassing votes of Uttaranchal migrants in his *Sabha Sad* (member) election.

By late night, more of Pushkar's friends gathered there and started motivating him to come out of the crowd of Lucknow leaders and go through the BJP's mainstream politics in Uttaranchal. But Pushkar was immersed in the atmosphere of Lucknow; it was not so easy to leave. But on the other hand, there was his birthplace. Dealing with this dilemma meant that, for a few days, Pushkar would feel extremely emotional when it came to the matter of leaving Lucknow.

'*Ka guru! Suna hai Uttaranchal jae ke plaan bana leehe ho* (Friend, we have heard that you have decided to go to Uttaranchal finally),' said Manoj Jaiswal, slapping Pushkar on the shoulder while he was standing outside the faculty of law. Startled by a sudden attack, Pushkar looked back and saw that Manoj was with his friends Sanjay Shukla, Tarunkant Tripathi, Pradeep Chandra and Pawan Upadhyay.

'*Yaar*, you have broken my shoulder, you hit me so hard,' Pushkar said, rubbing his shoulder, his eyes squinting in pain. But his expressions did not seem to have any effect on Manoj.

'*Ka Rumi* gate *ker khade takat ho sannate mein, jo hamre haath maare se tumhar burji toot jae rahi hai!*' Manoj, a resident of Hasanganj, again shouted in Awadhi, 'What are you looking at, standing in silence like the Rumi Darwaza, that just by placing a hand on your shoulder, your bones are cracking.

Pushkar, along with other colleagues, laughed at his sarcastic speech, although nothing could be understood!

'*Chala bhaee, Basanti chaachi ke adde par chalkar baithal jae, aaj na aeehain R.R. Singh sir, unki class na hoe aaj;* come on, brother, let's sit at Basanti aunty's tea stall because there is no class today as R.R. Singh sir is on leave.'

Pushkar understood the typical native sentiment and couldn't resist the influence of friends like these companions. He also joined in, embracing his pure Uttarakhandi roots.

'*Theek chh hit maathoo-maathoo, parantu dhyaan raakhiya, bhale pakaudee chaay kha ya samausa chaay, aaj bill main nee bharun.*' Okay, let's go, but remember, whether you all enjoy tea-pakodas or tea-samosa, I will not pay today's bill at any cost.

This unexpected comment was beyond anyone's grasp, so the entire group laughed and made their way to Basanti Chachi's tea point. The heat was so intense that the humidity had started making everyone feel suffocated. But the group happily settled down there, shooing away the hovering flies around the benches.

8

JOURNEY IN POLITICS : THE ENLIGHTENMENT OF POLITICAL OBLIGATION

The inertia spread along the path of action does not clear up until the steps towards action are taken!

The BJP in Uttar Pradesh faced a sudden split due to a conflict between CM Kalyan Singh and Atal Bihari Vajpayee. Only 13 months earlier, Atal Bihari Vajpayee had won the Lucknow parliamentary seat by a margin of 4,31,000 votes, while Kalyan Singh narrowly escaped a political conspiracy, winning by only 70,000 votes. In 1998, the BJP had secured 58 seats in the state, but in 1999, that number halved to 29. Kalyan Singh's strategy was aimed at sidelining Atal Bihari Vajpayee from the prime ministerial race, prompting strict state administration orders until the voting concluded.

This move drew criticism from two senior UP government ministers, Kalraj Mishra and Lalji Tandon. However, Atal Bihari Vajpayee, now serving his third term as PM, planned to oust Kalyan Singh within a month, garnering support from coalition parties. Discussions began on potential successors, with the name of Ram Prakash Gupta, a 76-year-old figure living a secluded life, emerging amidst key BJP figures.

The news of Gupta's possible selection spread rapidly across Lucknow, prompting student union activists like Pushkar to organize seminars, emphasizing the importance of recognizing individuals for their deeds rather than overlooking them. Anubhav, Amarendra and Pradeep, with some other students, joined in to ensure daily discussions shed light on such remarkable figures.

Dhami, emphasizing his point, said, 'We often repeat such mistakes in society, and calling them mere human errors would be foolish. Every individual should be remembered for their deeds. This not only upholds the morale of that person but also of many others who work for social, cultural and political welfare. The discussion about Ramprakash Gupta ji is significant because he was an extraordinary personality. Mathematics has always been my favourite subject, so it is natural for me to know that Gupta ji completed his M.Sc. in Mathematics from Allahabad University with first division. He also had a deep interest in literature and was actively involved in social welfare and educational upliftment. Not only that, but he was also highly interested in astrology and debates related to it.

During the Emergency, and just a year before my birth, he became the state president of the Bharatiya Jana Sangh. Most notably, from April 1967 to February 1968, he also served as the Deputy Chief Minister of this state. Therefore, it is both astonishing and regrettable that today, we hardly know anything about him.'

Eventually, Lucknow police managed to locate Gupta's residence after hours of effort, leading to debates about his luxurious estate in Charbagh. Amidst this, Gupta, unknown to journalists, enjoyed the morning sunlight at the PM's residence in Delhi. When BJP party president Kushabhau Thakre arrived and warmly greeted Gupta, journalists took notice. Thakre officially declared Gupta as the successor to CM Kalyan Singh, eliciting heartfelt gratitude from Gupta and his supporters towards PM Atal Bihari Vajpayee and the BJP for this unexpected honour.

It can be said that **politics is an open field of infinite possibilities where predicting what will happen at a particular time is beyond the reach of prophets and experts!** Throughout the day, all student leaders of Lucknow University wondered who would be fit for the CM's position, advocating for figures like Rajnath Singh, Kalraj Mishra, Keshari Nath Tripathi, Lalji Tandon, Om Prakash Singh, Vinay Katiyar, etc. Pushkar persistently endorsed Rajnath Singh until the end.

Finally, the auspicious moment arrived on 12 November 1999 when Ram Prakash Gupta, despite not being a member of any House, gained favour within the supreme leadership and was scheduled to be inaugurated as the eighteenth CM of the largest state.

Gupta had withdrawn from active politics 15 years before assuming the CM's role. He had spent his time within the confines of his home, blessing new leaders and recounting past anecdotes. Consequently, his withdrawal from society had diminished his oratory skills. His advancing age had started affecting his memory as well. Each day, his secretary prompted him for speeches, but Gupta only uttered words that immediately come to mind, without any premeditation.

Gupta found it challenging to handle the honour bestowed upon him by the BJP and its top leadership, overlooking many veteran personalities. Even Mayawati sarcastically responded to his remarks about the Ram Temple. 'Poor Gupta! He always seems forgetful... Perhaps he was advised not to articulate the party's views on Ayodhya, but he did so anyway!' Meanwhile, Opposition-leaning students teased Pushkar and other dedicated workers of Sangh, by beginning each observation of theirs with 'your government's Chief Minister, Gupta...'

Fed up with the comments, Pushkar silenced every one by asserting his respect for all but his preference for those who demonstrated the ability to fulfil assigned duties. He believed that Rajnath Singh was the only suitable person under the current circumstances to efficiently govern the state.

This scenario turned CM Gupta into the subject of daily discussions. The media shifted their focus from seriousness to intrigue, publishing captivating stories based on his statements. Several MLAs took advantage of CM Gupta's infliction with dementia, providing the Opposition with an opportunity to undermine and ridicule his position. 'The state's CM isn't contesting elections; on election day, he'll forget where he's standing,' remarked the Opposition.

Despite the top leadership offering ample opportunity to CM Gupta to govern effectively, he concentrated on the mantra of 'listening to everyone but acting on one's own accord'. Consequently, albeit reluctantly, the high command had to fulfil a prediction made 25 years ago in 1975 during the Emergency when Gupta, as the first Satyagrahi of Uttar Pradesh, was imprisoned alongside the district-level party worker Rajnath Singh. Gupta, who also practised astrology, had then examined Rajnath Singh's palm lines, smiled, and forecast, 'One day, you will become the head of your state!'

That is how CM Gupta came to resign from his position on 20 October 2000, acknowledging his inability to manage the system smoothly. The high command announced the same day that on 28 October 2000, Rajnath Singh was to assume office as the nineteenth CM of the state.

As soon as this news reached the students' union at Lucknow University, Pushkar began dancing with his colleagues of the student council. By evening, the campus was alive with fireworks. Disregarding the hostel dinner, which was replaced by a gathering hosted by party workers and well-wishers at the nearest hotel, everyone celebrated. Witnessing Pushkar's prophecy coming true, classmates applauded him, to which Pushkar responded with a smile, 'Brothers, it's written in your fate lines that one day your brother (referring to himself) will not only become the chief minister but also the prime minister!'

Anubhav, who had just come back from a date on his bike, spoke up, 'Why should your future depend on us, brother?'

Pushkar jokingly responded by pulling his leg. 'Forget it. First tell me, where are you coming from? Show me your cell phone, who was the last person you talked to, your mother or father?'

When Anubhav reluctantly showed his phone, the recent caller's name was 'Chhaggan Lali.'

Pushkar quipped, 'See, that's how it always is! Sometimes it's saved as Ramlal Halwai, sometimes as Maggan Chaggan...

Anubhav's friends would often make fun of him because of the bizarre contact names on his phone.

'That's what I want to say, my brother!' Pushkar continued. 'You are a lover. And it is written in the palm lines of a lover, no matter what happens, if she says yes then your life is made, otherwise there is a deafening lull.'

His friends teased him, playfully singing the lyrics of a song from the movie *Barsaat* (1995):

Ye jurm-e-wafa dil to sau baar karega,
Ye kab dara hai duniya se jo ab darega.

The lines represent fearlessness in love and loyalty. The lover declares that his heart will commit the 'crime' of true love countless times, as he has never feared the world before, so why fear now? It reflects deep devotion and unwavering courage in love.

At last they all visited the office of Uttar Pradesh Petition Committee member Bhagat Singh Koshyari, where it was discovered that the demand for the formation of a separate state of Uttarakhand was likely to be realized that week. He was blessed with a simple and humorous nature. He was also revered as an elder among both the youth and the elderly. Pushkar, along with all the students of the Hill Students Council, considered him their guardian and political mentor, with Pushkar being his closest student leader.

Prakash Pant, an Uttar Pradesh Legislative Council member known for his calm, gentle demeanour, was also there, he had called Pushkar next to him. That time Bhagat Singh Koshyari, seated on the sofa, eating bread and bananas, got up from his chair, patted Pushkar's back, and with a smile, said, 'Come on! Why keep studying forever? Let's take you with us too... Is that right, Pant ji? What's the task you've told Pushkar about, the one that remains incomplete?'

Pant smiled slightly as if he either didn't understand or was unaware of everything.

Meanwhile, Somesh Vardhan explained to Bhagat Da the story of Pushkar's relocation to Uttaranchal and the associated challenges.

'Yes, if Pushkar stays with me in Uttaranchal, I'll be comfortable. I need to engage in politics there, so having a capable person like Pushkar with me would be beneficial. However, since you are office bearers of ABVP, it's better to seek permission from Sangh's regional pracharak, Om Prakash ji. Visit Bharti Bhawan and meet him. If he permits, we can discuss our plans,' Bhagat Singh Koshyari replied.

The following day, Nagendra ji, along with senior ABVP office-bearer Udayveer, met regional pracharak Om Prakash ji at the Sangh office in Bharti Bhawan. Om Prakash ji warmly welcomed them and arranged the cane chairs nearby.

After a brief pause, Nagendra said, 'Brother, we've come to discuss Pushkar with you. Our officials want to involve him in Uttarakhand politics.'

After discussing the upcoming Assembly elections, Om Prakash said, 'I agree with you. His abilities and dedication will strengthen our organization in Uttaranchal. Tomorrow, Shri Vijay Agarwal ji, an area officer, is going to Dehradun to oversee the organization's work in the Assembly elections. Send Pushkar with him, as Bhagat Da holds him in high regard. In the future, Bhagat Da will play a significant role in Uttaranchal, so Agrawal ji will introduce Pushkar to the new state office-bearers. Our best wishes are with Pushkar.'

In a cheerful mood, Nagendra left the Sangh office, while Udayveer and Pushkar, accompanied by other colleagues, went to inform Bhagat Da about the permission.

'I'm travelling to Dehradun tomorrow. I have a reservation. How will *you* come?' Bhagat Da asked Pushkar worriedly.

Somesh Vardhan immediately quipped, 'Pushkar travels as comfortably as one would sitting in the train's engine. Everyone, from the loco-pilots to the security guards, knows him.'

Pushkar gestured to Somesh to calm down, but everyone laughed.

Bhagat Da remarked, 'Let's accept challenges. Challenges are great lessons, and life becomes dull without them.'

Leaving behind a Chapter of Life: Lost to Light

What we lose to the light is never truly lost—it merely transforms beyond our sight, where every ending becomes the dawn of a deeper truth.

It means that losing is not always destruction; sometimes, it signifies transformation to a greater state.

The day Pushkar was to leave, the veranda in front of room 119, ND Hostel, and the room itself were filled with Pushkar's supporters.

'Pushkar bhai, I'm thrilled that a strong young man like you is supporting Uttaranchal. I see a future politician within you. May God make you a successful politician soon!' said Somesh Vardhan emotionally, convinced that Pushkar was moving onwards and upwards, towards Uttaranchal.

Accepting everyone's good wishes with a heartfelt gratitude, Pushkar reminisced. He acknowledged that numerous well-wishers had given him an extraordinary identity at Lucknow University, lifting him up. Hence, moving away from such companions felt like the separation of Lord Rama from Shatrughna and Bharata. However, he understood that change was the ultimate law of life and that change of place paved the way for progress, just like flowing water. After all, like water, staying stagnant brought impurity.

At approximately 6.00 p.m., not only a large number of friends from the university campus and the students' council but also regional businessmen and political figures gathered at Charbagh railway station to bid farewell to Pushkar Singh

Dhami, who would board the Doon Express. The loco-pilot warmly shook hands with Pushkar. As he headed towards the door of his coach, he couldn't believe the crowd on the station of the city of Nawabs, where once he had arrived as a stranger, now seeing him off. He was leaving, rich with knowledge, achievements and the blessings of thousands of young people.

Hua tha aagman haath khaalee aur tha sabse anjaan main,
Is mitti se milee jo bhool jaoon kaise ye pehchaan main.

When I arrived on this land, I had nothing, but from this land, I have gained an identity that is impossible for me to forget.

The train blew its horn as a final warning to move towards Dehradun. Pushkar kept wiping his eyes as he hung by the door, all alone, waving at the crowd, as the train inched away, taking him with it.

Jaishanker Pandey, Somesh Vardhan, Anubhav, Diwakar Singh Chauhan, Prashant Singh Atal, Kuldeep Tripathi, Amarendra Pratap, Pradeep Chandra, Prabhakant Tripathi, Satopanth, Sanjay Shukla, Tarunkant Tripathi, Manoj Jaiswal, Ram Pratap Singh, Udayveer Singh, etc., are individuals who still, after years, get emotional remembering the scene.

The 'Uttaranchal Bill' sent by PM Atal Bihari Vajpayee to the Uttar Pradesh government in 1998 was passed by the State Assembly with 26 amendments suggested in advance. Consequently, after being passed by the Parliament and approved by President K.R. Narayanan, the Uttaranchal hill region became the twenty-seventh state of the country on 9 November 2000. This occurred despite all the struggles, just a week after Chhattisgarh was carved out of Madhya Pradesh as the twenty-sixth state and a week before the creation of the twenty-eighth state, Jharkhand, from Bihar on 15 November.

A total of 30 members, 22 from the Uttar Pradesh Legislative Assembly and eight from the Uttar Pradesh Legislative Council, were part of the Interim Legislative Assembly of Uttarakhand (then Uttaranchal). Apart from 23 BJP members, the Congress had one MLA, Karan Chand Singh Baba, and one MLC, Indira Hridayesh. Additionally, there were three members from the SP and two from the BSP. The responsibility of forming the government lay with the BJP. Bhagat Singh Koshyari, known for his sharp strategic insights, was named to lead the first interim government. The people of the hill region also desired progress under Bhagat Da's leadership. The Rajnath Singh government in Uttar Pradesh too supported him. However, as per Bhagat Singh Koshyari's proposal, Nityanand Swami, a member of the Legislative Council, was appointed as the first chief minister, with Bhagat Da serving as the Minister of Energy and Irrigation in his government. Prakash Pant, known for his cheerful and sociable personality, was appointed the Speaker of the Interim Assembly. Due to insufficient members, the Leader of Opposition's seat had to remain vacant.

When Bhagat Singh Koshyari took oath as the minister of energy and irrigation in the first Uttaranchal government, Pushkar Singh Dhami was given the opportunity to work as his political adviser due to his industrious nature. Dhami's responsible performance soon made him a ray of hope and confidence for many, from the cabinet to the general public. The week before, an incident left a positive impression when Pushkar was, acting as a political adviser of Bhagat Da, efficiently managed all records, office work, correspondence, and attended to various calls and complaints.

Once, the principal of a Shishu Vidya Mandir in a remote area of Garhwal division shared the challenges due to lack of electricity. He said that even after 53 years of independence, his village hadn't seen electricity. Dhami, in response to the principal's plea, promptly took action and instructed the chief engineer of the state electricity department to illuminate the school immediately, even before the principal could reach his house in the village.

The inertia spread along the path of action does not clear up until the steps towards action are taken!

Dhami's advocacy paid off so much that when the principal reached his village the next day, he found a hundred-watt bulb lit up in his school! Seeing this, he was thrilled with joy! The principal returned to the young man the very next day and thanked him for his kindness, along with a box of confectionery! This led to the news of his quick decision-making ability and a positive message of his relations with the public reaching the ground.

The state was expected to hold its first-ever independent Assembly election in February 2002. Soft-spoken CM Nityanand Swami, originally from Haryana's Narnaul, sought suggestions from senior leaders from the Centre to the state government to ensure that there was no hindrance in the electoral politics of Uttaranchal. The newly formed state was mainly influenced by the equations and dynamics such as those of mountain–plain, Kumaon–Garhwal, Thakur–Brahmin, etc. Nityanand Swami ji had grown up in Dehradun, the plains of Garhwal, along with his father. Therefore, following a certain logic, he voluntarily sent a proposal to the top leadership to make Bhagat Singh Koshyari the CM, keeping in mind the future of the party.

Born in Bageshwar, a hilly region of Kumaon division, Koshyari had been a contender for the CM post from the very beginning. And so, Koshyari replaced Swami on 30 October 2001, with the support of supreme leadership, including the cabinet.

Due to the many achievements of Dhami and his versatility, the newly appointed CM Bhagat Singh Koshyari appointed him as his officer on special duty (OSD). His responsibility had now increased more than before, while he also got a lot of opportunities to learn the nuances of politics from his political guru.

In order to campaign for Bhagat Da in the February Assembly elections, Pushkar had gathered every Uttaranchal BJP supporter, from the migrants in Lucknow to the remote villagers in his constituency, to prove his organizational ability. In this election, Bhagat Singh Koshyari was fielded from his home district Kapkot Assembly seat, which despite being a snow-capped high-altitude area, was a hot ground for the election atmosphere; Bhagata Da reached the Assembly with more than 8,500 votes with 61 per cent voting. But unfortunately, out of the 70-seat legislature, the BJP got only 19 seats, while the INC emerged as the single largest party with 36 seats. The party contested the first election in the state under the leadership of Bhagat Da. The party could not get a majority in this election, but Bhagat Da's political clout within the party remained intact.

The Congress contested its election under the leadership of the party's state president and veteran politician Harish Rawat. However, after a conspiracy by a lobby that was against Rawat, the party leadership and Sonia Gandhi, the veteran Congress politician, appointed three-time undivided Uttar Pradesh chief minister Narayan Dutt Tiwari as chief minister on Rawat's replacement. Bhagat Da played the role of Leader of Opposition of the Narayan Dutt Tiwari government! During this time, the administrative potential that Pushkar displayed made the party and the public realize that as an OSD he had sent a message to the supreme leadership of the party that the young Pushkar could garner great support among the youth.

Therefore, in view of qualities like skilled leadership, planning, managing the organizational structure and coordinating among workers, the party's national president Venkaiah Naidu issued instructions to appoint Dhami as the state president of BJP's youth wing Bharatiya Janata Yuva Morcha (BJYM).

While discharging this important responsibility, the BJYM was also engaged in the exercise of expanding the youth front. This was the reason that every month hundreds of youths were becoming members of BJYM on the behest of Dhami.

After the victory of 1999, the BJP successfully ran a government at the Centre for five years uninterrupted. Meanwhile, the ECI announced the election for the 14th Lok Sabha. However, the announcement of 'India Shining' and 'Feel Good' by BJP did not go down well with the new electronic voting machine, which had been introduced in the electoral field for the first time. The victory of the Congress proved to be a major setback for the BJP. It could understand that the throne had slipped away from its fingers. However what was strange was that the Congress party came to power with 145 seats, but the PM candidate Sonia Gandhi refused to occupy the position of PM. Therefore, Dr Manmohan Singh, a renowned politician and economist with a simple lifestyle, was unanimously appointed as the first Sikh and 13th PM of the country.

Pushkar received news that 29 people had lost their lives when a tunnel collapsed at the Tehri Dam. He hurried to assist the affected people on behalf of the youth wing. Impressed by his sociocultural and humanitarian efforts, the party honoured him again when he was made the state president of the youth wing of BJYM. This new title further boosted Pushkar's morale. He began overseeing the regional issues of Khatima, facilitated by his father Sher Singh and associates.

Encouraged by his efforts, the local community invited him to contest the upcoming elections during his visits for party-related purposes. However, Pushkar requested some extra time, committed to furthering his skills. But he felt time was slipping away faster than usual. He realized the importance of managing his own work style in a time-saving manner, as time might not always offer another chance.

Meanwhile, the prospects of marriage started appearing before him. As the only son in the family, his parents, Sher Singh and Bishna Devi, began pressuring him to consider getting married. Nonetheless, he hesitated to take responsibility for someone's sister or daughter without a solid foundation.

The time for the second State Assembly election was drawing nearer. After visiting the State Assembly constituencies, Pushkar urged regional people to support the party at the polls. Simultaneously, he highlighted the ruling party's anti-people policies and stressed that progress relied on the success of his party. 'Sometimes, ruling parties prioritize economic gains over public welfare, leading to the bureaucratic machinery being driven by the power hungry,' he told them.

'The collaboration of these three mechanisms, motivated by vested interests, is forming a detrimental triangle in the state, contributing to its internal decay. As a robust Opposition, it's our responsibility to question the ruling party and guide them towards greater awareness,' he further said.

Thousands of Pushkar's supporters rallied to field him from the Didihat Assembly constituency, his hometown falling under Pithoragarh. While there was support for some time, out of respect for Bishan Singh Chufal's strong influence, he chose not to contest. Instead, he gathered support through party rallies for all BJP candidates. When the BJP decided to contest the entire election under Bhagat Singh Koshyari's leadership, an enthusiastic Pushkar devoted himself to promoting his political mentor and the party.

Upon the declaration of results by the ECI, it was encouraging news for the state's workers that under the leadership of political stalwart Bhagat Singh Koshyari, the BJP had secured 34 seats, with Congress as the primary Opposition with 21 seats. The party also received support from Uttarakhand Kranti Dal (UKD) and independent MLAs. However, instead of Bhagat Singh Koshyari, the supreme leadership appointed Major General Bhuwan Chandra Khanduri, an active figure in central politics, as the CM. Despite dissatisfaction expressed by all party supporters, including Bhagat Da, with Khanduri's leadership, the supreme leadership armed the state with skilled governance and public-oriented schemes. Within a year, the party's national vice-president Bhagat Singh Koshyari surprised everyone by securing a Rajya Sabha seat from Uttarakhand quota. However, in the 15th Lok Sabha elections, the party lost all five parliamentary seats from Uttarakhand, placing CM Khanduri's governance under scrutiny.

Therefore, upon accepting this, CM Khanduri offered to resign just two days after the election results. However, senior party leader Venkaiah Naidu present in the state as an observer rejected his resignation on the grounds that 'those who try do not lose.' After ample discussion, an emergency meeting held in New Delhi called for a legislative party meeting, following which the state health minister, Ramesh Pokhriyal 'Nishank', was appointed as the CM, in line with Khanduri's proposal and with the approval of state tourism minister, Prakash Pant, and agriculture minister, Trivendra Singh Rawat. The Opposition parties took advantage of this instability and garnered support by describing Khanduri as a Delhi leader imposed on the state.

As the BJYM state president, Pushkar, active in political activities, had been continuously organizing unemployed youths across the state for six consecutive years, addressing their issues. Whether it was accessible education in new schools, colleges or job reservation, his State Infrastructure and Industrial Development Corporation of Uttarakhand Limited (SIDCUL) movement had secured 70 per cent employment reservation for the youth in regional industries. Impressed by his style, he was appointed as the vice-chairman with state minister rank of the urban monitoring committee in the state government.

At the same time, as he matured, relatives were pushing him towards a new relationship under the guise of family responsibilities! His friends also advised him by saying that youth only came to a person once in his life.

Therefore, on the guidance and persuasion of his parents, relatives and other elders, who explained the responsibilities of married life to him, Pushkar agreed to fulfil parental aspirations. Meanwhile, Dr Rastogi, while chatting with his friend Subedar Sher Singh in Nagla, began advising him, whose every word he always took to heart. But the thought of all those 'beauty queens' who had made a secret place in his heart since school and college days, although he never seriously thought about anyone like this, started hovering on his mind.

Meanwhile, while Pushkar was barely ready for marriage, Bishna Devi received news from some relatives that a decent family from Bogta Tola village of Pithoragarh, residing near Shripur Bichua Chowk, Khatima, the head of which was a certain Subedar Ramesh Guru was also seeking a suitable groom for his youngest daughter, Geeta. At the same time, in preparation for the upcoming Assembly elections, Pushkar was laying the groundwork to enter the electoral arena from Khatima, his home district, with the support of the public and party well-wishers.

Parents and insightful friends believed that marriage often unlocked fate's possibilities, therefore, Pushkar, the youth icon, should also believe in this adage. Bishna Devi was advised by a priest that if a young man's marriage is delayed or hindered, at least one mantra of Lord Shri Krishna should be chanted: *Kleem Krishnaye Govindaye Gopijanavallabhaye swaha.* She encouraged her son to chant the holy mantra with true devotion.

A multitude of questions swirled within his heart. On one hand, he aspired to commit to every possible political change, while evading the complexities of marriage, to be able to address the numerous issues faced by the regional populace. On the other hand, he was torn between fulfilling parental dreams in accordance with societal norms! How this fervent ambition would align with the contrasting reality remained to be seen. He stood at a crossroads, compelled to navigate both paths amid the limitations of time. Only time would tell.

9

PUBLIC ACCEPTANCE: FULFILMENT OF PUBLIC ASPIRATIONS

*Na hi kashchit vijanati kim kasya shvo bhavishyati,
Ataha shvah karaniyani kuryadadyaiv buddhimana.*

That is, nobody knows what tomorrow holds. So whatever tasks need to be accomplished should be done today—this is the hallmark of a wise individual.

Looking back, in the Uttarakhand Assembly elections of 2002 and 2007, Congress' candidate advocate Gopal Singh Rana secured victory from the Khatima Assembly seat. Pushkar wanted to reverse this equation. However, Pushkar, with his focus on regional development politics and adopting a strategic approach, believed that he would be able to shatter Rana's grip on locals and victory in the next Assembly elections would be all but ensured. Political deftness, discretion, ability to take wise decisions were his assets that he would use as weapons. He knew the ageless saying of Chanakya: 'Politics engaged in bloodshed is war, and war without bloodshed is politics!'

Hence, the young persona of Pushkar, even without a political family background or high connections, lacking the ability to spend vast amounts of money or indulge in exaggerated and fake grandeur, was intent on carving a niche for himself in development-oriented politics. The absence of conventional political tools like muscle power, money and hate speech might have seemed like a hindrance in his career. Yet, because there was passion, a principled man was driven to pursue bold actions through politics founded on integrity, duty, fairness, transparency and accountability.

Datritvam priyavaktritvam dhiratvamuchitagyata,
Abhyasen na labhyante chatvarah sahaja gunah.

Acharya Chanakya, in the first verse of the eleventh chapter of his *Chanakyaniti*, has described four qualities inherent in every successful person or good leader. He asserts that giving donations, making decisions, maintaining patience in difficult situations and speaking pleasantly are inherent traits that cannot be taught but are present in certain individuals since birth.

One day, Pushkar's father, Sher Singh, suddenly rang him at a time when he had just finished his speech and sat himself on the chair. Pushkar had a habit of not ignoring anybody's call unless absolutely necessary. And it was a call from his father, so he couldn't give it a miss. He exited the auditorium to pick up the call.

'Son, your mother and I have visited Subedar Ramesh ji's house and met his daughter Geeta. She's a beautiful, gentle, highly educated and cultured girl with all the qualities required in an ideal match for you. We even shared a meal prepared by her! If you agree, come home, see for yourself, and then let's proceed.'

The name Geeta touched the strings of Pushkar's heart and he felt pleasant emotions like a symphony that are elixir for any young heart. He replied, 'Father, if you both have seen the girl and like her, what role do I have now?... How many siblings does she have?... Your choice is my choice. Please decide. I know you won't choose incorrectly for me!'

Sher Singh responded, 'They are four siblings. There's an elder brother Rajesh working in the police department. Elder sister Anita is married, then Geeta, and a younger brother Pawan who is studying in an inter college.'

Pushkar exclaimed, 'If the girl is cultured, that's great, father! I don't have any special preferences. Hope she is intelligent and decent. Then you can proceed as you wish.'

Sher Singh added, 'No, son, you will have to come. It's not guaranteed that the girl will match your personality. And what if she also wishes to meet you and judge you before giving her consent? Come home on Saturday, we'll go there on Sunday. Meanwhile, talk to your mother.'

'Haan beta, kas hai gyo yo, bhaunt bhalee dekhan chaani cheli chhe, ek baar dekhiya baabu, theek-thaak laagali ta phir maag-phaagun mein lagn karunla,' Bishna Devi spoke from the other side, 'yeah son, you've become quite busy! There's a very beautiful girl; go and meet her once. If you like her, we can arrange the wedding in February–March.'

'Eeja, 2012 mein ta mera chunaav chhann kaisikai hol... Chal theek chha, main chhanchar baar byaakhul tak aa junlo phir baatacheet karnun,' Pushkar replied, 'Mummy, we have elections in 2012, how will I make time? Okay, I will come by Saturday evening, we will talk about it later.'

As soon as the call ended, one line started whirling like a sweet reminder in the young man's ears: 'If you agree, come home once, see for yourself, then let's go ahead...' Family happiness, political dreams, future concerns and challenges—these thoughts filled his mind. He was curious about many things and also suffered from indecision. But a smart and wise person kept remedies for every ailment or situation up his sleeve. For gregarious and jovial Pushkar, such remedy was his group of naughty friends...

Dhami invited almost all his friends who happened to be in the vicinity for an evening dinner. When he shared the conversation he had had with his father with his friends, everyone praised him and egged him to move forward towards marriage.

Meanwhile, Amarendra mentioned, 'My marriage is likely to be arranged by February. Nowadays, most of my time is spent on the phone.'

'So, it's good that you go first. And then we'll get to dance with the new Bhabhi ji,' Dhami said with a tinge of playfulness.

Somesh Vardhan, with respect, interjected, 'Hey, give us rational advice, brother, this is a very important time, what nonsense are you telling us guys! Listen, when both families give you a chance to spend time together, there's no need to panic. Stay calm and make the most of it.'

'I'm not a child; I know that much, hahaha...' Pushkar laughed.

'What's amusing you, Dhami ji?' Anubhav summed up all his experiences and revealed that it was not that easy, after all.

'You will get to know your worth, mister. The day I visited my would-be bride, I came to know how difficult it was,' Amarendra added solemnly.

Somesh Vardhan continued, 'Hey! Look! Just be plain, straightforward and simple so that she can feel comfortable.

When everything looks relaxed, don't forget to ask her questions about her likes, dislikes, preferences, education, and the like.'

Suddenly interrupting everyone, Anubhav said, 'Hey! Listen Neta ji, don't forget to ask for her number, otherwise you'll struggle like me day and night! Not only that, she'll tease you like Mishra's wife, saying, "Mishra ji, you didn't even think it appropriate to ask for my number?"'

Pushkar, for the first time, bought clothes of his choice and headed home. Late into the night, there were lengthy discussions with parents and relatives. It was finally decided that they would visit the prospective bride the next morning at 11 o'clock. If all terms and conditions go favourably for both sides, they would finalize an auspicious day for the wedding.

Throughout the night, Dhami kept gazing at the ceiling and the rotating fan, pondering deeply over his would-be bride and future marital life. It is shocking when one looks at the political landscape and evaluates one's economic situation. The house was built with his father's support, along with the education of four siblings and the marriage of three sisters. How many resources does a soldier have? He wished to invite all his close friends to the wedding if the marriage was confirmed, but the current situation didn't allow him to consider that.

Geeta was informed by her father that Subedar Saheb would visit with his son the following morning. 'Be careful, beta,' he advised. Upon hearing the news, Geeta took a deep breath and went to the kitchen, draping a dupatta over her shoulders. She hoped to discuss with her mother Radhika about who all were coming. However, due to her mother's busyness, this was not possible. Geeta tried to inquire with her Bhabhi (sister-in-law), but even she was not aware about the details. After dinner, everyone went to their respective beds.

Among all children, Geeta was the one who shared a special bond with her grandparents, Amma-Bubu, since childhood. She had taken on the responsibility of grooming her grandmother's hair, massaging her grandfather's hands and feet, and ensuring timely medication, tea and water for them.

Since her early years in primary school, whenever she received gifts or desserts from school events like Independence Day celebrations, Geeta always saved them for her grandparents. She cherished the joy of sharing these gifts with them, getting their heartfelt blessings in return: *'Bhalo jamai mili jyo eeja tukain Gopu! Khoob thool ghar mein tero bhagyo basi jyo...,'* her grandparents would give her heartfelt blessings, 'May you be blessed with the perfect match, Gopu! May you be as lucky as a queen.'

Geeta completed her schooling at Government Girls Inter College, Khatima. She often shared her food with neighbouring children, becoming their most beloved elder sister. Despite being successful in school competitions, she found it challenging to break societal norms in a male-dominated society.

Simple by nature, Geeta engaged in innovative activities. She enjoyed decorating the house, sewing, embroidery, crafts and cooking a variety of dishes to share with others. Alongside pursuing higher education from the Hemwati Nandan Bahuguna Post Graduate College, Khatima, she also showed a special interest in household activities.

As the darkness of night gradually faded with the first light of dawn, Geeta prepared herself for the auspicious moment for which she seemed to have awaited more than two decades.

Dressed in a beautiful silk Patiala suit, she eagerly awaited the arrival of the special guests, feeling a mix of excitement and apprehension about adapting to a new household and the potential challenges that might arise.

Amidst silent contemplation, Geeta, committed to fulfilling the responsibilities of an ideal Indian woman, assisted her sister-in-law and mother in preparing to welcome the guests. Despite her inner thoughts, she focused on hospitality, arriving in the living room with a tray of fresh juice, her hands trembling slightly.

Dhami captured this scene with his eyes.

As time passed, their eyes locked, and both were captivated by each other's charming and adorable personalities.

Dhami composed himself, speaking in a calm and polite tone, 'Geeta ji, there's no need to worry. Please, just be yourself. I come from a very ordinary family, and I understand everything.'

Geeta smiled gently and replied, 'Yes. There's no need to worry. I'm perfectly fine.'

'What are you doing these days? Are you studying?' he asked.

Geeta nodded in affirmation. 'Yes, I'm studying at Hemwati Nandan Bahuguna College.'

'Any plans for the future? Have you thought about it?' he inquired further.

'I don't have any specific plans as of yet. I'll go along with what you and my parents think is the best for me,' Geeta responded.

'My suggestion is that you continue studying. There's ample time, and if you keep planning, something fruitful will surely come out of it.'

He continued, 'My life revolves around the Sangh

and politics. I move from place to place. Sometimes here, sometimes there. Society and country are of utmost importance to me. Being the only son, it's my responsibility to honour my parents' wishes. Can you adjust to this lifestyle?'

Geeta replied confidently, 'Whatever I will do, it will be for the betterment of society. Since childhood, I've been passionate about contributing to the society in a constructive way and making sure that the helpless are assisted to move forward in life. Being your partner in life aligns perfectly with my aspirations.'

At the end, when Subedar Ramesh asked Pushkar for his opinion about dowry, he firmly expressed his opposition to such practices. 'The daughter whom you've educated and brought up—how do you expect to see her off with anything but love and blessings? Such thoughts should be abandoned for the benefit of both families and society,' he stated.

Impressed by the young man's words, Subedar Ramesh promptly discussed about finalizing the relationship.

After discussing other crucial matters, both families decided to conduct the marriage rituals three months later, during the auspicious time of *Magh* (January-February). Gradually, preparations for the wedding occupied both the families.

Amidst the political chaos of the '*Khanduri hai zaroori* (Khandoori is necessary)' campaign supporting former CM Khanduri, the BJP high command reluctantly accepted CM Nishank's resignation in September 2011, reinstating Khanduri just five months before the elections. Dhami, with thousands of supporters, dedicated all his efforts to the upcoming elections.

The workers, including the enthusiastic Dhami, were confident that he would secure a place in the Assembly, regardless of where the party positioned him in the electoral battlefield.

Several veteran leaders, including former CM Bhagat Singh Koshyari, lauded his regional development programs. However, politics is a battleground where favourable situations can quickly turn unfavourable due to selfish motives.

While preparations for the wedding were in full swing, Dhami was also committed to resolving the daily issues of the regional populace through public hearings. With the support of university and Sangh friends, thousands of wedding invitation cards were printed and distributed, urging attendance at the wedding on 28 January and the reception on 29 January. Dhami's three sisters—Nandi, Pushpa, Indra—had been preparing for their brother's wedding for about a week. The parents were eager to see their beloved son as the groom. The house, adorned with colourful decorations, *bandanwar jhalar* (door hangings) of various flowers, mango and peepal leaves, seemed to dance and welcome the newlywed couple and guests amidst the beats of the DJ.

Suddenly, fresh western disturbance during the night changed the weather from the plains to the hills. In the courtyard, hundreds of *baratis* (wedding guests) and *chhalia* (dancers) presented various dance forms to the tune of band-bajaa and dhol-damuo, local drum-like percussion instruments, in front of the groom.

For the marriage ceremony, it seemed as if the entire Nagla Tarai had showed up. The venue was filled with enthusiasm and echoed with laughter. Gradually, Pushkar and Geeta performed all the marriage rituals according to the holy Hindu religion with Vedic chants recited by the priest, considering fire as a witness, in the decorated wedding pavilion at Shripur Bichua Chowk.

Almost every acquaintance was present at the marriage ceremony; many uninvited individuals, viewing themselves as strong supporters of the groom, were witness to this auspicious occasion.

Classmates from Lucknow, Dehradun, Khatima, Pithoragarh, Delhi, Madhya Pradesh, along with veteran personalities like former CMs Bhuwan Chandra Khanduri, Bhagat Singh Koshyari and Ramesh Pokhriyal 'Nishank', former Speaker (state Assembly) Shri Prakash Pant, extended their love, blessings and good wishes to the newly married couple. With moist eyes, Geeta's brothers Rajesh and Pawan lifted her *shivika* or *doli* (palanquin) on their shoulders.

On the very first night of marriage, the newly-wed couple felt overwhelmed by a mix of shyness, hesitation and joy upon finding their lifetime partner in a secluded space! Adorned with a *gajra* (garland) in her hair, a golden *chandrika* on her forehead and a gold ring on the nose, hands adorned with mehndi and with vermillion nails, draped in a vermilion lehenga choli with her head covered, Geeta glowed in radiant youthful beauty. While Pushkar, taking a long sigh, felt lost in the beauty of the moment.

From early morning, the entire gathering began preparations to depart for Lohia Head in Khatima for the reception.

Once the wedding was over, Pushkar resumed his daily routine. Geeta, having had no prior involvement in politics, started to closely understand it with her husband's guidance. What she once considered a platform of allegations and counter-allegations, she now understood as a sacred platform for sociocultural welfare, enabling impactful steps for betterment of the society and the nation.

Like drops of water leaving their source, unsure of the

direction or destination, nature decided the course of their lives based on karma! Perhaps his Amma–Babu (grandparents) with their pure heart blessed him in return for his service to the nation. He believed that their blessings had landed him there.

As the sole daughter-in-law, and a blend of modern and traditional values, Geeta faced various challenges due to her parents-in-law's adherence to traditional methods of running a house, requiring her to manage social customs. Pushkar was prepared to fulfil her wishes and tackle all challenges. She observed how her father-in-law warned her husband about future challenges and fulfilled his duty as a parent without expecting reciprocity. It was reminiscent of our mythological scriptures describing a grand heaven where virtuous souls live eternally by virtue of their good deeds. According to Chanakya's policy, a person whose son is obedient leads a blessed life, akin to attaining heaven on earth itself.

> *Yasya putra vashibhuto bharya chhandanugamini,*
> *Vibhave yascha santushtastasya swarga ihaiva hi.*

Even on Diwali, Pushkar did not get the time to stay at home due to his political activities. Expressing her unwillingness to eat at night, Geeta asked for some water from her mother-in-law. Holding the filled glass with some discomfort, Geeta drank two or four sips intermittently. Bishna Devi kept talking nonsense by stroking her daughter-in-law's head for a while. The latter felt a bit feverish. Bishna Devi went to her room and requested the Subedar for a paracetamol tablet. Hearing this, a wave of fear and shame sparked in Geeta's body, who was sleeping in the adjacent room. Until late at night, somehow, she endured the silent agony. On waking up in the morning, Geeta noticed that the sun's rays had spread in all directions.

Embarrassed to have slept for a long time, Geeta threw the sheets aside and stood up. By noon, she had started working. But whatever breakfast she had had, she threw up. She felt a craving for the mango pickle placed in a box on the kitchen rack.

Seeing all this, Bishna Devi grew excited with wonder, her body tinkled like the strings of a stretched veena. She said to Geeta, 'Beta, all the symptoms of your illness seem to indicate the arrival of a new guest in our house! Are you feeling something?'

Geeta bowed her head in bashfulness.

'When Pushkar comes tomorrow, he will take you for check-up at the Jamuna hospital.'

Hearing this, Geeta's eyes lit up. She understood what her mother in law had meant—her words, meanings and expressions. But how could she say something to anyone?

Her mother-in-law too understood the untold, but did not say anything to anyone; she had patience! Getting lost in an imaginary world, she started thinking about the mischievous pranks of the new guest.

Political guru Bhagat Singh Koshyari was greatly impressed by the humility, skilful behaviour and discretion of his spouse, as a result of which Dhami was given many responsibilities one after the other. Fortunately, soon the party fielded him from the Khatima Assembly constituency, placing immense faith in him. At the same time, the Congress had also fielded its candidate Devendra Chandra to put up a tough fight against him.

'Now it is the responsibility of all of us to raise a hand of cooperation for Pushkar,' Geeta exhorted not only her family, but everyone in Khatima. She in fact became as active, if not more, as her husband. Along with her household responsibilities, she went to the people and met them personally and listened to their problems. By making a list of all the problems people of the constituency had been facing, she also started motivating her husband to solve them quickly.

In the first month of the new year, on 13 January, Dhami was involved in the field-election for a new responsibility in his political journey after worshipping his deity and receiving blessings from his parents. The meteorological department had predicted an extension of the polling date due to the possibility of snowfall and low temperatures. However, the Phase 1 polling was completed peacefully.

The fate of 788 candidates for 70 Assembly seats in the state was sealed through 1,806 polling stations from 8 a.m. to 5 p.m. A total of 67 per cent voting was recorded. The ECI stated that the results of the third Assembly would be declared on 6 March, along with the results of four other states. All candidates and workers were now eagerly awaiting the results.

Amidst all the busyness, Pushkar surprised Geeta with a special dress on the first anniversary (28 January) of their wedding. Geeta's heart was filled with pride when she saw the presence of her spouse on their very first anniversary! At the same time, the guest in the womb had completed seven months and was about to enter the eighth.

Geeta had also begun feeling the impatient kicks of the little guest in her womb, signalling its imminent arrival into the world. Day and night, there was a buzz of activity in the courtyard of their home. Some awaited the election results while others awaited Geeta's. Although the ECI had declared the result date as 6 March, the Gynaecologist Commission had marked the D-Day for the family as 23 March!

When it came to the election results, broadcasting stations made predictions following full-scale exercises to create an atmosphere favouring their preferred candidates, under the guise of government machinery.

The counting of votes, which commenced in the early hours, concluded by noon, revealing all results. Pushkar Singh Dhami defeated Congress candidate Devendra Chandra by a margin of 5,394 votes from the Khatima Assembly seat. The most interesting and hotly contested Raipur Assembly seat, established after delimitation in 2008, witnessed Umesh Sharma Kau on a Congress ticket winning the Assembly election, defeating BJP's veteran leader Trivendra Singh Rawat by a narrow margin of just 473 votes. The biggest surprise for BJP was that along with Khanduri, Nishank and Prakash Pant could not retain their seats either.

However, a political struggle was also evident within the Congress party. In the elections led by Harish Rawat, the Congress emerged as the largest party in the state with 32 seats. After prolonged deliberation, the Congress announced that Harish Rawat would continue serving as the union water resources minister at the central government level, and Vijay Bahuguna would form the government with the support of the BSP, UKD and independent candidates. Consequently, with 31 seats, the BJP was at the second spot and the main Opposition party. Even though the government was formed by the Congress, Pushkar Singh Dhami won his first election and made significant efforts to solidify his regional influence among booth workers to top leadership.

It was anticipated that if the BJP had formed a coalition government, he would have likely become a part of the cabinet at that time. His political mentors Bhagat Singh Koshyari and Rajnath Singh, along with all his friends and senior politicians, expressed their hopes for his bright future by congratulating him.

Friends started teasing their popular elected MLA friend by saying Geeta Bhabhi had brought him luck, attributing the success to her, and so on. Mother Bishna Devi and father Sher Singh were witnesses to this historic victory. Subedar Ramesh (Geeta's father) also seemed delighted that his son-in-law had been appointed as a member of the state Assembly.

Suddenly, Geeta began experiencing irregular and painful contractions. She went to the kitchen and in a low voice informed her mother-in-law Bishna Devi about her pain.

Interpreting this pain as labour pain, Bishna Devi asked her son Pushkar to be called immediately. Before this, Subedar Sher Singh did not want to disturb his son so he arranged for a driver and a car himself.

Bishna Devi, accompanied by two neighbouring women and her daughter-in-law, reached Jamuna Memorial Hospital. Sher Singh handled all formalities at the counter and alerted the doctor. Observing Geeta's critical condition, the doctors and nurses rushed her to the delivery room as she was convulsing in grave pain.

Seated on the bench outside, Bishna Devi prayed for her daughter-in-law's successful delivery, folding her hands in front of her beloved Harishchandra and Bholenath. Shortly after, a nurse appeared from the room and said in a serious tone, 'Who is with Geeta Dhami?'

Subedar immediately stood up, while Bishna Devi rushed towards the room.

The nurse exclaimed, 'Congratulations, you've become a grandmother. Geeta has just given birth to a son!'

An abrupt smile of joy appeared on their lips, accompanied by tears in their eyes! Bishna Devi, overwhelmed with happiness, blessed the nurse profusely while caressing her. After a while, Geeta was brought out on a stretcher. Bishna Devi was the first to catch a glimpse of the newborn's black-haired head.

Subedar informed his son Pushkar over the phone, 'You have another responsibility now! Geeta and you have become parents today. May you both have a bright future, son!'

The lively and enthusiastic Dhami asked, 'How is Geeta, father?'

'Both are absolutely fine, and the newborn is healthy! The doctor mentioned they would be discharged after a while.'

'Dad, I'm tied up with some important meetings. I'll only be able to make it in time for the naming ceremony. Take care, I'll be back soon!'

All colleagues congratulated Dhami at the Vidhan Sabha Auditorium in Dehradun, and Geeta eagerly awaited her husband at home. On the eleventh day, the naming ceremony was organized with great pomp. With the priest chanting mantras, the newborn lying in the cradle gifted by Nana ji was named Diwakar, and his horoscope indicated Pisces as his zodiac sign.

Upon reading the birth chart, the priest revealed that the child, Diwakar, had brought auspiciousness to the family, particularly to the father, ever since his inception in the womb. Born in the Pisces house, the second and final sign of the Jupiter cycle, he would grow to be compassionate. Though not instinctively proactive, he'd readily assist when called upon, leading a romantic life filled with progressive and philosophical ideas. He would communicate confidently and have a supportive circle around him. His generosity might sometimes lead him to miss several opportunities for success. Nonetheless, he was foreseen to become a successful administrative officer, doctor, engineer or social thinker with profound thoughts. The parents felt immense pride witnessing the charming presence of their little boy.

Meanwhile, shocking news arrived for the Dhami family, including Bishna Devi and Sher Singh. It was about the youngest daughter, Indra, who was found suffering from acute typhoid and jaundice. Despite doctors' efforts, she couldn't be saved. She left behind three young children in the care of her widower and in-laws. Dhami was deeply saddened by the passing away of his sister and found himself sinking in her memories for a long time. However, shouldering the weight of responsibilities, he gathered the courage to support her family as well.

As an MLA, Dhami never viewed the public from a caste or party perspective. Bharatiya Janata Party's worker and leader Vivek Saxena highlighted during a personal interaction with the villagers that Pushkar Dhami advocated strongly for the needy, speaking up for 70 per cent reservation for local unemployed individuals in regional industries under the SIDCUL movement of 2009. Sanjay Tolia, who had been by his side since 1999, credited Dhami's tireless efforts for the revival of the Tehri Dam project despite its closure after completion. Dhami wasn't swayed by appearances or symbols; rather, his focus was drawn to the hardships faced by the poor, vulnerable elders and women more than the urban elite.

As a result of his dedication to resolving regional issues and his efficient work ethic, he was awarded the title of 'Best MLA'. His swift actions and connections with numerous individuals in the community led to this recognition.

Not only this, Dhami, committed to the upliftment of Scheduled Castes and Scheduled Tribes, supported Kanhaiya ji, who ran a small shop at Melaghat Road, in a way that enabled him to win the election by 6,000 votes. Dhami always ensured the observance of every religious festival, be it Holi, Deepawali, Eid, Christmas, or the ones important to the Bengali community or the Purvanchali Chhath, or festivals related to the tribal community.

At the home front, Geeta gave birth to their second son on 8 November 2014, whom they named Prabhakar. Geeta was seen as the fortune-bringer daughter-in-law of the family. She was not only taking care of her family and children but was also actively engaged in social work alongside her husband. In their busy routine, two and a half years passed in the blink of an eye. Now, the state was abuzz with election fever. Every street was filled with debates, and rallies were being organized. For Geeta and her husband, this was a challenging time—balancing family responsibilities and social service. Yet, Geeta remained determined. She spent her days helping people and her nights with her family. As the elections approached, her enthusiasm only grew stronger. Not only this, the party leadership gave the green signal to contest the election for the fourth state Assembly from the same Khatima constituency.

Maintaining a healthy balance between personal duty and social responsibility is the true test of one's character.

This time, voting was to be held for 69 seats only. The voting in the Karnaprayag constituency had been postponed until 9 March due to the sudden death of BSP candidate Kuldeep Kanwasi in a road accident.

Elections were peacefully held on 15 February 2017 in a single phase. Upholding the wishes of the party high command, the vibrant Dhami handed over the victory certificate to the

BJP, defeating hardworking Congress candidate Bhuwan Chandra Kapri by 2,709 votes.

Under the leadership of CM Harish Rawat, the Congress had to face a crushing defeat. The BJP's victory was so substantial that senior Congress leader Harish Rawat himself lost the election from both Haridwar Rural and Kichha Assembly constituencies. The Congress party was reduced to just 11 seats from 32 seats. Harish Rawat commented on the unexpected victory of the BJP, saying, 'I salute the "Modi Revolution" and the miracle of EVMs! I take responsibility for not living up to the expectations of my party workers who worked hard despite a paucity of resources, and I believe that under my leadership, there must have been some shortcomings leading to the party's underperformance in the elections.'

It was evident that the Congress party overall had suffered several blows in the past few years. There was the issue of the national NPA (non-performing assets) crisis in which stressed assets or bad loans of public sector bank had kept mounting by the year 2017. Additionally, the 2016 political crisis in Uttarakhand had led to President's Rule being implemented for the first time in the state.[3]

Fortunately, in the Modi wave, the BJP secured more than three-fourths majority, i.e., 56 seats. Trivendra Singh Rawat was sworn in as the ninth CM of Uttarakhand by Hon'ble Governor Baby Rani Maurya in front of PM Narendra Modi and party national president Amit Shah at the parade ground.

It was speculated that Dhami might be included in the cabinet this time, since his name was on everyone's

---

[3]'President's Rule Imposed in Uttarakhand: What Is President's Rule and Why Is It Implemented', *India Today*, 28 March 2016, https://tinyurl.com/27dhvjsr. Accessed on 11 March 2025.

lips this time for a ministerial berth. But with a surplus of senior or veteran leaders, he had to commit to fulfilling his responsibilities solely as an MLA. Pithoragarh's renowned MLA, Prakash Pant was allocated the finance, commercial and entertainment tax ministry, while Satpal Maharaj received the irrigation ministry, among a total of 11 ministers in the newly formed cabinet.

With the support of his parents, wife and thousands of supporters, Dhami was growing stronger day by day socially, culturally, religiously and politically.

Seeing him busy, his elder son, Diwakar, would often say, 'Papa is never free, even on our birthdays. Every festival is celebrated by engaging with the public.'

Geeta sometimes wished for them to spend holidays somewhere with the children. But Dhami would arrive home late at night and depart for his various office programs early in the morning. Consequently, the children would go to bed early in the evening, and their father would head out for party activities before they woke up. However, on every festival, a lot of goods were distributed to all children of the Nagla Tarai region. Geeta would often jest with her mother-in-law, Bishna Devi, with a smile, commenting that over the years, Diwakar's father took her to Mumbai only once for two days in the name of Bharat Darshan and to Nepal border in the name of travelling abroad!

'*Aadim bachi roon chaichh ghuman-phiran ka bhaut mauka aal*,' her mother-in-law tried to pacify her by saying, 'If the person remains alive, there will be many opportunities for going on trips.'

Sarve bhavantu sukhinah sarve santu niramayah,
Sarve bhadrani pashyantu ma kashchid dukhbhagbhavet.

She pointed to this well-known Sanskrit shloka from the *Brihadaranyaka Upanishada*, which says, may all be happy, may all be free from disease; may all see auspiciousness, may no one suffer in any way. There's an extensive list of tireless efforts aiming to realize the essence of Dhami's 'Sarvey Bhavantu Sukhinah' or the philosophy of may all be happy.

Some of these efforts include: a network of link roads were laid in Khatima constituency, executed using MLA funds. Boundary walls in public places, additional classrooms in regional schools, furniture procurement and beautification had been completed. Major motorways like Majhola Main Road to Nandana Bridge; Lal Kothi Marg; Kala Bridge to Prabhat Marg, Nagla Tarai, etc., had been expedited through the public works department. The construction of the Khatima roadways bus station had been accelerated, along with the construction of passenger sheds at public places in most gram sabhas. Emphasis had been placed on the reconstruction and new construction of all damaged motorways in the area. An allocation of ₹5 crore had been made for BCom, MCom and Yoga classes, intended for the hi-tech auditorium of the B.Ed. building, library building in Hemwati Nandan Bahuguna Post Graduate College, Khatima. A long-awaited bridge over Praveen River in Nausar had been constructed. Proposals for overbridges at railway crossings near Melaghat, Rajeev Nagar and Lohia Head Road, along with one for unmanned and manned gates at other places, had been passed.

All possible benefits were being provided to beneficiaries through the CM, PM and other disaster relief funds. Efforts were underway to establish Kendriya Vidyalaya, Khatima, to ensure quality education. A new policy had been formulated, offering assistance of ₹10 lakh to each martyred soldier's family, with memorials, *shaheed dwar* (honorary gate), roads and schools reconstructed in their honour. Khatima Mahotsav was held to felicitate several regional talents, certificates were awarded to state revolutionaries, and continuous efforts were being made to promote sports by organizing national-level boxing and other sports competitions in Khatima.

To maintain religious faith, the tallest Shiva statue in Uttarakhand had been erected at Bankhandi Mahadev Temple, Chakarpur. The construction of a complex auditorium in the old tehsil premises and the establishment of a free mobile clinic were accomplished in collaboration with Bajaj Auto Limited and Jimmedari Foundation. Solar lights and hand pumps were being installed at various locations. A commitment had been shown to quickly address regional issues through various helpline channels like Jan Chaupal and Janata Darbar. The construction of bridges across several rivers in Khatima was underway to modernize and restore Lohia Canal No. 1 to 10, aiming to resolve flood and waterlogging problems. Additionally, a Canteen Stores Department (CSD) facility was set up at Khatima for the welfare of soldiers. Keeping the interests of regional unemployed individuals in mind, 70 per cent reservation was provided to regional youths in industries like SIDCUL, and their demands were advocated through various hunger strikes.

Uttarakhand, being a Devbhoomi, emerged as the most reliable, the most advanced, the best and the number one state in India based on all possible development standards. Keeping this dream alive, Dhami moved forward every day.

Unfortunately, the health of the family patriarch, Subedar Sher Singh, was deteriorating due to age-related pressures and unforeseen illnesses... Seeking treatment from prominent city hospitals like Prayas and Medanta, sensing the severity of the situation, he was admitted to Max Hospital in Delhi on

26 November 2019. Leaving no stone unturned, Pushkar was fully engaged with the family.

Doctors revealed a serious lung infection, prompting extensive chemotherapy and radiotherapy to improve the situation. Every possible effort, guided by doctors, was made to safely bring the father back home. From 26 November 2019 to 10 April 2020, the entire family and many others prayed and offered assistance day and night in an effort to save Pushkar's father, but the Supreme Being had different plans.

Until now, Subedar Sher Singh would counter storms by being a defender, guide, friend and hero to his son and family, often as a protector in the face of crises. But today, such a huge calamity had befallen them all.

In this situation, hundreds of outspoken guardians, including military friends Subedar Kafaliya ji and Captain Bhani Chand ji, were present. In such moments, they consoled the grieving Pushkar by directing his attention towards the shloka of Maryada Purushottam Shri Rama attempting to console Bharata while mourning for his father.

Sarvekshayanta Nischaya Patananta
Samuchhra Va Sanyoga Vipryoganta
maranaantan chan jeevitam...

The shloka says that all riches eventually dwindle away. Anything that rises eventually falls. Every relationship reaches its conclusion. Every life concludes with death.

The doctors handed over the mortal body of the father to the bereaved family for the final rites.

Amidst this sombre moment, Dhami's mobile suddenly started ringing. A man from Khatima named Kamil Khan was calling. With a heavy heart, Dhami answered, 'Hello! Yes, brother, how are you?'

Kamil Khan expressed great trust in him and requested medicine for his mother's cancer. District hospital doctors had asked Khan to procure them immediately, but the medicine wasn't available nearby. Despite his own unbearable agony over the unrecoverable loss of his father, Dhami, with his father's body lying in the ambulance, arranged and delivered the medicine to the needy.

As news of Pushkar Singh Dhami's father's demise reached Kamil Khan, along with the bag of medicines, he felt immense guilt while also experiencing pride in his benevolent leader. He prayed to the supreme being for the suffering family, seeking for them courage and patience.

Following his father's wishes, Pushkar, with moist eyes, conducted the last rites as per Hindu customs in front of a huge crowd in Nagla, Khatima, lighting the funeral pyre and letting the body disintegrate and merge into the Panchatatva.

◆

10

POLITICS: A LABYRINTH OF CONSPIRACIES

Is agitation a conspiracy, or conspiracy itself a form of agitation? The truth depends on who writes history and who suffers from it.

The political proxy war being played out in the hill state of Uttarakhand was yearning to peak. On the sixth day of March, suddenly, political corridors were abuzz with demands to replace CM Trivendra Singh Rawat. The BJP high command was being petitioned for that. The Opposition, taking advantage, fanned the dissent in BJP when it got wind of senior BJP leader and observer for the state of Uttarakhand Raman Singh meeting state's in-charge Dushyant Kumar. Singh was present in Dehradun. Meanwhile, according to constitutional traditions, CM Trivendra Singh Rawat arrived at Gairsain, the winter capital of Uttarakhand, to present the budget on 5 March. After this, there was a round of discussion on the budget in the House. Suddenly, at the behest of Raman Singh and Dushyant Kumar, all the party MLAs were made to return from Gairsain to Dehradun, postponing the budget session midway.

The Opposition pounced upon the opportunity and slammed the BJP and its government in the strongest remarks. Ministers and MLAs of the ruling party sulked from providing clear information about the swift development. Some said they were moving because of some personal work, while others said that they had urgent formalities to complete at the state secretariat, and so forth. One BJP MLA Khajan Das explained with a bizarre argument, 'The opposition has arrived at the end of the session. Our Trivendra government is doing a better job, so we thought, let's meet the in-charge and share with him the excellent works and achievements that belongs to the present government.'

But the reality was that the party was holding a meeting of its core committee at the CM's residence in the presence of 45 MLAs. Chief Minister Trivendra Singh Rawat, state party president Banshidhar Bhagat, MP Ajay Bhatt, Mala Rajlaxmi Shah, Minister of State Dhan Singh Rawat, Cabinet Minister Madan Kaushik, State General Secretary Kuldeep Kumar, Rajya Sabha MP Naresh Bansal, and many other veteran leaders were present. Newspaper journalists, novices and non-officials were eagerly waiting to know what the main agenda of the meeting was. But after coming out of the meeting room, all ministers and officials spoke in the same language and said, 'Our government has completed four years with efficient leadership focused on development. It is a matter of happiness for the people of the state, so further policies and schemes should also be successful on the same lines. Future public necessities were discussed in detail through this meeting.'

Wherever there is smoke, there is fire

Some time ago, more than a dozen MLAs and ministers had defied the unilateral decisions of their chief and sent a letter directly to the party high command to remove CM Trivendra Singh Rawat. After fleeing from Congress, the newcomers of the ruling party were not satisfied with Rawat's role. Therefore, speculations were being made by political analysts that just before the Assembly elections, which were due to be held the next year, the resentment of these leaders could shake the party. Several ministers and MLAs had made it clear to Raman Singh and Dushyant Gautam that Trivendra Singh Rawat's family had also been interfering in government work. If the high command did not dismiss Trivendra Singh Rawat, then they would not hesitate to resign collectively.

Therefore, the biggest question was that if CM Trivendra Singh Rawat was removed mid-term, then on whom would the high command put its trust and would that face be able to prove the backbone of the party's state leadership by commanding an unwavering following? The top leadership, at any cost, was not ready to invite any stain on its image before the upcoming Assembly elections. It could ill afford repentance in the next five years.

There was no clarity on the question of resignations by the MLAs and only the future could tell that, but the power-hungry were already busy in shenanigans of occupying positions of personal benefit even before a new castle had been erected. Lok Sabha MP Ajay Bhatt and Rajya Sabha MP Anil Baluni were the first to be named in this race through their supporters. Internal conflicts in the party were deliberately being made public. It was being alleged that CM Trivendra Singh Rawat was running the government through bureaucrats. That he had clearly told the bureaucrats, 'If you are pressured by any minister, MLA, or any such person, then come straight to me!'

When the matter was discussed directly with the CM, he clarified:

> I did not want to join politics. According to me, there should be some people in politics who have no political ambitions. It is true that in 2002, I got a ticket, but I kept refusing. Maharashtra Governor Bhagat Da [Bhagat Singh Koshyari] and co-organizing General Secretary Shiv Prakash ji are witnesses to this. I went to him and said don't make me a contestant of the elections; if I don't take responsibility for my candidature, I can get at least a dozen seats for the party. Therefore, there was never a question of expressing desire to become an MLA, minister or CM. According to the blessings of the people, supreme leadership and the Supreme Father, I became the head of the state. Let me tell you that on 10 March, I will submit my resignation to the Hon'ble Governor Baby Rani Maurya at 4 p.m. at Rajbhawan only because of the pressure from the party's few people. Seeing this dire situation, Trivendra Rawat remembered the lines of the great poet Tulsidas:
>
> *Dheeraj dharm mitr aru naaree,*
> *Aapattikaal parakhiye chaaree.*
>
> Patience, faith, friends and women are tested in times of difficulty.

After the announcement of the resignation was made by CM Trivendra Singh Rawat himself, different trends ensued to interpret its aftermath. Some were counting his political achievements, while others were calling all his rules and decisions controversial and unilateral! Yet others were caught in the net of indecisions, unable to understand how they should find an axis of balance that could portray the impression that they lauded the achievements of the former CM but were critical of his shortcomings. And thus, they would be able to anger none and please the future leadership. In politics, some people have an uncanny ability to exercise this craft of taking advantage in every situation.

Meanwhile, Trivendra Singh Rawat also went to the Rajbhawan and submitted his resignation to Governor Baby Rani Maurya. The Opposition made full use of it as this was such a crucial moment in which every decision taken at the time would also determine the contours of the upcoming Assembly elections.

Therefore, Congress leader Harish Rawat reiterated his point, 'I am feeling the winds of change of power in the state. This means that finally even the BJP central leadership has also accepted that their double-engine government is proving to be lethargic in the state. The public understands everything that has been happening. It doesn't matter who the party will bring to power now, but I give you in writing that in 2022, people will never want to bring such misrule to power.'

Trivendra Singh Rawat was at sea regarding how to respond to such a diatribe. He did not see anything except his opponents at this juncture. So, when he was asked questions, he made it clear with deep confidence that those who had objections should go to Delhi and find out. He said, 'The party gave me the opportunity to serve this state for four years. Now only less than a week is left in that. I discharged my duty with full devotion. I never thought I would get such an opportunity. The party has now unanimously decided that the opportunity to serve as chief minister should be given to someone else, whom I heartily welcome.'

Throughout the night, ministers and MLAs stayed restless. The power of opportunity always lurks around us. It is difficult to grab that opportunity, but it is not impossible. Therefore, one must be alert and prompt to notice and then take hold of the opportunity.

State minister Dhan Singh Rawat was said to be a strong alternative to Trivendra Singh Rawat. Uttarakhand MPs Ajay Bhatt and Anil Baluni were also being considered prominent among the contenders. According to newspaper reports, this time the party could also appoint a deputy chief minister to directly target the Kumaon region. For which, prima facie, the name of Pushkar Singh Dhami, the popular MLA of Kumaon Mandal, Khatima, had become a buzz. He was a youth icon and an energetic leader, and his name was slowly becoming a talking point. Even those who used to be busy in their fields, tending to their crops, etc, now knew that a young leader often visited them to take note of their well-being. As their legislative representative, he interacted directly with the public and took many important decisions in public interest regarding the burning problems of the area. The people of his region thanked him wholeheartedly. He also assured those who were affected by problems related to Sharda Barrage and disaster-prone areas of a speedy resolution of their problems.

It is said that if you conspire with a brave person, you'll boost their courage, but if you conspire with someone less resilient, it is certain that he will falter and weaken. According to political analysts, the biggest reason for the fall of CM Trivendra Singh Rawat was said to be the Char Dham Devasthanam Board built on the lines of Tirupati and Vaishno

Devi. Against this, senior BJP leader Subramanian Swamy himself had approached the Nainital High Court. But the reality was that there is a difference between heaven and earth.

The doors of Kedarnath and Badrinath, famous dham or religious sites in Uttarakhand established in the Bhakti period, open only for a few months a year. It has been a tradition for years that only hereditary priests serve the Lord in these dhams. A Badri-Kedar committee was also formed in 1939. Priests from Maharashtra come to Kedarnath, one of the twelve Jyotirlingas, located on the Kedar mountain range of the Himalayas, while Namboodiri Brahmins from Kerala come to Badrinath, one of the ancient temples on the banks of the Alaknanda River in Chamoli district, as head worshippers. The temple committee also paid salaries to these Brahmins and priests. Therefore, suddenly creating a board like the Char Dham Devasthanam Board at such powerful places of religious faith was a question quick to be questioned.

On the other hand, the announcement of making Gairsain Commissionerate was also inviting anger among the regional people, including the MLAs of Kumaon-Garhwal. They were asking why a Commissionerate was being set up, bypassing all issues like unemployment, inflation, employment, education, health, etc. Why did CM Trivendra Singh Rawat not even think it appropriate to take the opinion of any local MLA or MP before taking such a big decision?

From the CM office to a village tea stall, curiosity was pervading: everyone wanted to know who the next CM would be? Some said that the people would decide, some said that the legislature party would decide, while some others said that the remote-control unit from Delhi would have an answer to that question. Well, every MLA was dreaming of considering himself as the most qualified and the much-needed candidate for the development of the hill state in this seat. In the meantime, a meeting of the legislature party was called at the behest of Delhi and the name of the newly formed state's first education minister and an MP at the time Tirath Singh Rawat was approved.

On 10 March 2021, Tirath Singh Rawat was sworn in as the CM. Thousands of BJP supporters and Dhami well-wishers were surprised that the name of the deserving candidate whom they had been chanting in front of the high command day and night for the last several days was ignored.

Dhami was not offered any ministry either. His supporters would have settled for deputy CM, but that did not happen. They started openly expressing their displeasure. The party tried to placate them by saying that two MLAs from Udham Singh Nagar district had taken oath as ministers and that only two from a region could be adjusted in the cabinet, that there was no place for the third.

As soon as CM Tirath Singh Rawat came into power, he took several decisions one after the other. In his speech, he said, 'It is us who are holding key posts, but our party has a tradition of making collective decisions. We are for the people, we have come for the people, and we will do everything for the people. Modi ji's mantra *"Sabka saath, sabka vikas (inclusive development)"* is our basic principle. So we will try to take everyone along. I have made decisions in the interest of the people and according to their expectations.' Just two days after taking the oath, on 12 March, the new leadership started the process of reversing the decisions of the previous government.

Tirath Singh Rawat no doubt took the oath of CM and even took to his duties diligently, but he was to contest a by-election to be elected to the Assembly and his overall tenure was only for a year. This weighed heavily on his working style. He tried hard to strengthen the party's future path by reversing many important decisions of the previous government, but the critics made his life tough by targeting the plank of a double-engine government. At the same time, however, people across the state were listening to the new leadership interestingly because it was also the time to build the image of the party anew.

The new CM claimed to have expeditiously withdrawn cases registered for violation of rules during under the Epidemic Diseases Act, 1897 and the Disaster Management Act, 2005 during the COVID-19 pandemic lockdown. Such cases were registered against about 4,500 people from all over the state. At the same time, he claimed to have abolished the obligation for a development map to be passed by development authorities formed in the state after 2016. Within a few days, he also took a liberal approach to the COVID-19 restrictions imposed by former CM Trivendra Singh Rawat at the religious Kumbh *mela*, or fair, and said that the opportune moment had come after a long wait of twelve years, and that every COVID-19 protocol imposed on the devotees should be abolished with immediate effect.

The Tirath Singh Rawat government came into the limelight when he knowingly or unknowingly made a controversial statement about 'shorts and torn jeans' worn by girls in college. 'You've come to the university to study, and you're showing your body! What will happen to this country?'[4] Not

---

[4]'Uttarakhand CM Faces Storm Over Women's Clothing', *ETV Bharat*, 18 March 2021, https://tinyurl.com/yz24acfv. Accessed on 11 March 2025.

only the public at large, Rajya Sabha MP Jaya Bachchan and Delhi Women's Commission chairperson Swati Maliwal also strongly opposed this controversial comment.

Apart from being stung by an unwanted controversy, he was unable to manage time for his bypoll, even though the party had selected the Gangotri Assembly seat. Then suddenly he was called to Delhi. People who followed the political ideology and commoners alike began to feel that the CM's resignation was imminent, and soon it spread as half-baked news and rumour. It brought the gaze of all political analysts back to Dehradun.

Tirath Singh Rawat had to postpone all three-day programs of the state, as he was still stuck in Delhi. On Friday afternoon, BJP president J.P. Nadda clarified that Tirath Singh Rawat would have to step down as CM, citing constitutional hurdles in his Assembly by-election.

After this, CM Tirath Singh Rawat returned to his office in Dehradun after submitting a proposal for a resignation letter to Mr Nadda. Formally, he submitted his resignation to Governor Baby Rani Maurya at Rajbhawan late that night, clarifying that he would not contest the by-election. To retain the office, he needed to win the by-election by September, which was impossible under the current circumstances. 'According to Article 164-A of our Constitution, I was supposed to become a member of the Legislative Assembly within six months after becoming the Chief Minister. However, Article 151 states that if there is less than one year left in the Assembly term, by-elections cannot be held. Therefore, due to this constitutional obligation, I cannot become a Member of the Legislative Assembly within six months. Consequently, I do not want any crisis to arise for the party. Therefore, it is my compulsion to resign from the post of Chief Minister.'[5] As a significant step, CM Tirath Singh Rawat tried to boost the party's image by announcing a COVID-19 package of ₹22,000 crore and 22,000 jobs before his resignation.

Additionally, many unusual records were made during CM Tirath Singh Rawat's brief term. He became the first CM who did not become a member of the state's Legislative Assembly throughout his term. He was also the CM under whom not a single Assembly session was convened. In the political history of Devbhoomi Uttarakhand, his tenure was the shortest among all CMs, lasting only 114 days. Previously, this record belonged to Bhagat Da, the second CM of the interim government formed after the state's creation, whose tenure was only 122 days. The BJP government, with a significant majority, was seeking a third face under the same five-year Assembly term for a strong leadership. Most broadcasting stations were discussing the name of state government minister Dhan Singh Rawat in this race. But the opponents couldn't accept the recommendation of former CM Trivendra Singh Rawat, resulting in the removal of his name from consideration. Suddenly, the name of former CM Ramesh Pokhriyal 'Nishank', associated with the Anil Baluni faction, also emerged. After assessing the situation, the high command decided to entrust the responsibility to a neutral and experienced leader who could enter the fray with a clean and better image as the party's icon in the forthcoming Assembly elections.

Another legendary figure began to emerge like a twinkling star on the political firmament. As an MP and union minister,

---

[5]Mishra, Himanshu, 'Uttarakhand CM Tirath Singh Rawat Offers to Resign Months after Taking Oath: Sources', *India Today*, 2 July 2021, https://tinyurl.com/4hudb4dj. Accessed on 11 March 2025.

he was instrumental in the formation of the hill state; he persistently exerted pressure on PMs H.D. Deve Gowda and I.K. Gujral, and West Bengal CM Jyoti Basu. In March 2014, he departed from the Congress and joined the BJP. A trailblazer in political experience, noted senior politician Satpal Maharaj attempted but ultimately failed to catch the attention of the supreme leadership of BJP. Alongside, names of veteran and striving personalities like Anil Baluni, Banshidhar Bhagat, Harak Singh Rawat, Ritu Khanduri and Ajay Bhatt were also being mentioned successively. They were appearing on the horizon as the sun rays that are ready to be absorbed into the unknown future.

However, the high command was seeking an untarnished personality capable of making history within the BJP—a figure who not only becomes a research subject in Indian politics, particularly in Devbhoomi Uttarakhand, but also leaves a significant imprint globally. What the party wanted was that this individual should wield influence and devotedly propagate the party's ideology of cultural and political nationalism in the imminent Assembly elections across seven states.

11

CHIEF MINISTER: TRENDSETTER FOR HIS STATE

Swe swe karmanyabhiratah sansiddhim labhate narah.
Swakarmaniratah siddhim yatha vindati tachrunu.
Tribhirguna mayai bhavairebhih sarvamidam jagat.
Mohitam nabhi janati mamebhya paramavyayam.

True to the philosophical statement of Lord Krishna in the 45th verse of the 18th chapter of the *Shrimad Bhagavad Gita*, which teaches that a man achieves perfection by being engaged in his natural duties, and also says how one gets perfection by being engaged in duties, such a person ultimately appeared before the BJP under mysterious circumstances. Along with a coveted position, his forehead would illuminate to lead the party into the upcoming crucial Assembly elections. Besides Narendra Singh Tomar, the union agriculture minister, who came as a state observer, and the party's top leadership, no one even got a clue of his name. Who was this young child amid a galaxy of experienced members of this grand family known as the BJP?

By wearing the 'crown of thorns', he had to handle not only the leadership of the state in this hour of crisis but also organize the various factions that had formed because of animosity within the party. Not only this, he had to bring the faltering development agenda back on track and tackle the Opposition's allegations. However, the duration allotted for this main examination was limited, akin to that of a college student.

In the keen eyes of political analysts, such a person had been introduced as a batsman turned captain who had to score runs at the crease in the slog overs and must not lose his wicket as well. Born in the rugged mountains, raised in deprivation, coming from the land of martyrs who had been laying down their lives for the country, their families living amid tight border security, this son of a soldier began his journey into politics with dreams to contribute towards changing the national social landscape in the direction of progress and development.

Let's rewind into his background. Pursuing his educational endeavours, he initiated his political life with the RSS, ABVP and BJP. Playing a key role in Uttarakhand state formation, he easily accommodated future captains in his presence. In 2001, he drew the attention of the energy minister Bhagat Singh Koshyari (Bhagat Da) towards his versatile personality, becoming his confidant in a short time. Later on, he learnt the nuances of politics from his political guru by beautifying his position as Special Duty Adviser and OSD. He became a source of inspiration for all by securing a place in the political field for two consecutive terms in 2012 and 2017 as an MLA from the key constituency of Khatima. In 2017, his name came up for inclusion in the state cabinet, but the Almighty had not willed it yet. He was also in contention for the 2019 Lok Sabha elections but did not succeed. Consequently, he assembled all his belongings from the capital Dehradun and decided to devote himself for the development of his area. He thought when he would be able to work in his constituency Khatima, he might return to Dehradun once his party returned to power in 2022. Suddenly the legislature party meeting was called and it lasted for 20 minutes under the chairmanship of observer Narendra Singh Tomar. Towards the end, Tomar stood up, and the person whose name he announced as the leader of the legislature party was seen sitting in a corner, almost on the last seat, and was only busy in listening to others. Tomar began by saying, 'The one who works finally becomes visible, even if it takes some time...'

The person whose name he took was Pushkar Singh Dhami, who, on the fifth day of Ashadha Shukla Paksha, a Monday dedicated to Lord Bholenath, in the Magha Nakshatra of Siddhi Yoga, took the oath as the eleventh chief minister of the state under the direction of Hon'ble Governor, Lt Gen. (Retd) Gurmit Singh, and the efficient headship of the eminent PM Shri Narendra Modi. This peerless fortune of becoming the state chief was going to inscribe his name in the golden pages of history. Therefore, not only the position but also the Opposition was proud of such a versatile young leadership. For this historic win, thousands of his well-wishers showered congratulations and best wishes from the doorstep of the village to the legislature.

Former CM and senior Congress leader Harish Rawat said on his elevation to the post:

> 'It is our good fortune that the younger generation is moving forward. I have already congratulated Dhami for leading the state as chief minister. But today, I also want to give him advice. This is the last opportunity for him

and his party. So he should revisit his election manifesto from 2017 and understand it. A Chief Minister remains a Chief Minister, irrespective of the period for which he is appointed! If he has the determination to make decisions, then decisions can be taken. I myself made maximum decisions during a time when my government faced unnecessary imposition by the central government due to political instability. I may not have a soft corner for other BJP workers like him, but I am definitely supportive of the youth. As a youngster, if you have the opportunity, I want the youngster to shine a little bit, to ignite something!

Today, in the 21-year history of Devbhoomi Uttarakhand, Manaskhand Kurmachal (ancient names of the Kumaon region) has seen five CMs, including the current leader Pushkar Singh Dhami. If we talk about these extraordinary personalities, the names of the late N.D. Tiwari, former CM of Uttar Pradesh and Uttarakhand, along with Bhagat Singh Koshyari, Vijay Bahuguna, Harish Rawat, and now Pushkar Singh Dhami come to mind. N.D. Tiwari remains the only chief minister in the state's 21-year history who completed his five-year tenure uninterrupted.

As soon as Pushkar Singh Dhami assumed the position of the youngest CM of the state, he surprised political thinkers and senior party politicians with a strong display of announcements. This even startled those senior leaders of the state and the country who were somewhat cynical in accepting Dhami as the CM.

Undoubtedly, the young newcomer faced a grim array of challenges. However, within a few months, Dhami showcased not only skilled abilities in serving the party and the government but also made announcements that resonated with the public.

It appeared that Dhami held a lucky bat, constantly delivering metaphorical sixes. During the challenging period of COVID-19, which severely impacted the state's economy, especially tourism, Dhami approved a relief package of ₹200 crore, benefiting around 1.64 lakh individuals in this sector. Additionally, a gift of ₹205 crore was announced as an incentive and relief package for improved health and medical care, directly aiding about four and a half lakh people across the state. Around ₹140 crore was allocated for the medical colleges of Pithoragarh and Haridwar.

Plans to distribute tablets for students from tenth grade to graduation and free books for students from ninth to twelfth grade had been set in motion. Alongside increasing the honorarium of guest teachers, Shiksha Mitras, and medical interns initiatives for free applications in government job recruitments and a two-month helicopter deployment at Pithoragarh helipad for natural disaster relief had been announced.

Ensuring swift filling of around 24,000 vacant posts across various departments and allocating ₹34 crore for Uttarakhand Transport Corporation employees were among the measures for the youth and workforce. The initiative to provide micro-nutrients for children and the launch of housing for 16,472 people under the Pradhan Mantri Awas Yojana (Rural), starting in September, were other noteworthy steps of the young CM.

Furthermore, the young leader pledged to increase the pension to ₹10,000 per month for widows and veterans who were victims of World War II. Additionally, a commitment was made to augment the journalist welfare fund by ₹2 crore, along with considerations to simplify rules and rename the pension scheme for journalists as the Chief Minister Journalist Pension Scheme, discussed during a meeting of the Journalist Welfare Fund held in the Secretariat in the third week of July.

Therefore, it was surprising that Dhami had made all the important decisions in a wise manner upon assuming power. Despite this, there was no tension evident on his face, nor was there any sense of sadness apparent in his body and mind! While he chose to repeal the Devasthanam Act, he did not hesitate to execute significant decisions such as the UCC and state land laws, as mentioned in Article 44 of the Constitution. Additionally, special attention was directed towards challenges like inflation, unemployment, migration, education and healthcare.

On 19 November 2021, PM Modi himself stated while announcing the repeal of the newly launched farming laws, 'In the interest of the country's farmers, who have been encamped at Delhi borders for a year, we are giving the gift of the repeal of the agricultural laws. After consulting numerous agricultural experts, laws were enacted in the interest of farmers in an agrarian country. However, due to Opposition pressure, some farmers turned a blind eye to the true intent of the law and began opposing it. Consequently, in the interest of all farmers nationwide, it is being withdrawn today. This decision should not be viewed from a political viewpoint.'[6]

In response to this pivotal decision, Dhami also addressed the public, giving his reaction. 'I wholeheartedly welcome this decision by our esteemed PM Narendra Modi ji! He has

---

[6]'We have Decided to Repeal All Three Agricultural Laws: PM', *Narendra Modi*, 19 November 2021, https://tinyurl.com/ympttjxc. Accessed on 11 March 2025.

displayed remarkable courage by withdrawing the law with a 56-inch chest and a resolute heart, demonstrating sensitivity towards all our farming brethren.'

Overall, Dhami was adopting fair and transparent methods and carrying forward the state's command smoothly. Initially, many people in the state and across the country tried their best to discourage him by declaring him inexperienced. However, Dhami reflected wisdom and courage, evident in his mountainous persona, organizational capabilities and the unshakeable support of local youth behind him. The saying 'a pahari is honest, struggling and hardworking' was once merely a proverb, but Dhami ensured that it was a reality within the present society.

Notably, Uttarakhand, as a border state, holds unlimited possibilities for development but also faces equally unlimited challenges. Incidents like those in the Galwan Valley during the Corona period and the unprecedented tension on borders serve as a wakeup call not only for India but also for many Asian countries and partners. They highlight the need to anticipate the high-octane aggression of enemy countries in the coming time. Such incidents are also an opportunity for India to align its strategic interests more firmly and clearly, with the United States as a major strategic partner and to inject more energy into its relations with forms like Quad, G-20 and the Association of Southeast Asian Nations (ASEAN).

Dhami believes that our soldiers remain on continuous alert on the China–Pakistan borders. There is always an atmosphere of fear and urgency in states that approximate borders. Uttarakhand, being a mountainous state, also borders other countries and it is also one of those states that send the maximum number of army personnel to man such borders. Today, PM Shri Narendra Modi's transformative governance is witnessing radical changes not only in the social fabric but also in the political, economic, religious and cultural fields.

We know that the fervent personality of Dhami is such that no task, however risky or challenging, deters his determination to do it. He is among those whose belief is 'Janani janmabhoomishcha swargadapi gariasi,' meaning, for some, service of mother and motherland is greater than actual heaven, and they proceed on the path of their duty with this lofty spirit. In a span of just five months, right before the Assembly elections, the government bolstered its image among devout followers by dissolving the Chardham Devasthanam Management Board, appeasing discontented pilgrimage priests. These priests had long protested against this Act. With the dissolution of the Devasthanam Board, there was hope that the youthful government would promptly make crucial decisions under the committee led by former Chief Secretary Subhash Kumar, especially concerning robust land laws. Given the challenging geographical conditions of the state, establishing land laws akin to those of the hill state Himachal Pradesh was pivotal for the peaceful development of this mountainous region. The neighbouring state, established in 1971, introduced a provision in the State Tenancy and Land Reform Act, 1972, specifically prohibiting the sale of land or agricultural land for non-agricultural purposes under Section 118. Any fraudulent activities falling within the government's jurisdiction are to be swiftly addressed and incorporated into governmental actions. Additionally, non-residents of Himachal Pradesh are restricted from purchasing land there, although they may acquire land for commercial use.

Well! Bidding farewell to the passing year just before the implementation of the code of conduct in Uttarakhand for the next 2022 Uttarakhand Legislative Assembly elections,

PM Shri Narendra Modi reached the famous city of Kumaon, Haldwani. While playing a brilliant innings in the friendly cricket match between teams CM XI and BJYM XI, Dhami had suffered a small fracture in the ring finger. Despite this, he arrived with a plastered hand and was seen welcoming his special guest amidst a huge sea of crowd. The large crowd was filled with delirious joy, cheering loudly 'Modi! Modi!'. It seemed as if a divine power was keeping its commitment for their welfare, and the devotees were expressing their gratitude. Earlier, PM Shri Narendra Modi had laid the foundation stone and inaugurated 23 development schemes worth more than ₹17,500 crore in Manaskhand Kumaon. Referring to those, he said, 'All these projects are going to provide better connectivity and better facilities to all companions of Kumaon. Today, when I had the privilege of coming to Kumaon, many old memories have been refreshed. I feel proud to wear this Uttarakhandi cap that I have been wearing with great affection, and I also realize my responsibility that I have to continue making every effort to realize the dreams of the region.'

In accordance with constitutional traditions, the ECI announced the dates for Assembly elections in five states of the country (Goa, Uttarakhand, Uttar Pradesh, Punjab, Manipur). As many as 18.34 crore voters would decide the fate of eligible candidates in 690 Assembly constituencies in these five states. Especially for the elections to be held on 14 February on 70 Assembly seats in Uttarakhand, the ECI provided relief from the chaos by implementing the model code of conduct in the first week of the new year itself.

Scrutiny of nomination papers were to be held on 29 January, and 31 January was to be the last chance for withdrawal of candidature.

With the announcement of the election, former and new parties active in the state entered a hyperactive mode. In 1994, the UKD, a regional party, first raised the slogan of creating a new state by cutting off the neck of Uttar Pradesh, as seen on the map, which was Uttarakhand. But today, this regional party was looking for solid ground by at least winning a single seat. While the party successfully bet on four seats in the first Assembly elections of 2002, in 2007, it was reduced to three seats, and in 2012, to just one seat.

This time, the state's largest regional party boldly decided to field its candidates in 56 out of 70 seats in the State Assembly. Most of the focus was on Dwarahat and Didihat Assembly constituencies, from where party president Pushpesh Tripathi and party's founding member leader Kashi Singh Airi were to try their luck, respectively. If we look at the original ground of the downfall of the party, we come to know that the biggest reason was that the majority of UKD candidates shifted to Congress in 2012. These turncoats led to confusion for the general public, which was in a quandary whether to support the regional party or the national ones.

Almost all the parties had started the nomination process and announced their prospective CM faces. Three faces had been sealed for the post of CM. The first was the Kirti Chakra, Shaurya Chakra and Vishisht Seva Medal awardee, army officer Col Ajay Kothiyal, who was a son of Tehri. The second face was the seventh CM of the state, a five-time MP, Harish Rawat, son of Almora, and one of the veteran Congress leaders, very rich in sociopolitical experience. And finally, the third face was that of the youngest CM of the state in its political history and someone who was known for bold and awe-inspiring decisions. He was Pushkar Singh Dhami, son of Pithoragarh.

This time, the Aam Aadmi Party (AAP), a new entrant from the national capital, seemed active in the region since the COVID-19 period. Party supremo, Delhi CM Arvind Kejriwal and Deputy CM Manish Sisodia were touring the area constantly, promoting their Delhi model. In each visit, CM Kejriwal and Deputy CM Manish Sisodia would advocate for free facilities in Uttarakhand. Their manifesto included free electricity, free water, the Delhi health and education model, ₹1,000 per month to women and ₹1 crore to martyr families.

The BJP was also keen on targeting Opposition parties this time. A significant number of BJP workers assembled in Khatima, the stronghold of Dhami, to signal that he was the strongest contender for the CM's post once the BJP came into power.

Dhami was to engage with his candidates in a three-day regional public program from 26 to 28 January. On 27 January, after completing his nomination process as a candidate from Khatima, he targeted the Opposition and said, 'As it is well known, my party has fielded me from Khatima seat this time too. The people of Khatima will support me in the 2022 elections and we will emerge victorious! We focus on development and pay no heed to baseless allegations. I am confident that the people of the area will continue to support me as they have in the past. I reaffirm my dedication to the ongoing development of Khatima. Also, I request all the residents of Devbhoomi to uphold the ideal of *Atithi Devo Bhava* (a guest is akin to God) and extend a warm and respectful welcome to these tourists (Aam Aadmi Party) who have come from Delhi. These guests will stay for a few days, relishing the enchanting beauty and clean air of the mountains, before departing.'

Like it had done in the past, the Congress again fielded Bhuwan Chandra Kapri in the electoral battle against Dhami. Seeing these two veterans face off, it was going to be interesting to see who would emerge victorious on 10 March, ultimately earning the people's trust! After meeting with many important personalities in Khatima until late night, Dhami stayed in his home district for the night. He shared his plans and strategies with his workers, providing them election tips amidst the election fervour. Encouraging the workers to identify with their candidate, he also attended a Tharu family wedding ceremony. There, he sat with the mother of his childhood friend Manoj, sharing a meal and reminiscing about his childhood, recalling unforgettable moments of days when they used to study in the fifth grade in Nagla Tarai village and would have fun with classmates at Sharda Barrage.

The Khatima Assembly seat was considered the most hotly contested in the state. Aam Aadmi Party candidate S.S. Kaler, contesting for the first time from this seat, was filing his nomination and claimed to form a government in the state with a significant majority, by dint of the popularity of the so-called Delhi model. Public frustration persisted over the main election issue even after 22 years of state formation: migration. The government's Rural Development and Migration Prevention Commission, referred to as Migration Commission (2017), itself revealed that migration from rural areas in Uttarakhand has reached alarming proportions.[7] A comparison of census data between 2001 and 2011 reveals a stark decline in population in most of the state's hilly districts.

---

[7] Sethi, Narendra, '24 Years on, Uttarakhand Struggles to Hold Its People Together', *The New Indian Express*, 8 September 2024, https://tinyurl.com/4ta4xn7y. Accessed on 21 March 2025.

A significant drop in population in Almora and Pauri-Garhwal districts between 2001 and 2011 points to a massive exodus from the state's hill regions. On the other hand, many villages have become sparsely populated, some even labelled as 'ghost villages'.

If we go through the census of 2011, around 1,000 villages in Uttarakhand have become vacant, with the maximum migration taking place from Pauri and Almora districts. Unemployment was rampant, and poverty, hunger and educated unemployment continued to plague the region. While every party had consistently highlighted these issues in their manifestos for the past 20 years, the situation remained unchanged for the impoverished population.

The Congress actively released its lengthy manifesto through a virtual rally of Congress General Secretary Priyanka Gandhi from Dehradun, promising the people that if the Congress formed the government in the state, 200 units of free electricity and an annual grant of ₹40,000 would be provided to five lakh families, etc.

The BJP too released the list of its star campaigners. The list released by the party office included PM Narendra Modi, BJP national president J.P. Nadda, Defence Minister Rajnath Singh, Home Minister Amit Shah, Uttar Pradesh CM Yogi Adityanath, and many other prominent personalities.

The BJP also released its manifesto named 'Uttarakhand Vision Document' from Dehradun in the presence of former Union Minister Ramesh Pokhriyal 'Nishank', Union Ministers Nitin Gadkari, and Pralhad Joshi. It included several pledges such as providing three LPG cylinders to the poor, ₹6,000 annually to farmers, establishing a fund of ₹500 crore for the establishment of dairy cooperatives, constructing two 3-star hotels in every district of the state, granting ₹3,000 per month to unemployed youth for one year, and increasing Jan Aushadhi Kendras from 190 to 400. Union Minister Nitin Gadkari was seen personally speaking with a manifesto in his hand. 'If our government comes to power again in Uttarakhand, 50,000 government jobs will be provided. I assure you that this year we will endeavour to complete the work of Char Dham. A project worth ₹1,600 crore in Gangotri Dham alone has been completed. If I did not receive the support of MPs and the people of Uttarakhand, I could not have completed all this work alone. Despite all the obstacles, I had the courage and completed the work. Now, no matter how many clouds burst or floods come, these roads will not be affected!'

Campaigning was at its peak in all five states of the country. With lukewarm sunlight, PM Narendra Modi addressed a huge public meeting on 10 February 2019 in the holy land of Srinagar, Garhwal, the city of beautiful natural valleys. He mentioned that he had suddenly come on the orders of Baba Kedar by applying the soil of the Devbhoomi to his forehead.

On the last day of campaigning, i.e., Saturday, 12 February, election rallies continued one after another from early morning and until dusk. At the end of the day, every candidate across the state halted campaigning as per the rules of the ECI, making every effort to attract the public.

The Uttarakhand Assembly elections were ongoing since the early hours amid the heated fervour of Valentine's Day, in a single phase. Observing the crowd gathering at booth after booth, it was speculated that those celebrating the international festival of love and those who would be restricted by their families to do so might come to booths merely to get a glance of their beloved. The direct benefit of exercising their voting rights would ultimately fortify the dilapidated building of democracy.

The future of the candidates was sealed from the polling stations within the stipulated time before the day progressed any further. A voter turnout of 65.10 per cent had been recorded across the state's 70 Assembly seats this time, slightly lower than the 65.56 per cent in the last Assembly elections. Upon closer examination, it was evident that this election saw a tough fight between the world's largest party, the BJP, and the country's most senior party, the Congress. However, in some seats, BSP and independent candidates were also providing strong competition, alongside AAP.

Equipped with modern technology, the fate of future policy-makers had been monitored with strict vigilance until 10 March. As a result, the entire campaigning and voting process in the peace-loving state had been entirely peaceful. Hence, the attention of all political parties was now shifting from Devbhoomi Uttarakhand to Uttar Pradesh. Its vast geographical area and the highest number of Assembly seats (403) have a direct impact on the Centre's politics. Therefore, it is always considered crucial that a party must secure a substantial majority to influence the politics at the Centre. This is why political competition there revolves around factors like public support, financial resources and influence. Consequently, a web of many immoral incidents and activities of mafias seemed to be spreading in Uttar Pradesh, but strongman CM Yogi had been gradually addressing all these issues.

While the entirety of North India was engrossed in painting houses to welcome Holi, South India also basked in the glory of the spring season. On whose forehead would the vibrant hues of the Holi colours leave an enduring impression akin to a coronation (*mashtakabhishek*) for the next five years?

The semi-final decision-making had commenced with the evaluation of postal ballot papers. Ballot papers were being sorted from all ballot boxes. Amidst the ongoing COVID-19 period, this time the postal ballot facility was extended to senior citizens, disabled voters and service voters. Consequently, considering the sheer number of postal ballot boxes, they would act as a potential game-changer. The time required for their assessment too would be expectedly higher in comparison to previous elections.

Upon the ECI's public release of postal ballot trends, all attention was fixated on these trends, which were poised to potentially alter the game.

Firstly, through these trends, there came relieving news favouring Dhami, as he secured 923 votes, nearly double compared to his rival Bhuvan Chandra Kapri's 551, his future boding well. Simultaneously, the initial EVM trends indicated Dhami trailing by margins of ones and tens. However, a sudden surge was observed in the subsequent phases of counting, reflecting Dhami's ascent. In this intriguing contest, until noon, Dhami trailed by 2,300 votes, while the main rival, Kapri, steadily maintained his lead. By evening, Dhami had garnered 41,598 votes while Bhuvan Kapri had crossed the figure of 48,177.

In an unexpected turn for the ruling party, their chief ministerial candidate suffered a substantial defeat to his main rival, Congress' Bhuvan Chandra Kapri, by a significant margin of 7,000 votes. Additionally, in another surprising development, Congress' own chief ministerial candidate, Harish Rawat, was defeated by the BJP candidate Mohan Singh Bisht from the Lalkuan seat, with a wide margin of 14,000 votes. Speaking of the third chief ministerial candidate, AAP's Col Ajay Kothiyal, his figures seemed to affirm his defeat.

Therefore, it was apparent that all three chief ministerial faces from the state had been rejected by the people.

It was a shocking result that the CM, who led the party to a major victory across the entire state, lost his own seat. However, this occurrence isn't entirely unprecedented. Several reasons could be attributed to Dhami's loss in the election. He did not prioritize his Assembly seat, instead focusing more on ensuring victory for the entire state and the party. According to political analysts, a crucial factor contributing to Dhami's significant defeat was the decisive role played by the Tharu people, after the hill people were almost equally divided between the BJP and the Congress. As the head of the state, Dhami's attention towards policies for the entire state overshadowed the limited focus on a specific constituency like Khatima. Plus, anti-incumbency sentiments towards the CM and internal discord within his party might have influenced the outcome.

12

BY-ELECTION: ENDORSEMENT OF THE ACCOMPLISHED WORK

'Dhriti kshama damosteyam shauchamindrianigraha,
Dheervidya satyamkrodho dashakam dharmalakshanam.'

Maharishi Manu outlined 10 characteristics of dharma: patience, forgiveness, strength, *asteyam* (non-stealing), purity or lack of malice, control of the senses, avoidance of arrogance, knowledge, truthfulness and freedom from anger. One possessing these traits is deemed a religious person.

Despite the unprecedented defeat, the historic win had disrupted the centuries-old prevalence of an adage in the mountainous region: 'Everybody salutes to the rising, nobody cares about the drowning'. A number of MLAs from Devbhoomi, spanning the Opposition and neutral factions, rose above selfish interests and favoured giving another opportunity to Dhami, despite his defeat.

Not one, not two, but six MLAs publicly announced their intent to vacate their seats for Dhami, displaying genuine dedication. Finally, BJP's winning candidate Mohan Singh Bisht surrendered his Lalkuan seat, which is a constituency of high significance in Uttarakhand politics. His victory was not against any ordinary candidate but against the former CM and veteran Congress politician, Harish Rawat, by a margin exceeding 14,000 votes.

Lalkuan had become a significant contest ground ever since Harish Rawat, an influential figure in Congress and one of the most well-known politician of the state in recent years, shifted from the Ramnagar Assembly seat to contest from Lalkuan. In the face of Opposition and internal conflicts, the BJP fielded Mohan Singh Bisht, a formidable candidate, bypassing the incumbent MLA Naveen Dumka.

Bisht, hailing from the Halduchaur area of Haldwani, had previously contested as an independent candidate in the 2019 election, securing election results from Haripur Bachchi zila panchayat constituency against his own elder brother, BJP candidate Inder Singh Bisht. However, after defeating Congress' heavyweight candidate in Lalkuan, Mohan Singh Bisht made a remarkable gesture by publicly declaring his willingness to relinquish the Assembly seat for Dhami, who was for his supporters a figure synonymous with development of the state.

Moreover, Harak Singh Rawat, who had defected from Congress in 2016 to join the BJP, along with Haridwar district MLAs Pradeep Batra and Kunwar Pranav Singh Champion, also joined the BJP. Pradeep Batra's committed politics led the BJP to field him as a key candidate in 2017, where he secured a tremendous victory. This time, he defeated former mayor Yashpal Rana, contesting on a Congress ticket, by 2,277 votes, albeit with a narrower margin than before. Pradeep Batra of the BJP received 36,986 votes, while Congress candidate Yashpal Rana obtained 34,709 votes. Meanwhile, Cabinet Minister Harak Singh Rawat, who was turning rebellious, was expelled from the BJP.

The very important Roorkee Assembly seat of the newly formed state existed as an equally important seat of the Uttar Pradesh Legislative Assembly even before the formation of Uttarakhand. In the 2002 and 2007 elections, Suresh Chandra Jain had won this seat on a BJP ticket. However, in the 2012 elections, Pradeep Batra had won it by contesting on a Congress ticket. Batra's journey had been through trials and tribulations. He too felt that he should hand over the reins of the bright future of his state to Dhami.

Pradeep Batra announced that he would dedicate his Assembly seat to Pushkar Singh Dhami with an open heart, saying that if Dhami wished, he would immediately resign from his seat and begin efforts to ensure CM's victory with a huge margin.

Umesh Kumar, who had entered the electoral field as an independent candidate and won by defeating staunch politicians, had been a journalist by profession. Umesh Kumar's name came into the limelight in the year 2016 when he claimed to have exposed the horse-trading of MLAs by conducting a so-called sting operation on the then CM, Harish Rawat.

On 27 March 2016, the then president, Pranab Mukherjee, dismissed the Harish Rawat-led Congress government on the recommendation of the then governor, Krishna Kant Paul, amid reports that Uttarakhand Assembly Speaker Govind Kunjwal had disqualified nine rebel Congress MLAs out of 36 from the party due to political turmoil and suspended the Assembly on the recommendation of the union cabinet. Due to being surrounded by new controversies, this time the BJP had given Kunwar Pranav Singh Champion's ticket to his wife, Rani Devyani. But unfortunately, Rani Devyani was reduced to the third place in the election results.

Independent candidate Umesh Kumar defeated BSP's Ravindra Singh by a margin of 6,900 votes. He presented himself as the true voice of the people by dedicating the huge Jashn-e-Fatah to the respected people. Umesh Kumar said that the people of Khanpur had elected him for development, and that the people did not want an arrogant king but a humble servant in the form of their elected representative.

One interesting thing about Umesh Kumar was that he was popularly known as the 'Helicopter Leader' in this area, because he seemed to be addicted to helicopter rides and had also provided an unforgettable opportunity to many people of his constituency to travel by helicopter. This was the reason that he had adopted the helicopter as his election symbol.

When the news of the election results of the young CM Dhami reached Umesh Kumar, he also willingly offered his support and his seat for Dhami's election in the by-poll. He had made up his mind that Dhami could give a new direction and identity to the development of the state. Needless to say, such support and sacrifice by not only one's own party legislators but also independent leaders would humble any one; and so it was for Dhami. His enthusiasm to serve people and lead with pride was at its peak.

Mohan Singh Mahara, the newly-elected MLA from Jageshwar Assembly seat, requested the party high command with confidence that they should make Pushkar Singh Dhami the CM, and that if the party indeed unanimously agreed to do so, then he would willingly vacate his seat for him. Not only this, Mahara also claimed to ensure Dhami's victory from Jageshwar with a huge margin.

Even after a long struggle, the BJP was barely able to finalize the ticket from Jageshwar Assembly seat because there was an army of eligible contenders there, all vying for a single ticket. Fortunately, Mohan Singh Mahara, who had rebelled against the Congress and joined the BJP, managed to convince the party. For years, Almora's Jageshwar seat was considered a Congress stronghold. This was the same seat from where Congress leader Govind Singh Kunjwal was elected MLA four times. The BJP wanted to breach such a fortified citadel of the Congress. The BJP pulled out a card from Congress' own oeuvre to checkmate it in politics. The result was that many leaders who built Congress in the state by their contributions were now up in arms with one another.

The constitutional obligation required that Dhami be elected to the state legislature within six months so that he could lead Uttarakhand into the future. It was well known that the Didihat Assembly constituency was within his own district area. Most political analysts had started expressing a strong possibility that Dhami would contest the by-election on this seat, considering that his ancestral villages Hadkhola and Tundi were situated in the region.

One more reason behind this seat being most likely to be selected for Dhami's by-election was that the BJP had always had a stronghold on that seat since the inception of Uttarakhand. So, every well-wisher and top leadership, including Dhami, while scouting for the safest seat, zeroed in on Didihat. This sparked speculations in the masses and the media. the idea was both welcomed and feared. Some felt that it would open the routes of state's as well area's development when the CM himself would represent the area. At the same time some were fearful of the fact that someone new would represent the area in the sixth term and it might not go down well with the locals.

While all of this was happening, on another front, some internal conflicts had also surfaced, due to four senior leaders, including BJP state president, Madan Kaushik, not being given a place in the new cabinet. Not only the state president, but the hopes of experienced politicians like former education minister Arvind Pandey and the seniormost MLA of the state from the BJP, Banshidhar Bhagat, who have consistently secured victory in the same seat since the formation of the state, were dashed.

Out of the total eight faces of the newly formed cabinet, while some old faces were retained, some were shown the way out. In this context, the name of senior BJP leader Bishan Singh Chufal was under intense discussion and scrutiny because he had had a hold on the Didihat seat for six consecutive Assembly elections. Given BJP's unassailable hold, newspapers and broadcasting houses indiscriminately circulated the news that Didihat's MLA Bishan Singh Chufal had announced to give up his seat for Dhami.

The baffling revelation surfaced when MLA Chufal himself denied this fact, by stating

> With the blessings of the public, after the withdrawal of the Trivendra Singh Rawat government, I had the privilege of becoming a minister in the Tirath Singh government. Following that, in the first Dhami government, I served with the portfolio of the Pey Jal Ministry (water ministry). I am a grassroot-level worker. For the past 30–40 years, we've made every effort to strengthen the party. I've stood firm for my party. I've never acted in a way that would make the people or the party hang its head. My work has been selfless. Due to my efforts, I won the Uttar Pradesh Assembly elections for the first time in 1996. Since then, I've remained undefeated from the Didihat seat. Once again, I've been elected to the Assembly for the sixth time by the people of Didihat, who believe

in the all-round development of the area. No one has directly asked me to vacate the seat. Why is pressure being created through the news? There's no question of leaving the seat or not because I cannot betray my voters by compromising my principles for the political ambitions of a few.

Finally, after not securing a place in the cabinet, the internal discontent of former minister Bishan Singh Chufal became evident in this statement. Gradually, the aggrieved MLA, brimming with confidence, raised many logical questions about his exclusion from the new cabinet. While speaking to a private TV channel, Chufal also expressed his desire to understand from the party the basis on which he was ultimately dropped from the cabinet. He clarified that there were some supporters within the party who did not wish to see him in the cabinet. However, it wasn't clear from this statement whether he was referring to Pushkar Singh Dhami and his political mentor Bhagat Singh Koshyari or any other individuals within the party.

Chufal continued to voice his internal conflicts in public. He emphasized that the baseless or absurd arguments regarding his exclusion from the cabinet, suggesting it was due to his old age, were unfounded. He pointed out that if age were the real reason, then his political colleague Satpal Maharaj (born 21 September 1951) was close to him in age (born 13 May 1950). He questioned how Maharaj was included in the cabinet while he was excluded. He highlighted his unwavering support for the party during challenging times, expressing confusion as to why an honest, decent and diligent personality like himself had not been favoured by the party.

On 26 March, MLA Chufal stood alongside his supporters and openly expressed his dissatisfaction after not securing a place in the Dhami cabinet. Furthermore, he categorically denied any intention of relinquishing his seat for Dhami, a surprising and unexpected twist for political analysts, including Dhami himself. Addressing the media, he spoke of a soul burdened by sorrow. When pressed by journalists about any distance or tension in his relationship with the former CM and present governor of Maharashtra, Bhagat Singh Koshyari, he did not deny it.

In their personal lives, both held mutual respect for each other. Analysts, in their role, continued to observe that Koshyari maintains significant involvement in the government and politics of Uttarakhand.

Suddenly, among the 46 seats left by Dhami's political supporters, the second-most secure Assembly seat began to be sought after for Dhami. This seat was adjacent to Dhami's home district, attracting significant attention. Moreover, there was a substantial population of migrants from the mountainous region who directly supported Dhami, which boded well for his prospects. It was known that while the state chief had delivered a tremendous majority for the party based on a developmental agenda and a youthful appeal, he himself couldn't secure his own seat for some reason, giving the Opposition an issue to target him and the BJP with.

In such a state of turmoil, it was natural for an average individual to feel frustration. However, it could also be perceived as a golden opportunity in life. Such moments can awaken one's conscience and become a catalyst for a new beginning. A wise person shouldn't overlook such moments of self-awareness. With strong intentions and determination, one should confine their troubled mind to a corner and open themselves up to a transcendent dimension. Scriptures also advocate executing two formulas in this situation.

The first reverence is to have full faith in one's self-nature! It involves being completely dedicated to a life guided by supreme consciousness. The second principle is *saburi*, which signifies endurance.

If these two principles are embraced by someone, while patiently waiting for the new path that transcends the mind to emerge, one's life is sure to transform unexpectedly, eliminating the need to look back. Consequently, the spiritual practices, knowingly or unknowingly performed by that individual, the reverence bestowed upon the practice by him or her, and the person's endurance will lead to the pinnacle of his or her supremacy. Hence, great individuals perceive themselves fortunate during times of sorrow and adversity. Moving forward with dedication and a joyful spirit while holding on to hope is crucial in this test of time. It's a natural law that after every night, there emerges a bright morning; that nothing on this earth is perpetual. Sometimes the mind is defeated, while it triumphs on other occasions. While one path closes, thousands of new paths open up.

In a scenario where Dhami may have become unhopeful and distracted, something occurred that made him remain unwavering in his journey. Upon MLA Chufal's refusal to vacate the constituency seat, the words of another individual suddenly came to the forefront and echoed in Dhami's mind. This person's enthusiasm for Dhami was like that of an elder brother. His offer also coincided with the party's approval. This person's dedication was so profound that he didn't even ponder over his own political future.

The spirit of cooperation, support and sacrifice has been ingrained in Indian culture and civilization for years.

Consider Maryada Purushottam Shri Ram, who endured 14 years of exile, relinquishing the entire Kosala kingdom, for the coronation of his younger brother Bharata. Also, think of Panna Dhai, who didn't hesitate to sacrifice her son for the kingdom and the king.

Continuing this tradition, this person understood the challenging circumstances that Dhami was facing and he acted as a lifeline to resolve it for him. This person was Kailash Chandra Gahtori [who later died from a prolonged illness (mouth cancer) at the Government Doon Medical (College) Hospital in Dehradun, on 3 May 2024], the victorious and hard-working MLA of Champawat seat located on the banks of the Champawati river. The party wholeheartedly trusted his assertion and, with a unified decision, directed Dhami to contest from the Champawat seat.

Gahtori decided to formally resign from the legislative position on Thursday, 21 April 2022, and personally embarked on a tour of his Assembly constituency, assuming the role of an elder brother. During regional public meetings, he would engage with supporters, well-wishers and the public, discussing CM Dhami's candidacy in the by-election. He would passionately appeal to the voters to make Dhami victorious, highlighting the importance of his agenda, which was safeguarding and developing regional social, economic, cultural and religious diversity.

Gahtori arrived at the official residence of Assembly Speaker Ritu Khanduri Bhushan in Yamuna Colony, Dehradun, at 8 a.m. on Thursday to formally resign from the Assembly membership. After submitting his resignation letter, he devoted himself to rallying support among the regional populace, confidently projecting an overwhelming victory for Dhami. He boldly claimed that this time, CM Dhami would certainly become an MLA from his home district on 3 June.

When questioned about his motive for vacating the seat, Champawati Kailash Chandra Gahtori responded emphatically, 'I harbour no desires for personal status; my sole and utmost goal is the all-round development of my area.' He emphasized the importance of not leaving anyone disheartened in the region. He stressed that the government should strive to ensure justice for every individual, especially those deprived of essential amenities.

In the 2017 Uttarakhand Assembly elections, Kailash had secured victory on a BJP ticket, highlighting his focus on public welfare and developmental strategies. He had fiercely competed against Congress veteran politician Hemesh Kharkwal. In the subsequent 2022 Assembly elections, Kailash had once again triumphed due to his robust regional development initiatives. For the fifth consecutive time, the Congress had fielded their seasoned candidate, Hemesh Kharkwal, against him. Despite this, Kailash had clinched the Assembly seat with a lead of approximately 5,304 votes. He obtained 50.26 per cent of the total votes cast, totalling 32,547 votes, while Hemesh Kharkwal had secured second place with a 42.07 per cent vote share, equivalent to 27,243 votes.

The Champawat Assembly contest had been a battleground between the BJP and the Congress since the state's formation. Traditionally, the people of the region had alternated their support between the Congress and BJP. Moreover, a deeper analysis revealed that initially, the hilly regions of Champawat and Khatima were earlier parts of Pithoragarh constituency. Ever since the state was formed, it has been a tradition that the winning party in the newly established Champawat constituency during Assembly elections had coincidentally formed the state government.

Following Gahtori's resignation, the Champawat Assembly seat was declared vacant, and this information was relayed to the ECI via the chief electoral officer's office. Promptly taking notice of this development, the ECI itself issued the election notification within a fortnight, specifically on 4 May. The ECI, through its notification, specified that the deadline for filing nomination papers for the elections was 11 May, followed by the scrutiny of nomination forms on the subsequent day, 12 May. Therefore, the final date for withdrawal of nominations was set for 17 May, while voting was scheduled for 31 May, with counting of votes and result announcements planned for 3 June.

The prompt action taken by the ECI faced sharp criticism from Opposition parties and political critics regarding its impartiality and lack of accountability. They pointed out a significant delay when by-elections were supposed to occur in seven Assembly seats of West Bengal. Allegations were made that the ECI had deliberately disregarded this matter for several months. As a result, the TMC government sought refuge in the Calcutta High Court. At that time, their primary concern revolved around CM Mamata Banerjee's need to win the election and secure a seat in the Assembly within the stipulated six-month period, as failure to do so would cost her the CM's chair. The petition urged the Calcutta High Court to direct the ECI and the union ministry of home affairs to conduct the by-elections within the prescribed constitutional time limit of six months.

A petition has been filed by the Trinamool Congress in the Calcutta High Court, requesting the Election Commission to conduct elections within the prescribed time frame. Ramprasad Sarkar, the lawyer representing the West Bengal government, stated that Sections 150 and 151 of the Representation of People Act mandate that elections or by-elections should be held within six months.[8] Their main concern is why there is a delay in announcing by-elections for seven assembly seats in the state. Trinamool Congress leader Tapas Roy stated that assembly elections were held in the state during the COVID-19 pandemic, and now the situation is largely under control. He mentioned that according to the Constitution, elections should be held within six months, but the Election Commission has not taken any initiative in this regard. He added that the Election Commission's duty is to conduct elections, but it is not fulfilling its responsibility.

However, the double engine government of Uttarakhand, renowned as the land of gods, had seemingly influenced the ECI in its favour. This scenario raised substantial questions about the transparency, impartiality and accountability of the ECI itself.

Acknowledging the limited time available, all BJP workers and top leadership swiftly began contributing to strategizing the blueprint for star campaigners, extensive public meetings, regional tours and election rallies. This proactive approach aimed to ensure no complacency in the campaign process. Following Dhami's nomination on 9 May, the Congress party, after careful deliberation, also revealed the name of its candidate. The Congress party, on 11 May, nominated Nirmala Gahtori, a prominent advocate for women's empowerment and equality in the region.

---

[8]Tiwari, Anshuman, and Monika, 'TMC–BJP Face to Face on the Issue of By-elections in Bengal, Threat to Mamata's Position' (in Hindi), *Newstrack*, 4 September 2021, https://tinyurl.com/529uwexe. Accessed on 21 March 2025.

Before his nomination, CM Dhami visited the temple of his *kuldev* or family deity in his village Nagla Tarai, Khatima, seeking the blessings of, first, his mother Bishna Devi and then of *Param Shakti Aaradhya*, the Supreme Being, in order to maintain unwavering faith in religious beliefs and solicit good luck for his election.

Congress leaders also gathered in large numbers at Kharkwal Garden on Tuesday to show support for Congress contender Nirmala Gahtori in the election. Member of Parliament (Rajya Sabha) Pradeep Tamta and Mahila Congress State President Jyoti Rautela appealed to the people to vote overwhelmingly in favour of Nirmala, a hard-working candidate dedicated to women's empowerment. Referring to the activities of the former regional MLA of the party, Tamta mentioned that former MLA Hemesh Kharkwal had done significant work in the area, and the development work done by him could not be forgotten at any cost.

Drawing energy from his statement, former MLA Hemesh Kharkwal broke his silence. 'We will back Nirmala Gahtori in the election, and Champawat will witness a passionate campaign by the Congress. We will put up a spirited contest to our opponent and the locals will see astounding results.' The Congress established a management committee of senior leaders to ensure the success in the by-polls. In this committee, the party appointed former Champawat MLA Hemesh Kharkwal as the convenor for the Assembly by-election. Additionally, MLA Manoj Tiwari from Almora was designated as the chairman of the management committee. The MLA who defeated Dhami from Khatima, Bhuwan Kapri, and MLA Khushal Singh Adhikari of Lohaghat had been appointed as convenors of the committee.

State Congress Committee General Secretary Vijay

Saraswat said, 'Soon the party will form several more important committees, and the responsibility for these committees will be unanimously handed over to hardworking MLAs and senior leaders. Additionally, we plan to divide the entire Champawat Assembly constituency into four sectors, where our workers will collaborate with senior leaders up to the booth level.' Meanwhile, the Congress party broadcast shocking news, releasing a list of 30 star campaigners. These campaigners aimed to provide faster and better direction to the election campaign over several shifts and from various places in the region.

As the election date neared, BJP workers hadn't seen a moment's leisure. Everyone was busy fulfilling their responsibilities as faithful and conscientious workers. By Tuesday evening, the BJP surprised the Congress by releasing a list of its 40 star campaigners. Union Women and Child Development Minister Smriti Irani, UP CM Yogi Adityanath, Union Ministers Anurag Thakur, Tejasvi Surya, Ramesh Pokhriyal 'Nishank', Anil Baluni, Dushyant Gautam, Rekha Verma, Madan Kaushik and Ajay Bhatt were some of them. All these 40 star campaigners from the Centre and the state were to play a crucial role in presenting the state and central government's excellent work to the people in the region and apprise them about the party's upcoming strategies. They would address publicity rallies, meetings and road shows in the valleys of Champawat, supporting BJP contender Pushkar Singh Dhami. Overall, this by-election held immense importance for every political enthusiast.

Bharatiya Janata Party contender Dhami had addressed two election meetings himself. Continuous village-to-village and door-to-door regional tours were ongoing with the support of thousands of activists and supporters. However, the main

Opposition party (Congress) was still eagerly awaiting its star campaigners. So far, no strong Congress leader had been seen in the area, and no special election rally had been organized.

When questions arose about the laxity of Congress members, Congress leader Puran Kathyat stated, 'We do not believe in the politics of appearance! Our party high command has prepared a list of 30 star campaigners who will spearhead the campaign on 20 May.' The Opposition alleged that the BJP was in danger of losing the by-polls, hence it was gathering ministers and MLAs in the area, but this was not going to affect the Congress' morale and neither would it bring BJP any favourable results.

The people of Champawat were to cast their votes based on local issues like inflation, unemployment and migration, which could directly benefit the Congress. Congress State President Karan Mahara also claimed that the BJP was contesting the Champawat by-election in panic. He further added, 'Our candidate (Nirmala Gahtori) had established election offices at two locations in the last three days, which the BJP forcibly closed by threatening the owners, and it was despite the written permission obtained from the Election Office to open these offices.'

Furthermore, Leader of Opposition Yashpal Arya on Sunday and former CM Harish Rawat on Monday entered the campaign field, fiercely targeting the BJP. Simultaneously, from 24 May, Congress' state in-charge Devendra Yadav was to stay in Champawat for three days, adding momentum to the election campaign. Meanwhile, the BJP's rallies were in full swing, recording substantial public support daily. Veteran leaders from both the BJP and Congress continued their relentless campaigning from early morning till dusk, reaching every street and corner of the village.

At the same time, strategic meetings were taking place until late at night, where Opposition parties would devise diplomatic strategies against each other. Review meetings were being convened, gathering feedback from workers who returned late in the evening from the campaign. Bharatiya Janata Party cabinet ministers Ganesh Joshi and Chandan Ram Das had left no stone unturned during campaigning. To support women empowerment, the BJP organized a massive women's conference. Ganesh Joshi, the agriculture and social welfare minister, said, 'The state government is continually working in the best interests of women. By recognizing Dhami's dedicated leadership, the party had offered him a ticket from Mussoorie too, but the allure of Golu Devta had pulled him towards Champawat.

Early in the morning on 25 May, Wednesday, as a star campaigner, actor Hemant Pandey, a pride of Devbhoomi, canvassed for votes in favour of Dhami, reaching out to mountain dwellers. Before the day ended, an opulent stage was set up for poets, including well-known modern poet and litterateur, widely known as 'yuga kavi and Ram kathavachak', Dr Kumar Vishwas, the valorous poetess Kavita Tiwari, and other renowned poets, with the help of two institutions: Digital Khidki and the Devbhoomi Vichar Manch at the legendary Champawat's Goral Chaud Maidan.

Dr Kumar Vishwas enthralled the crowd of thousands with his ghazals, imparting profound thoughts to everyone present. 'The people of Devbhoomi Uttarakhand are hardworking, straightforward, truthful, simple and conscientious. For centuries, Uttarakhand, the land of the almighty, has been a comforting haven.

'It is an immense honour for me to be in such a sacred land of Golu Devta. I have a special bond with this place of penance. That's why I make it a point to visit Devbhoomi at least once a year. History bears witness that poets like Vedavyasa, Valmiki, Sriharsha and Kalidasa unveiled the enigmatic tableau of their inner selves in the golden expanse of nature. The primordial essence of nature resides in every particle here, which foments crafting of literature in such a serene and tranquil environment. It is an astounding experience in itself.'

Talking about Uttarakhandi dishes, such as pahadi raita made of cucumber and mustard seeds, *gahat ki dal*, bhang and pudina chutney, bal mithai, chapati made of ragi or rice etc., Dr Kumar Vishwas also discussed the simple and gentle personality of Bhagat Da, the Governor of Maharashtra and the pioneer leader of Uttarakhand, calling him a saint and the identity of the mountains.

In 1999, when the mortal remains of Kargil war martyr Major Rajesh Adhikari had reached Nainital, Kumar Vishwas had hummed the lines of the poem that he had composed in Nainital itself, leaving each one present with tears in their eyes that how this happened untimely.

> 'Hai naman unko ki jo is deh ko amaratv dekar,
> Is jagat mein shaurya kee jeevit kahaanee ho gae hain,
> Hai naman unko ki jinke saamane bauna Himalaya,
> Jo dhara par gir pade aur aasamaanee ho gae.

Salute to those great individuals who, through their selfless sacrifice and valour, created immortal stories of heroism. They are the ones whose contributions have left a lasting impact on the world, and whose strength and courage make even the most daunting challenges seem insignificant.

—Kumar Vishwas, *Koi Deewana Kehta Hai*

Meanwhile, the Opposition's blame-game continued. It made accusations that the BJP and the administration were working under pressure. That a situation akin to the murder of democracy had arisen in the state. The Congress state president also stated that the Char Dham Yatra was being publicized by the BJP to take political advantage. Fifty-six people had died in only 19 days of travel. The condition of the all-weather road was dilapidated. The health services of the state, including the districts, were crumbling. There was a shortage of doctors everywhere, and there are no toilets, parking or medical facilities along the way—these were all charges of the Congress.

So overall, the BJP was in trepidation. Amidst the fervour of the election festival, they had failed to realize that the common voter was grappling with issues like rising prices of diesel, petrol, gas, soaring unemployment, etc. The voters had been feeling incapacitated to voice their concerns. Former Uttarakhand CM and Congress stalwart Harish Rawat arrived in Champawat on 24 May and addressed a massive public gathering at Champawat Haat in support of Congress candidate Nirmala Gahtori. He appealed to the people to ensure a significant victory for the Congress candidate Nirmala Gahtori in the Assembly by-election and strongly criticized the ruling party.

Harish Da, giving vent to his inner turmoil, targeted the BJP and exhorted locals to support a woman candidate. He said that the BJP was misusing money power and administrative machinery to win the by-polls. He appealed to the BJP, urging them to not create a façade of false promises. Further emphasizing that Nirmala Gahtori was a local woman, he encouraged the people to ensure her resounding victory and ensure her journey to the Assembly. According to him, the development of the region and the state could only be achieved with the support of the Congress. He highlighted that the public at large was suffering due to inflation, unemployment, lack of adequate and affordable healthcare and education. He also said that the leaders and ministers were prioritizing state leadership campaigns over the people's development and misusing government funds recklessly.

Giving a fitting response to the Opposition's allegations made through covert means, the BJP shot back saying, 'How could we misuse government funds? Are the Opposition's intellectual leaders unaware of the country's investigative agencies? Would the Election Commission and CAG [Comptroller and Auditor General of India] allow any irregularities in elections? It's evident that the Opposition lacks faith in the Constitution and its institutions, the cornerstone of the country's democratic ideals and principles. We believe that if they lack trust in these institutions, they have no right to contest elections. It's a public event, and there's no question of irregularities. We are peacefully conducting our programs, adhering to all constitutional, administrative and COVID-19 guidelines and regulations, and strategically planning our activities.

> 'Apnee burai par chadhaakar achchhaee ka naqaab,
> Ham par daal rahe ho tohmatgee ka naqaab.'

> You are disguising your flaws with a mask of goodness while falsely accusing us and defaming us.

To cut a long story short, the Opposition was trying to save its own face, due to the non-cooperation of the star campaigners from the high command and inadequate public support, by laying blame on the ruling party.

Geeta Dhami, wife of Pushkar Singh Dhami, also broke her silence and said, 'The Congress, which has already accurately estimated its weakness and inability, has made Nirmala Gahtori into a "scapegoat". Therefore, she is being used due to a lack of strong candidates, and by making meaningless and senseless allegations, they are soothing themselves.'

Geeta Dhami's use of the term 'scapegoat' didn't sit well with Congress candidate Nirmala Gahtori. She openly expressed her discontent, airing her anger by posing a series of questions. 'If I am considered a weak candidate, why did the ruling party need 40 star campaigners? Why are these troublemakers afraid of women's power and our honest politics? I will not allow the mafia system to enter this area at any cost. Geeta is much younger than me, both in age and in politics. She should consider that despite being a two-time MLA and CM, why couldn't he save his own seat... So, I want to ask them, besides promoting hooliganism, are they ready to make real sacrifices now?'

> *'The mystery of the cosmos and the*
> *foolishness of man are limitless.*
> *Yet, man seeks to explore the mysteries of*
> *the cosmos rather than his own folly.'*

While responding to a journalist's question, Gahtori added, 'The Bharatiya Janata Party has presented me with many temptations; I can disclose the names! Today, I have been denied the permission to open the office and hoist the party flag (Congress) on the house. The Bharatiya Janata Party aims to establish a monarchy within a democracy. Alongside Nirmal Pandit, we have enforced a ban on liquor in the area—'neither alcohol nor money'—these are the only two tools of my election.' Moreover, Nirmala Gahtori didn't hesitate to compare CM Dhami with Ravana, referring to his pride, and likened Geeta to the Sita Haran episode.

The BJP saw her utterances as a case of *'khisiani billi khambha noche'* (A frustrated cat scratches the pillar) and rebuffed her frustration-filled statements.

Chief Minister Dhami addressed the final public meeting for the by-election amidst dwindling time and concluding moments of the election campaign. During this address, he earnestly urged voters to observe Tuesday, the voting day, as a festival dedicated to Bajrangbali Hanuman and ensure a 100 per cent voter turnout. With this conclusion, the election campaign for the polling scheduled on Tuesday, 3 May, culminated on the evening of the weekend (Sunday, 29 May), as the last rays of the sun eagerly sank into the horizon.

The election campaign for the by-election, conducted for the only seat in the state, spanned a total of 26 days, generating significant enthusiasm in the area. The nation's attention was eagerly fixed on the polling day of 31 May and the subsequent results on 3 June. A total of 96,213 voters, comprising 50,171 males and 46,042 females, were to determine the fate of four candidates, including CM Dhami. However, widespread speculation suggested that the primary contest would unfold between BJP candidate Dhami and Congress candidate Nirmala Gahtori only. This assumption arose as Manoj Kumar Bhatt of SP and Himanshu Gadkoti, an independent candidate, had displayed minimal zeal or interest for campaigning.

The cacophony of several birds chirping filled the air. The sun's radiant crimson hue blanketed the surroundings, casting a therapeutic warmth from the heavens to the earth. The cool air, carrying a gentle smile, seemed to greet the competing candidates, welcoming them with colourful flowers that were nestled on various plants strewn here and there. The mountain valleys witnessed a leisurely stroll. Voting, commencing with the sunrise, persisted until the sun dipped below the horizon. The ECI had arranged 151 polling stations to facilitate peaceful polling.

Dhami seemed as preoccupied as usual, following his daily routine. Every employee had to undergo comprehensive security checks in readiness for the vote counting process. Wherever one glanced, a sizable assembly of party workers and supporters was deeply engaged in forecasting the victory of their respective candidates.

The trends from the ECI in the first round of counting showed a surge favouring Dhami. He had secured 3,856 votes, while his closest rival, Congress candidate Nirmala Gahtori, only received 164 votes. As the trends progressed to the third round, Dhami had amassed 10,000 votes, while Nirmala Gahtori had to settle for just 425 votes. By the sixth round of counting, Dhami had soared to 22,693 votes, while the primary Opposition candidate appeared to barely cross the 1,000-vote mark. Local political analysts anticipated that the Champawat by-election would break all previous election records this time.

This remarkable turn of events sparked intense debates across the country's media houses and news broadcasting stations. Everyone exhibited unwavering confidence in their newly initiated debates. Suddenly, news began circulating about the 2017 victory of BJP candidate Kailash Chandra Gahtori by a margin of 17,360 votes. However, it became the party's good fortune that their current candidate had set a new record, surpassing the previous one.

In the 2007 Assembly elections, Veena Maharaj from the BJP had emerged victorious with 22,928 votes. Reflecting on previous results, Congress candidate Hemesh Kharwal had won with 15,870 votes, securing a margin of 7,058 votes. Dhami's astounding performance seemed as though all four directions were channelling positive energy towards him. One might even say that this day was Dhami's day!

The latest figures from the ninth round, as circulated by the ECI, portrayed Dhami leading by a significant margin of 31,966 votes. Party workers had begun their preparations for the impending celebrations. Congratulatory gestures, sweet distributions and fireworks were not limited to party offices but were evident on every street and in every household. With each successive round, the astonishing trends continue to widen the margin of victory. By the tenth round, reaching 40,384 votes, Dhami and the country's largest party exhibited clear signs of a record-breaking triumph. Joy radiated from every member of the party.

Political analysts, stunned by the current turn of events, found themselves revisiting past electoral differences. They recalled how Congress candidate Hemesh Kharwal, in the 2002 elections, managed to defeat independent candidate Madan Singh Mahrana by a mere 395 votes—a notable event since the state's formation. Observing the exponential growth in the vote margin on this day, everyone was compelled to contemplate deeply. As the figures from the 12th round revealed Dhami leading by approximately 51,000 votes, it seemed nothing could hinder this mountainous triumph now. From family homes to party offices and even the CM's office, the air was filled with an atmosphere of celebratory fervour.

> *Tamistra ko cheer kar phailee preet hoon main,*
> *Sangharshon kee tapish se mili jeet hoon main.*
> *Ret ke mafik na miloonga mitte mein yoon hee,*
> *Tapkar nikhre us kanak kee reet hoon main.*

The above lines signify the success gained through struggles and hardships. It emphasizes the victory achieved through love and struggles. One should not dissolve like sand in the earth, rather, like gold, one should shine after enduring hardships and gain lasting value.

It's remarkable that CM Dhami, the BJP's candidate, not only secured victory in the Champawat Assembly by-election with an unprecedented margin but also managed to negate the Opposition's divisive politics by rallying the people around his honest nationalist and developmental agenda. This by-election, perhaps a historic one, witnessed the confiscation of deposits or collateral from all candidates except the winner. If a candidate gets less than one-sixth of valid votes, their deposit is forfeited. For example, if a candidate gets less than 16,667 votes out of a total of 1 lakh, it leads to forfeiture of the deposit. Candidates deposit this amount with the Election Commission during nomination. Thus, Dhami had now become a contender for achieving a record-breaking victory in political history.

Securing the political ground of Maa Purnagiri and Champawati river, Dhami attained a staggering lead of approximately 54,121 votes. In contrast, Nirmala Gahtori, the Congress candidate representing the largest Opposition, only managed to secure 3,147 votes. Out of the 61,000 eligible voters, Dhami garnered a total of 57,268 votes, which accounted for a remarkable 97 per cent of the votes.

In this context, the Congress candidate Nirmala Gahtori secured only 3,147 votes, while the SP candidate Manoj Kumar received 409 votes, independent candidate Himanshu Garkoti garnered 399 votes, and NOTA recorded 372 votes. All of them, as per rules, having failed at getting one-sixth of the total valid votes, with hearts full of dissatisfaction, had to forfeit their security deposits.

The previous largest victory in the history of Devbhoomi Uttarakhand belonged to former Congress CM Vijay Bahuguna, who had secured a margin of 39,954 votes in the 2012 Sitarganj Assembly by-election. However, on this day, Dhami had etched a new record in history. The testimony to this milestone were the EVMs used for 13 rounds of vote counting at the Van Panchayat Bhawan Auditorium situated at Goral Chour Maidan in Champawat, the district headquarters.

To convey the joy of victory achieved through record votes had become a challenge for Dhami. Overwhelmed with excitement and emotion, he expressed his feelings publicly, saying, 'I am astonished by the early trends and overwhelmed by the affection and blessings bestowed upon me, a common candidate, by the divine people of Champawat.

My heartfelt gratitude goes out to all the people of this district. I find myself inadequate in expressing my feelings and gratitude in the face of such immense blessings. Before donning the crown of victory, I attribute this historic win entirely to you. I was certain I would receive your support and blessings, but I had not anticipated receiving your adoration in such multitude. The existence, name and essence of rivers remain unchanged despite the constant influx of new water streams; they just continue to progress in a more refined form. Similarly, with the prayers of all divine people of our state, I am committed to moving forward in serving the public with equal dedication. It is now my responsibility to prioritize the comprehensive development of Champawat as my foremost commitment. There is immense developmental potential here, and together, we will explore all those possibilities in great detail! Within the next few years, we aim to construct a healthier and more prosperous Champawat and a stronger and better Uttarakhand!'

Pravar man pravar jan devabhomi ka adhaar hoga!
Pravar Uttarakhand ka pratyek svapn sakaar hoga!

The pure-hearted and virtuous people will form the foundation of Uttarakhand's glory. Uttarakhand, known as the land of gods and goddesses, will see all its dreams fulfilled.

ACKNOWLEDGEMENTS

This book traces Pushkar Singh Dhami's life history from his birth in the lap of the hill state of Uttarakhand, encapsulating all important events from his childhood, till now. For the successful writing of this book, I would like to first thank the holy land of Devbhoomi Uttarakhand itself, where Pushkar ji descended like a sacred pond of water, still with peace and laden with natural beauty. It has been a privilege for me to narrate the glory of Pushkar on these beautiful pages!

When I ventured to pen the life of a young and dynamic leader for thousands of eager readers, I was assisted by a number of people at every stage—they included CM Pushkar ji's ardent supporters, well-wishers, literature lovers, scholarly personalities and journalists from both the digital and print media. Whenever I felt the need for their guidance, I found myself free to contact them. And it was humbling that they themselves were excited to help me every time! So now I consider it my utmost duty to express my gratitude to all those great helpers. Some names may not have found a place in print due to human error. I apologize to them and request them to accept my indebtedness.

Each fact and event has been described in this book exactly in the way as it might have taken shape in real life. However, we all know that no other published or collected material on the person on whom this book is centred was available. Therefore, bringing all the events together into a vibrant form was a bit of risk and a challenging task. But with your blessings and cooperation, this job became easy for me. Hence, it is incumbent upon me that I accord credit to you for this.

I would like to thank Sahishnu Samrat who supported me in the craftsmanship of writing down this biography at every formative stage. Not only this, he kept my confidence high and encouraged me through the process. I am happy to share that the foreword of this volume has been inscribed by him.

I would like to thank Additional Superintendent of Police, Lucknow, Uttar Pradesh, Trigun Bishun ji, who apprised me of some light but precious moments of his marriage when many dignitaries, including Pushkar Singh Dhami, Anubhav and Amarendra, became witnesses to his nuptials and danced to the rhythm of the wedding DJ. Besides, he also helped me in getting access to many important sources.

I would like to express my gratitude to respected Anubhav ji and Amrendra Pratap ji who with great enthusiasm gave me their valuable time as per the orders of the CM at Starbucks, Hamilton House, Delhi, and introduced me to many incidents of their Lucknow University days.

I would also like to thank all those people of Harkhola, Tundi (Pithoragarh), Khatima, Lucknow, Dehradun and Sagar (Madhya Pradesh), who have been direct witnesses to all important and interesting episodes in Dhami ji's life that have been duly mentioned in various parts of this book.

First of all, Dhami ji's parents—Bishna Devi and Subedar Sher Singh—deserve kudos and deference; they gave birth to a worthy son and devoted him to the all-round development of the Devbhoomi. I am especially indebted to Dhami ji's elder sister Nandi ji, who took me around every room of their parental house, which is nestled amidst the natural beauty of Nagla, Khatima. Chief Minister Pushkar Singh Dhami ji had spent his childhood in this modest but beautiful house, indulged in naughty mischiefs and delighted in innocent games. She showed me Sharda Barrage in front of the house, where she would go to take dips after a rebellious banter with her family members. She said she was quite fond of doing that. I also owe a debt of gratitude to dear Bhabhi ji, Geeta Dhami, who has always been ready to step forward to contribute from her end in the sociocultural development of her people. She reserved precious time of her life for me at the CM's residence in Dehradun, and shared with me interesting anecdotes of her childhood, school days and then married life. I also express my heartfelt gratitude to all those family members who are directly and indirectly associated with CM Pushkar Singh Dhami ji.

I extend my heartfelt gratitude to Inspector Atul Srivastava ji, presently an SHO, who is not only a decorated protector of our lives by virtue of his duty, but also nurtures an enduring love for literature and creative pursuits. He provided me with guidance during every step of this book's writing stage. He facilitated my writing journey by removing the pebble stones that came in the way; whatever amount of gratitude I can express to him would be insufficient. He was instrumental in helping me to make contact with Dhami ji's classmates, friends, journalists and teachers. He even assisted me in traversing the campus of Lucknow University and introduced me to various student leaders and contemporary journalists so that I could understand the past and present, and all other contours of student politics at Lucknow University.

I would like to express my gratitude to the gurus (teachers) who provided primary education to Dhami ji. Balkrishna

Pandey ji and Mohan Ram ji are two prominent names in this regard. Dhami ji's childhood friends Ram Singh Kholiya, Madho Singh, Govind Singh and Subedar Bahadur Singh Dhami, who have been observing all key developments in Dhami ji's life and who also showed interest in the compilation of this book, also deserve gratitude. I am especially grateful to Vivek Tripathi ji, chief correspondent (Lucknow) of the news channel ABP Ganga. He kept aside time from his busy routine and considered the progress of my work important.

I am also thankful to respected Pawan Upadhyay ji, who is a devoted practitioner of celibacy and someone who has dedicated his life to the Indian judiciary. He shared those important moments of Lucknow University that proved to be turning points in Dhami ji's political, social and cultural life. My gratitude to Rajesh Srivastava ji, assistant editor at the Lucknow office of the *The Times of India*, is also due. He made me understand the politics of the BJP and ABVP from close quarters.

It is not an easy task for me to express my gratitude to Somesh Vardhan ji, a government advocate in the Lucknow division bench of the Allahabad High Court, who strived to polish my writing from the very start in a way that it would narrate more in a few words; and he did it through Inspector Atul Srivastava ji. Similarly, Bhuvan Tiwari ji, who was working as a review officer in the chief minister's office, tried to sharpen my writing with many untouched memories; I say thanks to him. My gratitude to respected Bansidhar Tiwari ji, director at information and public relations department, who has been committed to improve the quality of education in the state. He did not hesitate to reserve his valuable time in the Uttarakhand House (Delhi) and at the chief minister's office (Dehradun) for me. I am also thankful to all the officers and sub-staff of the chief minister's office, especially Rajendra Bisht ji, Bhupesh Basera ji, senior officer Sanjay Tolia ji, and others.

I express my sincere gratitude to fibre industrialist Rakesh Rastogi ji who not only appreciated me for compiling this book from day one but also helped me tour Dhami ji's area by providing his valuable time and a driver. With this assistance, I was able to collect information by meeting many important people.

I am thankful to Dr Ajay Prabhakar ji, agricultural scientist of GB Pant University, Pantnagar, who obliged me with information about the initial steps, regional challenges and achievements in Dhami ji's political journey. Special thanks to Rajpal ji, who also visited my residence in Dehradun. He not only shared with us valuable memories but also those unforgettable moments that he had spent with Dhami ji. He used to be with Dhami ji in every election campaign. Not only this, he also played an important part in bolstering BJP's image through various public meetings. Despite severe pressure from farmers, he took Dhami ji to tour the disaster-hit areas in a tractor.

I am also thankful to BJP district president Vivek Saxena ji of Khatima and Kanhaiya Lal ji, who represents the Scheduled Caste section of Khatima and shared many regional problems with me. Kanhaiya ji also shared important perspectives, such as the display of hurt sentiments of the local people due to the defeat of Dhami ji in the by-election through a collective *jalsamadhi*, a demonstration of a symbolic 'atonement' by standing in water for several hours.

I am grateful to all businessmen and other personalities committed to BJP, who gave me courage and proper guidance.

FELICITATIONS FROM WELL-WISHERS AND POLITICAL LEADERS

Political Leaders

Hon'ble President Droupadi Murmu: I have been hearing and seeing for years that the people of Uttarakhand are hardworking, honest, decent and friendly, but the determined diligence seen in Chief Minister Pushkar Singh Dhami is rare. My heartiest wishes for the development of the mountainous region under the able guidance of Prime Minister Narendra Modi and the leadership of the youth!

Hon'ble Prime Minister Narendra Damodardas Modi: I am confident that our influential Chief Minister Pushkar Dhami ji is making every possible effort for the progress of Uttarakhand and the accomplishment of the dreams of the youth! Through the BJP, he is committed to the all-round development of Devbhoomi for the year 2025 with his mantra of *Vikalp Rahit Sankalp* (Resolve without Alternative)! I thank the people of Champawat for reposing faith in the leadership of this young man and appreciate the hard work of our workers! Dhami is an unblemished personality; may his future be bright and may my blessings always be with him!

Former President, Hon'ble Ramnath Kovind: Pushkar Singh Dhami is a man who, having grown up in the inconveniences of the mountainous region, embodies humility with his simple lifestyle, honesty and hard work. We are confident that as per his commitment of all-round development of the state, under the guardian-like guidance of respected Prime Minister Narendra Bhai Modi ji, he will be able to make Devbhoomi the number one state in 2025. I pray for his good health and long life.

Shri Amit Shah: Bharatiya Janata Party's double engine governance system has brought development on all fronts. The state was formed by the Atal government, and under the guidance of the Modi government, the successful Dhami government of the youth is working to improve it. It is a promise that with Dhami ji's *Antyodaya Sankalp* (welfare of the people at the bottom of the pyramid), the wheel of development will roll forward and Uttarakhand will be rejuvenated. Dhami is a hardworking, honest person, a fighter who will prove to be a milestone for Devbhoomi. I am confident that under the guidance of Prime Minister Modi, he will continue to serve the people with this dedication and devotion to take Devbhoomi Uttarakhand to new heights of development.

Shri Rajnath Singh: I have been familiar with Pushkar Dhami ji's work excellence for a long time. Exhaustion and failure are words absent in his dictionary, so that's why I had said, 'Our Pushkar is a flower as well as fire; he will never bend, nor will he stop.' *Dhaakad* Dhami, like the Dhoni of the 20-20 matches, is a successful batsman and a finisher, and deserves to play his innings continuously for five years. With the able guidance of Prime Minister Narendra Modi and the leadership of the youth, Devbhoomi will emerge as the number one state. My warm blessings for his bright future!

Hon'ble Governor Gurmit Singh: India is a Vishwaguru, a world leader; many good leaders were born here. Among them, illustrious Prime Minister Narendra Modi ji and Dhami ji are also one, under whose leadership the country has made the path of progress easier at every step and who have also established new dimensions of progress in many other areas. The state is progressing under the able leadership of Dhami ji. My blessings and guidance will always remain with the young leadership.

Shri Jagat Prakash Nadda: A multifaceted talent, educated youth Pushkar Singh Dhami is determined to reach out to the last person in society. It has always been his endeavour that the benefits of the schemes be available to all equally. He is always ready to take the affection of elders and the love of others. His working style for the welfare of soldiers, martyrs, women and children makes us proud. I wish that the state continues to get the blessings and guidance of the BJP family under his leadership!

Shri Mohan Bhagwat: Chief Minister Pushkar Singh Dhami, who is always dedicated to establishing an egalitarian society, is moving forward with humility and decency. Devbhoomi is a newly formed state with limited resources. The more the population of the state, the greater the burden; hence, if the population is used properly, only then it becomes a means. Under the guidance of the Prime Minister, the illustrious Chief Minister Dhami ji will also have to reflect deeply on it, so that he can have the all-round development of the state materialize on ground.

Mr Ramesh Pokhriyal 'Nishank': Pushkar Singh Dhami is a very mature, simple, genuine and gentle leader. Under the guidance and leadership of Prime Minister Narendra Bhai, we have broken the myth of alternating governments between Congress and BJP in the state. My eternal best wishes are that the BJP's victory chariot advances under his leadership and ensures the development of the state!

Mahant Shri Yogi Adityanath: Chief Minister Pushkar Dhami, my younger brother, is a young and hardworking leader. Under his leadership, we have to together facilitate inclusive development of Uttar Pradesh and Uttarakhand. The reconstruction of Baba Kedarnath is taking place at a fast pace under the resolve of Hon'ble Prime Minister Narendra Modi. Under the humble and friendly relationship of an elder and younger brother, we have made the division of 21-year-old assets successful. In Dhami ji's determined resolve to make Devbhoomi number one state, I am always with him and the people of the state with dedication and integrity!

Hon'ble Bhagat Singh Koshyari: I took over as chief minister of the state. I was also the minister of energy, irrigation, law and legislative affairs in the Nityananda Swami government. Pushkar Dhami ji always impressed us with his talent and versatility during his time at Lucknow University. His disciplined style of working and selfless service sometimes amazed us. As our deeds shape our destinies, Dhami ji has become a source of inspiration for both the nation and the state. He is doing excellent work under the guidance of top leadership, and I am also with him as a guardian forever!

Swami Ramdev: Chief Minister Pushkar Singh Dhami is a man who has come out of struggle and deprivation, and who also understands the pain of people at the very bottom. He is the most sharp and powerful chief minister ever. Dhami ji is a person associated with yoga, so his government has resolved that Uttarakhand will be made the cultural and spiritual capital of the world. My best wishes to this young leader.

Shri Lal Krishna Advani: Pushkar Singh Dhami is humble and committed and always ready to get guidance from the experiences of seniors. May the state experience an all-inclusive progress under his skilled leadership! My best wishes for his successful and long life!

Shri Murli Manohar Joshi: Be it Garhwal or Kumaon, most leaders do not forget to seek my blessings whenever they visit Delhi. Pushkar Singh Dhami is a very popular and unblemished personality. The state has put faith in his style of functioning. My blessings are with him. He is doing a better job in the state, and I am sure he will continue to do so!

Shri Harish Rawat: Dhami is a sober and mature person. There are endless possibilities for the development of the state in his hands. Four important points that I would like to point out—age, disposition, support and time. Only if a fifth thing, 'understanding', could be merged with these four, on the strength of these five principles alone, no power could stop him from achieving sky-high success. He should hone himself more. Devbhoomi is a land of intelligent, honest and hardworking people. My love and blessings are with the young Dhami and I hope that he can reinstate the state's lost identity.

Shri Satpal Maharaj: Under the leadership of Chief Minister Pushkar Singh Dhami, the BJP government of the state is continuously preparing a series of development works. In Champawat election, we had said that if you elect Chief Minister Dhami, development will happen automatically here.

Therefore, the state is achieving day by day new milestones on the path of development.

Swami Chidanand Saraswati (President, Parmarth Niketan): Pushkar Dhami ji is a young thinker, young at heart and a young leader of a young state. His every effort will lead to unity and integrity spreading to the entire nation. His courageous decisions like the Uniform Civil Code will make the nation turn a new leaf. This is not the time for doubts or suspicions, but for achieving what is right through his actions. May God bless such a talented young man!

Shri Chandra Prakash Pant: Blessed with a simple and gentle personality, Pushkar Dhami ji is a source of inspiration for all of us. He has not only changed history in the state but has also made the public conscious of their abilities. Under the guidance of the Hon'ble Prime Minister and the able leadership of Dhami ji, we are confident that we will move forward on the path of progress and Dhami ji's resolve will make 25-year-old Uttarakhand the number one state in the country in 2025. On behalf of the entire Pant family, I wish him well. May he move forward ever!

Shri Kailash Gahtori: Pushkar ji, the young leader of a young state, has written a new chapter in the history of our state. As a chief minister, he exhibits immense potential for the development of the state. He is an affable and inclusive person. Even after becoming the head of a state, he has ensured that he gives due respect to the senior leaders of the party. His image as a clean leader is why he was Prime Minister Modi's first choice to be the chief minister.

From the Chief Minister's Office

Shri Bhupesh Basera: Dhami ji is a simple, intuitive person who thinks of the welfare of one and all. It is not common for a common person of humble beginnings to reach such great heights. He has no airs about his achievements. He always treats every person with humility. Today, he is a role model not only for Pithoragarh and Khatima, but also for the entire country. My best wishes to him, may he be entrusted with even better responsibilities!

Shri Sanjay Tolia: I have known Dhami ji since 1992. When the state was formed in 2000, the Uttar Pradesh Public Service Commission came here from Allahabad; since then, we have been friends through thick and thin. His moral conduct and visionary thoughts, which I saw when we first met in Yamuna Colony, remain intact till date. It is his progressive thinking, committed to the progress of the state, that makes Dhami what he is today. May my love and blessings always be with such a progressive personality!

Teachers

Balkrishna Pandey: A three-and-a-half-feet tall boy would always be found scribbling away on his wooden slate in the Barmon Primary School. He was the one who would give the calls of 'attention' and 'at ease' to the students in the school assembly, whilst his loud voice echoed in the mountains. After assembly, the same loud voice could be heard reciting tables and poems. We often used to say to the staff that he should be sent for addressing big election rallies. I am proud that our child, who grew up in deprivation, has shouldered the leadership of the state today! May my blessings be with him forever!

Shri B.C. Mehta: From 1986 to 2021, I was a teacher at Tharu Government Inter College. Meanwhile, Pushkar was also like other children. But he came to the fore as he was always ahead in every competition, school programs, etc. He gave a new identity to the pride and glory of the state. He was a child who gave due respect to everyone, from his ancestors to his teachers, and from his friends to the Almighty. This unique journey of a student from a small school makes us all proud. Our blessings! May our child keep progressing in life!

Principal R.N. Tripathi: When Pushkar was a student at DNCB, I used to teach him science. He was different from his classmates not only in appearance but also in activities and thoughts. We were very proud when we came to know that Pushkar Dhami had become the chief minister. We always present him as an example in front of the students in the school. Pushkar's journey has just begun; our prayers are with him.

Prof. Nishi, Lucknow: Pushkar Singh Dhami has always stood out among his teachers and peers for his humility, simplicity and honesty, even as a student. Today, despite holding a high office as chief minister, he has retained these qualities, which are the hallmark of his personality. A man of the soil—his commitment to the welfare of the underprivileged is exemplary. My affection and blessings to my promising disciple and skilled politician!

Prof. Vinita Kachar, Lucknow: I used to teach management (HRM) to Pushkar. He was an average student but remarkably engaged outside the course. He had great respect for teachers. May the political field bring him even more success; it would make our university proud to count Pushkar Dhami among its great personalities!

Family and Friends

Mata Bishna Devi: Our son respects everyone a lot. Since childhood, he has never done anything that would make us bow our heads in shame. Not only us, the entire nation is proud of him. He will certainly think of better ideas for the development of the state. The only regret is that his father could not see his work; he had a dream that Pushkar would lead and develop our state, which Pushkar did realize, but...

Geeta Dhami (Wife): He is not just my life partner but a devoted servant of the nation and a visionary leader. His every thought reflects patriotism, and every decision serves public welfare. He may be a steadfast warrior in politics and yet is a pillar of love and values at home. His sacrifice and dedication are for every citizen's prosperity and not just for mine.

Diwakar and Prabhakar (Sons of CM Dhami): Papa is always very busy. He returns late at night; by then we are already asleep. And in the morning, Mummy and Dadi send us to school. When Papa became chief minister, we told our friends about it. They wrote us a letter saying, 'Ask uncle to install swings in Khatima as a gift.' So Papa built three parks there.

Govind Ballabh Pant (Father of the Author): Pushkar Dhami ji is a multifaceted person, a quality that sets him apart and makes him effective in comparison to other leaders. Being the son of a soldier, he comprehends the essence of responsibility, a hallmark of a true leader. Moreover, his passion for work and self-awareness are commendable. Under his leadership, comprehensive development of our state is certain. I pray for his enduring health and well-being.

Anuradha Paudwal (Singer): It has been an honour for me to have met Shri Pushkar Singh Dhami. He is a remarkably humble individual, loved by all. I extend my best wishes to him for a bright future and for the development of the state.

Amarendra Kumar: Pushkar Bhai is a very friendly, happy person who is adept at helping others quickly get rid of troubles. He has always respected his seniors and juniors. Before exams, my notes used to be a panacea for him. With his sixth sense, he used to sense every activity on the university campus. I reached for his wedding two months in advance. Even today, his behaviour has not changed at all. We are very proud that an ordinary friend of ours is the state head today. We are confident that he will go a long way because his leadership ability is of another level!

Anubhav Singh: In Pushkar ji's eyes, I was often a mischievous student. Because of my scooter, I was seen as something of a Don Juan by everyone. He always showed us the right direction. He would often call us to his room and treat us with *paneer* and *dal-chawal*. I had somehow managed to gift him a T-shirt worth ₹70 at the Mumbai convention. He was very pleased. Then, times were difficult, but our spirits remained high. Dhami ji was a tremendous Kabaddi player and part of the college team, but he loved doing commentary on the field. We were always sure that he would reach where he is today, but that it will happen so quickly is a bit amazing. He will soon make his mark at the Centre. Wishing him a bright future!

Dr Jaishankar Pandey: I would like to give him the first credit for the expansion of the council (ABVP). I was a little sad about his Khatima election result because we, along with

Dr Manjul, had prayed at the Pancheshwar pilgrimage site that if Dhami won and became the chief minister again, we would return to thank Him. He, however, healed our wounds in such a way that history was made. If Pushkar manages to manoeuvre petty conspiracies, he will go a long way. Our eternal best wishes!

Somesh Vardhan: We, along with Dhami ji, had created ABVP units by making inroads among the delegacy students in almost all localities of Lucknow. With tireless efforts of the organization, the ABVP office in Gomtinagar was also opened. Dhami ji is a person who deals with all kinds of risks with a smile. Friendly behaviour and disciplined conduct with everyone are his two powerful weapons. Our brother is the chief minister today, what can be more fortunate than this for us!

Advocate Pawan Upadhyay: We, his friends from Lucknow University, were the happiest to see him become the chief minister. Naturally, a grand welcome ceremony was organized for him in Lucknow. As soon as he saw me, saying 'oh brother', he pulled up a chair for me. When I told him, 'There are some other friends who want to meet you', Dhami swiftly said, 'Oh, do call them!' Hardly anyone these days exhibits such friendly behaviour after reaching such a high position. This quality makes him remarkable. We wish him a bright future!